KING HUSSEIN AND THE CHALLENGE
OF ARAB RADICALISM

STUDIES IN MIDDLE EASTERN HISTORY

Bernard Lewis, Itamar Rabinovich, and Roger Savory,
GENERAL EDITORS

THE TURBAN FOR THE CROWN
The Islamic Revolution in Iran
Said Amir Arjomand

LANGUAGE AND CHANGE IN THE ARAB MIDDLE EAST
The Evolution of Modern Arabic Political Discourse
Ami Ayalon

ISLAMIC REFORM
Politics and Social Change in Late Ottoman Syria
David Dean Commins

KING HUSSEIN AND THE CHALLENGE OF ARAB RADICALISM
Jordan, 1955–1967
Uriel Dann

EGYPT, ISLAM, AND THE ARABS
The Search for Egyptian Nationhood, 1900–1930
Israel Gershoni and James Jankowski

EAST ENCOUNTERS WEST
France and the Ottoman Empire in the Eighteenth Century
Fatma Müge Göçek

THE FERTILE CRESCENT, 1800–1914
A Documentary Economic History
Edited by Charles Issawi

ESTRANGED BEDFELLOWS
Britain and France in the Middle East during the Second World War
Aviel Roshwald

OTHER VOLUMES ARE IN PREPARATION

KING HUSSEIN AND THE CHALLENGE OF ARAB RADICALISM

Jordan, 1955–1967

URIEL DANN

In cooperation with
THE MOSHE DAYAN CENTER
FOR MIDDLE EASTERN
AND AFRICAN STUDIES
Tel Aviv University

OXFORD UNIVERSITY PRESS
New York   Oxford

Oxford University Press

Oxford   New York   Toronto
Delhi   Bombay   Calcutta   Madras   Karachi
Petaling Jaya   Singapore   Hong Kong   Tokyo
Nairobi   Dar es Salaam   Cape Town
Melbourne   Auckland

and associated companies in
Berlin   Ibadan

Copyright © 1989 by Oxford University Press, Inc.

First published in 1989 by Oxford University Press, Inc.,
200 Madison Avenue, New York, New York 10016

First Issued as an Oxford University Press paperback, 1991

Oxford is a registered trademark of Oxford University Press

Library of Congress Cataloging-in-Publication Data
Dann, Uriel, 1922-
King Hussein and the challenge of Arab radicalism : Jordan
1955-1967 / Uriel Dann.
p.   cm.—(Studies in Middle Eastern history)
Includes index.
ISBN 0-19-505498-9
ISBN 0-19-507134-4 (pbk)
1. Jordan—Politics and government.   2. Jordan—Foreign relations--
Arab countries.   3. Arab countries--Foreign relations—Jordan.
4. Hussein, King of Jordan, 1935-   . I. Title. II. Series:
Studies in Middle Eastern history (New York, N.Y.)
DS154.55.D35 1989
956.95'043—dc19   88-29104

1   3   5   7   9   8   6   4   2

Printed in the United States of America
on acid-free paper

In memory of Zeev Bar-Lavie, "Biber," 1927–1985

However much one may admire the courage of this lonely young king, it is difficult to avoid the conclusion his days are numbered.

Anthony Nutting, former British minister of state for foreign affairs, *New York Herald Tribune*, 31 July 1958

Preface

The epigraph has proved to be wrong. I myself pronounced King Hussein's days "numbered" before Sir Anthony Nutting did; today—perhaps wiser than I was thirty years ago and certainly under no pressure to pontificate—I predict nothing. Yet I cannot say that my earlier evaluation was founded in ignorance, and certainly not in wishful thinking. There were valid reasons for discounting the odds on Hussein and on the polity for which he stood.

Since this book is not an occasion for self-justification, the best I can do is exchange the role of forecaster for that of historian and find out how Hussein survived, and why. I have assumed as little as possible. It is true that the foundations of Hussein's rule were charged with problems. It is also true that between 1955 and 1967, Hussein faced a challenge and an onslaught from Arab radicalism personified by Gamal Abdel Nasser and those who followed his lead, although challenge and onslaught intensified or receded with the circumstances, dramatically diminishing after the Six-Day War. I had to assume one constant—that Hussein was determined to stay the course, although fluctuating moods are discernible.

Among my sources, first place goes to primary materials—official publications, newspapers, periodicals, broadcast monitorings, pamphlets—which have again proved to me that they may serve as mines of understanding, not merely of information. Secondary sources are multiplying, and I have used them as best I could. I have utilized originally classified material as it became available; the liberal practice of declassification that prevails in the United States carries the researcher far closer to the present day than the thirty-year rule would allow. Interviews have given me some confidence that I was on paths that led somewhere.

It is difficult to apportion acknowledgments for a work that has been with you for more than thirty years. My debt to the Moshe Dayan Center is in its totality greater than the sum of its parts—academic, secretarial, financial—important as they are. The head of the center, Professor Itamar Rabinovich, has been a friend indeed. Among the members of the center who have helped me, I owe special mention to Ms. Lydia Gareh, Ms. Edna Liftman, Ms. Amira Margalith, Dr. Asher Susser, and Mr. Haim Gal. Mr. Daniel Dishon, Professor Bernard Lewis, and Mr. Yitzhak Oron read the draft of the manuscript before I submitted it to the publisher; I cannot sufficiently stress the value of their suggestions. I also talked to persons who were involved in the events described in this book. Since not all wish me to mention their names, I have done so, when permitted, in the notes. My colleague Professor J. L. Wallach collected archival material for me when he was on research leave in the United States.

I owe much to the assistance and good will of the directors and staff of the Library of Congress; the John F. Kennedy and Lyndon Baines Johnson libraries; the Department of State Library; the Classification/Declassification Center, the Department of State; the Defense Intelligence Agency, the Department of Defense; the Middle East Centre, St. Antony's College, Oxford; the Public Record Office, London; the Political Research Center, the Israeli Foreign Ministry; and the Israel State Archives. Maddy and Bernard Reich, of Wheaton, Maryland, and the Rector, Fellows, and staff of Lincoln College, Oxford, made our sojourns pleasant and profitable. The Ford Foundation (through Israel Foundations Trustees) assisted me with a grant. My daughter Naomi's involvement meant more to me than she realized. At Oxford University Press, Nancy Lane and Irene Pavitt were invariably helpful.

My gratitude goes to all.

My wife shared the burden and the joy.

Tel Aviv
June 1988   U.D.

Contents

KING HUSSEIN AND THE CHALLENGE
OF ARAB RADICALISM

Introduction: The Jordanian Entity

Jordan is a hereditary monarchy of the Hashemite family, with the prince as its cornerstone.[1] The monarchy has been characterized by a conservatism wary of radical notions, no matter where they originated. Instead, it has adhered to that brand of Arab nationalism that first came to attention in the "Great Arab Rebellion" (or "revolution," *thawra*) of Sharif Husayn bin 'Ali, the amir of Mecca, during World War I. According to this view, the Hashemites had a historic claim to Arab national leadership. Their mission was to work for Arab political unity under their own guidance within the Arabian Peninsula, paying lip service to existing territorial interests there, and the Fertile Crescent. (Egypt was not genuinely "Arab" according to their perception, and the Maghreb was too far away.) This mission was first claimed by the Hashemites as male descendants of the Prophet's daughter Fatima and through their guardianship of the holy places at Mecca and Medina for almost a millennium. Unlike his grandfather Abdallah, who sought territorial aggrandizement,[2] Hussein never attempted to expand his domain beyond what he had inherited. It is clear, however, from Hussein's recorded opinions that his faith in Hashemite excellence was that of his forebears.[3]

It is important to realize the physical disadvantages under which Jordan labored: even before 1967, it was an area of less than 40,000 square miles, hardly one-tenth of which were arable, with about 2 million inhabitants, one-third of whom were refugees. It had no important mineral resources and no historical frontiers, only a natural frontier to the east and south of doubtful location and political validity. Jordan's Arab neighbors—ignoring for the moment the special problem of Israel—are Syria, Iraq, Saudi Arabia, and (except for the thin Israeli wedge) Egypt, each surpassing Jordan in area and population and each bearing a special relevance to the kingdom's very existence.

3

Traditionally, the Hashemite Entity was allied with the "West." It had a strong standing army that was based on personal allegiance to the ruler and was known officially in English as the "Arab Legion" until 1956, and unofficially called so even later. Those who supported the Entity were the ruler and the members of his extended family, the Hijazi descendants of the Prophet, the sharifs; a circle known as "the king's friends," perhaps a score of individuals of differing origin who usually held key positions in the king's retinue and the court; the beduin, who were in the process of settling but who were maintaining their social cohesion and identity; the villagers and the small-town dwellers in the East Bank, especially in the south; and, finally, those from the outside who supported the Entity, for differing reasons and on different levels: Britain and the United States, the Arab monarchies, the majority of non-Arab Muslim states, and an uneasy political consensus in Israel. Those who opposed, or at least mistrusted, the Entity were the Palestinians when they organized as such; a stratum of intellectuals in the East Bank; and "radicals," whether pan-Arab nationalist (*qawmi*), Communist, Muslim-fundamentalist, or unspecified "progressives." The supporters of the Hashemite state generally showed a greater degree of consistency, resilience, and readiness to run risks than did its opponents. While on the side of the Entity, attention centered on the king, it is less simple to find a focus on the opposing side. Gamal Abdel Nasser comes to mind, and on the impersonal level, rejection of "the West," passionate and honest.

Although the foundation of the Jordanian Entity changed remarkably little over the thirty or so years before 1955, between 1955 and 1967 its constituent elements each attract particular attention.[4] The Hashemite rulers aimed at authoritarianism and usually were successful. They did not want a totalitarian society like that of Abdel Nasser of Egypt in the mid-1960s, Saddam Husayn of Iraq in the late 1970s, and Ayatollah Khomeini of Iran in the early 1980s. Rather, the Hashemite detachment was based on the acquired instincts of an ancient dynasty deeply conscious of its right and ability to rule in an environment of finely balanced forces, including the natural limitations of the ruler's power.

Jordan was governed according to the 1952 constitution and its later amendments.[5] The constitution was not overly conservative or rigid, and the regime generally obeyed it. The constitution's continued validity was due in no small degree to its open-ended provisions for emergencies in which the Entity might find itself: "except for cases provided for by law" was a phrase frequently appended to provisions guarding the citizens' liberty. (This squaring of the circle was not the least of the services to the Hashemite monarchy of Tawfiq Abu'l Huda, the prime minister who steered the constitution through a skeptical Chamber of Deputies.) The regime also occasionally used the sweeping 1939 "Defence Regulations" of mandate times, which were never repealed.[6]

The Jordanian throne belongs to the family of King Abdallah. (The 1946 constitution, the first of the independent kingdom, refers to Abdallah's father, King Husayn of the Hijaz, thus leaving open the possibility of switching to the Iraqi Hashemites.) The king's constitutional position is as expected in a parliamentary monarchy in which by custom he plays an active part: he is the supreme commander of the armed forces,[7] alone possesses the executive authority, and shares the legislative authority with a parliament consisting of an appointed Senate and an elected Chamber.[8] As the embodiment of the executive, the king has the exclusive right to appoint and dismiss his ministers, including the prime minister. He has extensive rights regarding the convening, prorogation, and dissolution of parliament, and of legislation by royal ordinance when parliament is not in session. The civil service is essentially outside the constitution; it is "royal" as a matter of course. But the constitutional clout of the king's powers derives from the constitution's paragraph 125, which provides for the declaration of martial law (more correctly "emergency administration") by royal decree in case of a "serious emergency," "notwithstanding the provisions of any law in force."

The Senate's membership (half the number of the Chamber) served as a sinecure for faithful politicians in semiretirement.[9] The eight-year (later four-year) term was a reasonable guarantee of continued good behavior. The Chamber of Deputies was a very different body. It was based on general male suffrage.[10] The West Bank and the East Bank each returned an equal number of representatives from their territorial constituencies, a total of forty until 1958, fifty until 1960, and sixty by 1967. The Chamber's constitutional powers were considerable. Until 1967, in session for four months each year unless dissolved, it could force the government's resignation by the vote of an absolute majority. In addition, legislation by royal ordinance was restricted—in theory—in certain respects.[11] In practice, however, the king could have his way by applying its defense and military-law sections or, alternatively, by persuading a two-thirds majority of the Chamber to expel a member or an absolute majority to consent to a member's arrest and trial. Although such majorities could not be taken for granted, it was proof of Hussein's skill that they were available when needed. Another necessary skill was ensuring the chief precondition for managing the Chamber: making sure that as few members as possible were elected who were of doubtful loyalty. Yet, by and large, the Chamber (as distinct from the Senate) played an active role between 1955 and 1967. It was a platform on which the proponents of clashing views and interests thrashed out their opinions and demands. On one occasion, in April 1963, the Chamber even caused the government's resignation.

Because of the ban on political parties since April 1957, we should mention that political parties were expressly legalized in the constitution, "provided their objects were lawful, their means peaceful and their rules do not infringe upon the constitution." The Communist party has never been found to qualify under these provisions. It has been forbidden since mandate times, and even when it did enjoy relative freedom of action, in 1956 and 1957, it operated under the cloak of a National Front (al-jabha al-wataniyya).

The constitution provided for the adult male suffrage of Jordanian citizens, by secret ballot. (For the beduin, another system was in force.) This was liberal (apart from the exclusion of women), as the Palestinians, including the refugee population, had been granted Jordanian nationality from the beginning. In practice, however, the situation was rather different. First, the ostensibly fair division of parliamentary constituencies between the two banks in fact doubly favored the East Bank; two-thirds of Jordan's population from 1949 to 1967 were Palestinians, and the East Bank constituencies were defined in order to give "Transjordanian" conglomerations an advantage. Second, the authorities always interfered in the elections. However, the degree, the method, and the effect varied from case to case. Generally, government interference advanced over the years from crude tampering with voters and the vote to manipulating candidates. Usually the interference was remedial. An early example was the stationing of army units for election day in doubtful constituencies where they then voted. At a later stage, the inofficial evaluation of prospective candidates by district authorities, and security officials especially, became something of an art. Threats and coercion or, in difficult cases, preventive arrest were in use too, and a code of communication that spelled out the risks to unwanted candidates was developed. At the other end of the scale, the outright falsification of results was not unknown during the early 1950s, and obstreperous deputies have been removed from the Chamber, when necessary, since 1957. To what extent this supervision was loosened—and declared in advance to be loosened—twice depended on the personal decision of King Hussein, in 1956 and 1962. The outcome on both occasions indicated at the time that the king had taken an ill-considered risk. A more rounded view now suggests that he was gifted even then with his usual feel for the right choice in difficult circumstances, followed up by his usual courage and good luck.

It is a mistake to apply Western notions to Jordanian parliamentarism without caution. Jordanian society was by no means monolithic. But it was still governed largely by traditional perceptions, and traditional perceptions in this political context meant respect for customary authority and obedience to the rulers of the state. It was neither force and fraud nor the free choice of the engaged citizen, in the Western democratic sense, that ensured the government of its normal predominance at elections. Rather, it was a sense of appropriateness, to a greater extent than foreign observers recognized or enemies of the Hashemite Entity nearer home cared to acknowledge. Rebels, malcontents, visionaries, and plain mavericks all played a role, but a much smaller role at the polls than between elections, when they tended to monopolize attention.

Political society in Jordan before the Six-Day War fell into four vertical sectors: the villagers and townspeople east of the Jordan River; the beduin (most, but not all, east of the Jordan); the Palestinians in their towns and villages west of the Jordan; and the Palestinian refugees on both sides of the Jordan, in camps or mixed in with the resident population. Among the 1.2 million inhabitants of the kingdom when newly constituted in 1950, the number of settled Transjordanians roughly equaled that of indigenous Palestinians in the West Bank and again that of refugees in either bank, plus 100,000 beduin. The population growth from then on was fabulous and by 1967 may have amounted to 70 percent, but the proportions hardly changed.[12]

It is important to realize that these four sectors did not have rigid boundaries. They played distinct political parts as actors and as objects, and to this extent their categorization is justified and indeed necessary. But there were also shadings at the fringes, and thus it is often difficult to place individuals and families, and reactions to given situations varied.

The backbone of the state were the settled Transjordanians, the *hadari* population east of the Jordan. In 1948, they were living in about 300 villages and a dozen towns; among the latter, only Amman, al-Salt, Kerak, and Irbid could be considered urban centers like those in neighboring Palestine and Syria. They included nomads who had turned sedentary and become peasants generations before; immigrants from west of the Jordan, from the Hawran and the Djebel Druse; and descendants of Ibrahim Pasha's army and its followers in the 1830s—on top of the substratum rooted in its home ground. The Syrian admixture was particularly strong in the north around Irbid, the Palestinians in the center around al-Salt, and the former nomads in the south around Kerak and Maʿan. Ethnically, the settled Transjordanians were Arabs, in the modern sense of the term. (In the late 1940, "Arabs" would still have meant beduin to some.) Circassians and Chechens—displaced from the Caucasus by the Russian advance and settled by the Ottoman authorities along the edge of the desert in geographical Syria in the late nineteenth and early twentieth centuries—were still identifiable, but their ethnicity was steadily paling. A few thousand Armenians had settled in the larger towns in the wake of World War I. By religion, the' vast majority was Sunni Muslim. However, a minority of nearly 10 percent was Christian, most of them Greek Orthodox, who lived in their own quarters and villages. They were descendants of the resident population at the time of the Muslim conquest who had remained true to their faith. In life-style, they differed little from their Muslim neighbors.[13] Until the mid-1920s, cleavages among the settled Transjordanians had been bitter; they were loyal to their clan and the local community and considered outsiders to be "foreigners" and often enemies. The south—Kerak, Maʿan—close to the Hijaz and its beduin culture, differed from the north—Salt, Irbid—which lay wide open to Syrian influences.

The central government and its agencies, whether at Constantinople, Damascus, or Amman, might bribe or penalize; it might provide protection from a common and recognized enemy like the beduin. That was largely the extent of its influence. The last twenty years of the amirate, when the habit of peace and orderly government was taking root, had produced some changes, but still the people's identification with the state was passive at best. It was the addition of twice their own number of Palestinians as nominal cocitizens that turned the mass of settled Transjordanians into conscious supporters of the Hashemite Entity. On the rational level, the Palestinians were competitors to whom their recent past had given an advantage in the struggle for what little Jordan had to offer. But their political past, their prolonged exposure to modernization, and their recent misfortunes stamped them as different beyond their geographical extraction. Their conduct in the 1948 war led to accusations of military ineptitude; at best, it did not inspire respect when compared with the record of the Arab Legion. In any case, the Palestinians were strangers who provided a rallying focus for group antipathies. Still, the Transjordanian south remained more solidly conservative than the north, and a growing stratum of Transjordanian intellectuals became "Palestinianized" in their social and political attitudes. All the same, it remains true that the 1948 war was a trauma that affixed the non-beduin population of Transjordan more closely to the Hashemite kingdom.

There is no valid definition of what constitutes "beduin" in Jordan. As mentioned, nomads had been absorbed into the settled community throughout the generations, as individuals, families, and subtribes, and they became, for all intents and purposes, part of village or town society. But there were macrofamilies, "tribes," that were often classed as beduin, even though they had been residents for generations of towns as large as Kerak; the Majali were a prominent example. The best criterion was still self-identification, together with a political position that fitted the stance adopted by the tribes toward the Entity. Nomadism was no test: the beduin were becoming sedentary in increasing numbers without, thereby, ceasing to regard themselves as beduin or ceasing to be so regarded. Nor was religion: Greek Orthodox beduin tribes existed, even if their religious practices did not stand scrutiny (the same obtained, *mutatis mutandis,* for the Muslim beduin). Their political culture was a mixture of the traditional and the modern and included pride in being beduin—as belonging to humankind's true nobility, with its corollary contempt for the *hadari,* hewers of wood and drawers of water—which was still genuinely felt and arrogantly expressed.

At the same time, intertribal jealousies were much in evidence and demanded careful watching from Amman. They might be nurtured in order to ease tribal management, but they might also erupt in brawls that might harm the Hashemite state. The king was something of a paramount shaykh: he dispensed largesse and patronage, judged disputes, settled priorities, and identified with the collective values and images of tribal society. In return, he received loyalty and service, particularly when these matched the ingrained antipathies of the tribespeople. Hussein was good at living up to this role—better perhaps than his grandfather Abdallah had been—for it suited his peculiar gift of showmanship as well as his inclinations. Economically by the mid-1950s, the beduin were prosperous. Their old economy, based on goat and camel rearing and the exaction of protection money, had been dead for a generation. In its place was government employment, chief among which was service in the army.

The army was based entirely on regular, often long-term, service. The first beduin units in the originally "antibeduin" Arab Legion were established in the 1930s. World War II, the war of 1948, the birth of "Jordan" on both banks of the river, and the abrupt "Arabization" of the army command after Glubb's dismissal in 1956 had put a premium on beduin manpower. The beduin were conditioned and eager to fight (or at least to find their pride in soldiering); receptive to the material rewards the army offered and dangerously quick to resent disappointments, as the king was well aware; and, in sum, loyal to the basic prescripts of the Hashemite Entity. By 1955, the army had absorbed practically all the young men of the tribes, beduin or near-beduin, inasmuch as they met the rather strict criteria of health (and freedom from the taint of subversion). Even so, the army could not avoid mobilizing *hadari* as combat troops, let alone for support and service units. But the army's key units—royal guards, armor, and the desert police—were beduin, the "other ranks," and, since 1956 and 1957, the officers as well.

As with the Transjordanians, it was impossible to identify the Palestinians in Jordan with certainty, whether as opposed to the Transjordanians or within their own group, resident versus refugees, and refugees in camps versus refugees dispersed among the settled population. Palestinians had migrated to pre-1948 Transjordan for a variety of reasons: intermarriage, economic pressure, and the pursuit of administrative careers. Migration in the opposite direction, from the sparsely populated East Bank to the densely populated West Bank, was comparatively rare, though Palestinian families sometimes returned, their original objective achieved. A number of educated men who had left their homes in mandated Palestine to help build up the administration of the amirate in the 1920s had founded "official" families and were by 1955 among the Entity's prominent supporters: the Rifaʻi, from Safad; the Hashim and branches of the Touqan, from Nablus; and Abu'l Huda, from Acre. On the West Bank itself, Abdallah had powerful allies and clients long before 1948; they were joined during the first days of the enlarged kingdom by prominent personages who had until then been allies and clients of Abdallah's archenemy, the former mufti of Jerusalem, Hajj Amin al-Husayni.

Although the older generation of notables (including many in early middle age) may be described as generally supporting King Hussein, the same cannot be said for the younger intelligentsia. (The Arabic *muthaqqafun* has a fairer connotation, as the term *intelligentsia* sometimes has a pejorative flavor in Middle Eastern contexts.) Teachers, journalists, lawyers, and professional and would-be professional politicians—the whole gamut of university graduates in the humanities and social sciences, with little prospect for employment or advancement—became the natural nucleus of discontent in a society in crisis. The Hashemite Entity meant to them nothing, or worse.

The authorities, on their part, were anxious to assimilate the troublemakers, potential if not actual, into the state. But suitable carrots were few, and the stick was the more common means of control. Supervision by the various government agencies was close[14] and efficient by the only yardstick that counted—the preservation of the Hashemite monarchy. Sanctions were harsh, up to a point: dismissal, enforced idleness, or blacklisting; trial before the regular or, more frequently, the military courts, often entailing long prison sentences; detention in desert camps without trial; and "encouragement" to decamp from Jordan (the constitution forbade the exiling of citizens). However, in no case did the king put to death a political opponent—as opposed to, occasionally, those convicted of espionage for Israel and, once, the perpetrators of a particularly bloody act of terrorism that claimed the lives of Majali clansmen, self-styled beduin whose goodwill was vital to Hussein.

The mass of West Bank residents were normally not much interested in politics. Their sympathies undoubtedly lay with the antagonists of the Entity: the menace of Israel was near, and their faith in the capacity—and even the will—of the Jordanian state to protect them was shaky at best. The state, or so they believed, subordinated their interests to those of the East Bank, and thus they had no ingrained tie of loyalty to the Hashemite house that might counteract their grievances. (The south—Bethlehem and Hebron—was more conservative and hence easier to rule than was the north—Ramallah and Nablus.) Superimposed on these reflexes of neglect and impotence was the Palestinians' sense that they were inherently superior to the Transjordanians in intellect, education, and political experience. But the significance of these attitudes must not be distorted. The struggle for existence was hard and unceasing for the great bulk of West Bankers and left little time and energy for active politics, let alone for political activism. Moreover, the Hashemite state enjoyed reasonable respect: although it visited its wrath on offenders, it was not strikingly inefficient, corrupt, or despotic. It could and did provide for the deserving. And it was, when all is said, both Muslim and Arab, although it is doubtful whether Hussein's claim as a descendant of the Prophet had a measurable effect.

The refugees in both banks, whether cooped up in camps or dispersed in villages and towns, had a political significance for the Hashemite state—as distinct from their social, economic, and psychological situation as such—that differed from that of their more fortunate brethren in degree rather than in quality. They were more cowed, disoriented, and leaderless, and they were also more distrusted by the authorities. At the same time, they were usually concentrated in groups and hence more easily controlled. All refugee camps—even veritable townships like Aqabat Jabir, near Jericho, and Zerqa, near Amman—were closely guarded by armed forces, whether police or army, that regulated the refugees' communications with the outside world. For all these reasons, refugees played a smaller part in disturbances until 1967 than did nonrefugee Palestinians, and a far smaller part than Western onlookers believed.[15] Party politics were open to refugees, as to other Palestinians (and Transjordanians). But here, too, the refugees—again for the reasons just enumerated—were even less active in organized politics than were their Palestinian nonrefugee compatriots. The authorities also had a particular interest in preventing the refugees' political consolidation. The General Refugees Congress, convened in 1949, withered away in the early 1950s, largely because of obstruction from above, and a delegation from that congress was prevented from stating its case before the United Nations Palestine Conciliation Commission at Lausanne in 1949.[16]

It has been said that the refugees were the wretched among the Palestinians, as among the population as a whole. However, a clarification is necessary. The refugees came under the care of the United Nations Relief and Works Agency for Palestine Refugees in the Near East (UNRWA), established in 1949 and financed chiefly by the U.S. government.

The importance of UNRWA in Jordan during those years can hardly be overestimated. Its official ration cards were to some degree an identification superimposed on Jordanian citizenship papers, although not entirely so, as the ration cards were not only traded, but also issued only to refugees recognized as "needy." UNRWA supplied basic relief to hundreds of thousands of them: food and shelter, education and health care.[17] However basic the food and shelter, and deficient the education and health care, may have been, they were dependable and often superior to those available to the resident population in either bank. (This argument did come up in domestic debates, and it did not serve to make the position of the refugees any easier.) Although the relief afforded by UNRWA was politically acceptable—who else would have kept the refugees alive?—rehabilitation was not, as it would have entailed a backhanded admission that Israel was there to stay. Hence, evasions, apologies, and controversies accompanied the constructive work of UNRWA, and even sabotage was sporadically attempted and constantly feared. UNRWA and the government treated each other somewhat like independent powers, whose relationship was regulated by formal agreements.[18]

UNRWA's dependence on the government—for protection, for support, and for the fundamentals of legality that the state dispensed—needs no elaboration. But the Jordanian authorities, even the Entity as a concept, needed the goodwill and cooperation of UNRWA. Without it, Jordan would have lost financial resources vital to the survival of the state. Finance apart, it is highly doubtful whether Jordan then had the administrative and technical ability to deal with a mass of humanity larger than the population of Transjordan in 1948. Also, UNRWA served the kingdom in two matters that were not advertised. The authorities used UNRWA's financial and organizational capacity in their policy of strengthening the East Bank at the expense of the West Bank. And UNRWA was a lightning rod—less in moments of political crisis than in the enervating atmosphere of everyday frustration in the camps.

It remains to outline the practical lessons that the leaders of the Entity, the king in particular, drew from the composition of the Jordanian population. As might be expected, the principles were clearer than their actual application.

The beduin were the fighting material par excellence. Their educational handicaps (of which they were well aware) put some limitation on their rise to senior command positions and sophisticated technical postings, although less so as time went on. The beduin were not especially suited to service appointments or general administration. They were the faithful of the faithful, but there occasionally were mavericks on all levels of this intricate society. Also, their tendency to be carried away by tribal and personal jealousies was ever present, and their loyalty entailed no willingness to make material sacrifices. In fact, they were desperately poor and, in the past, predatory in order to survive, and so they always had to be propitiated with largesse. It is not known whether the beduin had a clear concept of Jordan as a state, as distinct from their attitude toward the king; events showed that it is a question that need not be answered.

The settled Transjordanian population also posed problems. As already mentioned, they were the *staatsvolk* if there were any in Jordan, and yet they were by no means homogeneous for the purposes of the Hashemite state. The result was that the settled Transjordanians as a sector were considered suitable for any employment; in the armed forces up to any level of command, in the police and the security services, in the civil and diplomatic services, in parliament, and in the media as far as government influence carried. But although it probably goes too far to say that the people from the north—'Ajlun and the Belqa—carried an automatic handicap, it is still true that anti-Hashemite winds from Nablus and Damascus blew stronger there than in the south,[19] and that vigilance was indicated. Nonetheless, there still were exceptions. The Tall family of Irbid supplied both the archtraitor of independent Jordan—'Abdallah— and its outstanding statesman—Wasfi—and apparently neither was impeded in his calling by his regional roots. Instances like this can be multiplied at a less dramatic level. Even so, members of established families from the southern provinces of Kerak and Maʿan had an inborn advantage in the struggle for office and advancement.

By a similar token, the Palestinians—nonrefugee and refugee—should have been denied government favors. To some extent that was true, but again, the situation is complicated. There were notable families in the West Bank who had been Abdallah's associates or clients since the 1930s, if not earlier, and who had a right to be treated as supporters of the Entity. More important, however, was an ideological issue: there were no "Palestinians" in any sense that touched on the official self-view of the state; there were only Jordanian citizens.[20] And because the law had not merely to be observed but also to be seen to be observed, it was doubly important to give Palestinians a fair deal. Hence, some Palestinians could be found in the highest and most sensitive offices of the Entity. But in general, the authorities considered caution the better part of policy as far as Palestinians were concerned. To reach those highest and most sensitive offices in the Entity, Palestinians (unless particularly favored by their family connections) had to prove themselves as individuals in a way not expected from Transjordanians, and not only in security matters. Senior officials in local administration—district and subdistrict governors—were not permitted to officiate for long in one locality, especially in the West Bank.

Economically, too, the state gave preference to the East Bank, to the point of brazenness. Indeed, development centered on the East Bank as far as it lay in the power of the government to direct. The showpiece of those years, the East Ghor Canal Authority, was in the East Bank; an envisioned West Ghor Canal, running parallel to the East Bank canal and fed from it, never got past the preliminary planning stage. The strength of UNRWA in finance, labor, and international connections was manipulated to divert resources from the West to the East Bank. Migration eastward was encouraged, despite the political risk involved.

The refugees were Palestinians. Compared with the nonrefugee population of the West Bank, they were a greater threat to the Entity; they had less to offer; and they were miserable. Many were intellectuals. They seemed to have much to gain by violence and disobedience and less to lose. The common impression that the refugees lived in camps needs correction. About two-thirds were dispersed among the settled population, equally in both banks. In the West Bank, they had moved to villages as well as towns and cities. In the East Bank, because of the villagers' and townspeople's dislike of the masses of destitute strangers, the Palestinian refugees settled in an area around Greater Amman that rapidly acquired a "Palestinian" majority, although the character of Amman continued to be determined by its being the hub of the Hashemite monarchy. Much of the disfavor and the suspicion with which the authorities regarded the refugees must be understood as the gut reaction of an alien regime, at once conservative, authoritarian, and frightened. The authorities had no panacea for the resulting security problems. The camps could be guarded closely and efficiently at not too great an expense of highly trained forces. The normal means of supervision had to suffice for the refugees outside the camps, which they usually did. Beyond this, the regime's policy regarding the refugees was unconstructive (disregarding the uneasy license granted to UNRWA to try its hand at rehabilitation, as far as UNRWA could and dared). The government made no attempt to reconcile the refugees to the Entity except by propitiation with the usual catch phrases. With few exceptions, refugees were not accepted into the armed forces in any capacity; nor were they trained for the National Guard, the village militia (chiefly in the West Bank), if this could be circumvented. The camps offered no weapons training, despite occasional promises to do so. The reluctance to employ refugees in the public sector was much greater than that to hire other Palestinians. The refugees' absorption into Jordan's rural economy, primitive in any case, was unfeasible, and the urban economy did not start to pick up until the 1960s.

The captains of the state held that the best politics for its citizens was abstention from politics, whether realized by political parties or otherwise. This preference can be traced back to fundamental concepts of Muslim society. Abstention from politics was one of the dividing lines between the traditional regimes in the Middle East and the mobilizing ideology of radical regimes, such as Nasser's Egypt and Syria. But as these authorities also cherished an image as "modernists," they had some difficulty in expressing their preference in terms that would not brand them as reactionaries in contemporary Arab opinion. Hence state instruction in "citizenship" always remained unsophisticated, even though the state continued to demand it.[21]

　　The kingdom was governed from Amman according to unitary and centralist principles inherited from the Ottoman Empire, where they had been circumscribed during the empire's last hundred years only by the difficulties of their realization. Such principles matched Abdallah's desires and policy, with the same proviso, and they suited Hussein's personality—his desire for a federated state dates strictly from the Six-Day War. Whatever the roots of centralization, historical or otherwise, it was held to be vital to maintaining the Entity. Occasionally, attempts were made in the Chamber of Deputies, in the West Bank press, and at local meetings to achieve a West Bank entity within the Hashemite kingdom. The verbal responses from Amman, including the king's in person, were often sympathetic, especially in times of tension, but nothing of consequence was ever done. Between 1955 and 1967, there was no "West Bank" as an administrative concept.

Naturally, Jerusalem was a focal point. Tradition and repute made Jerusalem the pearl of the kingdom, immeasurably outshining Amman. Abdallah responded to its call, although not in the field of administration. By the time of his death in 1951, he had taken away from Jerusalem whatever superiority he had accorded it during the first months after the end of the British mandate. During Hussein's reign, calls for proclaiming Jerusalem the second capital, for transferring to Jerusalem at least some ministries and central offices, and for holding parliamentary sessions there also found a sympathetic reception—verbally. But again, nothing was done that would detract from the status of Amman. Hussein's visits to Jerusalem were few. It is significant that a royal palace, whose first stone was laid in the northern outskirts of Jerusalem in 1963, was still unfinished in June 1967.[22]

The Hashemite Entity also did not welcome the development of political parties, less even than Egypt, Syria, and Iraq did, whenever the regime in power in those countries gave political parties a chance. Yet political parties legally existed (except for the Jordanian Communist Party) until April 1957, and they went underground afterward. They suffered, to varying degrees, the problems affecting political parties throughout the Arab East: weak roots in the society's political tradition, no dependable mass following, no adequate bureaucratic apparatus, and a leadership manifestly unsuited to enduring adversity, with the Communists and Muslim-fundamentalist groups as significant exceptions.

Until their suppression in 1957, political parties were regulated by the relatively liberal law of 1954, superseded in 1955 by more stringent legislation.[23] Most of the parties had parent organizations outside Jordan. The Ba'th (Arab Socialist Resurrection) party was run from Damascus, which was until 1920 the seat of administrative authority on the East Bank and until the rise of Abdel Nasser, the recognized center of pan-Arabism. The Arab Nationalist Movement (harakat al-qawmiyyin al-'arab, or simply the Qawmiyeen)—a political party in all but name—started in 1949 as a Palestinian nationalist association that by the mid-1950s professed total allegiance to Abdel Nasser. The Jordanian Communist Party was strictly loyal to Moscow, although its dependence on daily instructions from the center should not be overrated. Usually it reacted to local impulses, by necessity but also by an instinct of sturdy self-reliance. Party members had always been subjected to suppression by penal legislation. The Muslim Brothers remained part of the Egypt-oriented mainstream of their movement, which gave them a peculiar importance in the political history of Jordan between 1955 and 1967. Much as the Muslim Brothers hated the Western roots and trappings of the Hashemite monarchy, their even greater hatred of Abdel Nasser precluded them from joining the assault on the regime in predominantly "Nasserite" company. But this was not true for the other Muslim-fundamentalist organization in Jordan (and elsewhere in the Arab East): the Tahrir (Liberation) party, without historical and personal strings tying it to Cairo, rejected the Hashemite Entity unconditionally and on all occasions.[24] The two or three loyalist parties that turned up at election times until 1957 were insignificant, even by Jordanian standards.

The most authentic expression of party life in Jordan was the National Socialist party (al-hizb al-watani al-ishtiraki), founded under this name in 1954. The party had the deepest roots of all in the political history of Jordan. It had a stake in the country. Most of its leaders belonged to respected families in the East Bank and in Nablus who were prosperous landowners and merchants. By the 1950s, their opposition was traditional: dating back to the disappointed hopes for national freedom and personal careers at the end of World War I, to Arab nationalism suppressed by the French on the other side of a frontier that to the Arabs was worse than meaningless, and to Abdallah's petty persecution and the contempt of a peculiarly unsympathetic British resident, Lieutenant Colonel Henry F. Cox. Although the National Socialist party had many noted members, it had few leaders and no true demagogues. The members' interest in social progress was unconvincing. For all these reasons, the opposition of the National Socialists to the Entity was bound to be erratic. They certainly lacked a desire for sacrifice. But their relative weight within the body politic as well as their ingrained self-importance made them unsuited as mere fellow travelers to more devoted or more ambitious radicals. All these aspects came into play when their historic chance arrived in 1956.

Jordan from 1949 to 1967 was a poor country.[25] It had been desperately poor as the Amirate of Transjordan, and the addition of the Palestinians, half of whom were refugees, greatly aggravated the situation. The British and, since 1957, the American subsidy for the upkeep of the army should not obscure the fact that the Hashemite state had depended on foreign handouts all along, sometimes dressed up as "development." Funds from the U.S. Point Four program, as well as from UNRWA, helped balance the Jordanian budget in the early 1950s. Politically, however, the sub-sidies were not critical. Abdallah and Hussein (the grandson, through a changed situation, even more than the grandfather) pursued their own policies and assumed that the basic community of interests would continue to secure foreign funds. No doubt, they were wise. After 1960, the economic situation became, or appeared, less bleak, mainly because of the rapid growth of tourism. Still, economic independence never came into sight between 1955 and 1967.

I

FIRST TRIALS

1

Last of the Beaten Track

If 1955 was a turning point in the history of the Middle East, 1954 set the stage for this drama. At the periphery, Turkey and Pakistan concluded a defense treaty that aimed at bridging the North Atlantic Treaty Organization (NATO) and the Southeast Asia Treaty Organization (SEATO), a move inspired by Great Power politics and as yet of no direct interest to the Arab world. But in August 1954, Nuri al-Saʿid resumed power at Baghdad and at once set out to engineer Iraq's inclusion in the treaty, and in doing so turned the alliance into a lever to achieve Iraq's dominance in the Arab world.

In Damascus, the Shishakli regime, relatively staid in its policies, gave way to unstable constellations that amplified the convulsions soon to shake the Arab world under the battle cry of *qawmiyya ʿarabiyya* (or simply *qawmiyya*), pan-Arab nationalism.

In Amman, where King Hussein had assumed his constitutional powers on 2 May 1953, his eighteenth birthday (lunar reckoning), the king became disillusioned with the liberal urges that marked the first year of his reign and returned to a rejuvenated version of his grandfather King Abdallah's maxims, and also to Abdallah's trusted servants.[1]

In Cairo, Gamal Abdel Nasser set the stage for "the hero in search of his role," by assuming power for all to see and by signing the agreement that ensured Egypt's freedom after seventy-two years of British occupation.[2] It was this achievement that allowed Abdel Nasser to implement a long-term objective of his leadership. The decision came to him without apparent soul-searching: he appeared in public for the first time as the champion of Egypt's active involvement in Arab nationalism within a week of the "Heads of the Agreement" signed with Britain in July 1954.[3] But it took the seminal events of 1955 to bring home this promise—in

21

both senses—to the public, and as late as December 1954, furious masses demonstrated in front of the Egyptian embassy in Amman against Gamal Abdel Nasser, persecutor of the Muslim Brothers.

On 21 February 1955, King Hussein arrived in Cairo for a six-day visit in Egypt. He was received by Abdel Nasser, who invested him with the Grand Cordon of the Order of the Nile, a distinction dating from the British protectorate.[4] At the end of the visit, its outcome and its purpose were announced: Hussein's bethrothal to his distant cousin, the Sharifa Dina 'Abd al-Hamid, a Cambridge University graduate then living in Cairo and a university lecturer of English literature there. The marriage took place two months later. A more suitable match could not have been conceived. Tradition and modernity were admirably united in the bride's person: she was a Hashemite princess (the Hashemites customarily married within their extended family), strictly brought up but with the best education the West had to offer. Her maturity—she was twenty-six, the bridegroom not yet twenty—added an aura of dignity. And in the background hovered the benevolent figure of Abdel Nasser, who, although obviously not the matchmaker, blended into the picture as associated with the couple's bliss. Hussein's first marriage forms no recognizable part of his or his country's political history; yet it has its poignancy all the same. Hussein divorced Dina a little more than one year after the marriage and three months after the birth of their daughter. He probably did so at the prompting of his mother, Queen Zayn, with whom Dina was on bad terms.[5] An underlying reason may have been Dina's lively interest in the social concerns of her new country, which did not meet with her young husband's approval.

Hussein's visit of 1955 was the only time that he met with Abdel Nasser without stress and strain. In political terms, it was the end of Hussein's age of innocence, for 1955 is the year that created Abdel Nasser as he is now known in the history of the Middle East. The mileposts dispersed throughout 1955 are many. On 28 February, an Israeli raid in the Gaza Strip, in retaliation for Egyptian-sponsored fedayeen incursions,[6] exposed to the world the feebleness of Egypt's defense or—in an interpretation less damaging to Egyptian self-respect—the culpability of the Western powers in leaving Egypt powerless against an aggressive enemy. The Gaza raid came a week after David Ben-Gurion's return to power as Israel's defense minister, from his self-imposed exile in the Negev. It has been argued ever since that the Gaza raid ended any real chance of an Israeli–Egyptian *modus vivendi*, but it also has been contended with equal conviction that it did nothing of the sort. Subsequent developments that have little to do with the Palestine conflict tend to support the latter conjecture, for conjectures they both remain. However that may be, the traumatic impact of the incident on Abdel Nasser is a matter of record.

On 4 April 1955, Britain joined the Turkish–Iraqi alliance of 24 February—soon to be styled the Baghdad Pact—and thereby served notice that it had added its weight to a regional, and in fact a global, arrangement that was designed to tie the Arab world anew to the West and that would place Hashemite Iraq into an Arab leadership position. Both results were equally abhorrent to Abdel Nasser and the new spirit of independence and populism that he represented.

On 15 April 1955, Abdel Nasser arrived at Bandung in the company of Indian Prime Minister Jawaharlal Nehru to attend the conference of Afro-Asian states there. Abdel Nasser returned thirteen days later as a leader of what became known as the Bloc of Positive Neutralism, the nonaligned countries of later decades, with a personal image less stellar only than those of Tito, Nehru, and Zhou Enlai. This outcome may have been a surprise even to Abdel Nasser. But the time was ripe for the concept of a Third World outside the struggle of the superpowers but, through its history and value systems, "neutral against" the West, and Egypt was a superpower in the Arab world, where other contenders for leadership at the time were unimpressive. Yet there is no doubt that Abdel Nasser's triumph at Bandung was also very much his own triumph: his presence and his way with the media. His testing as a statesman was still to come, and as we now know, he proved to be deeply flawed. But when he returned to Cairo in 1955, he had gained a stature all his own in the Middle East. The photograph of the closing reception at Bandung, in which Abdel Nasser is seated at one table in the company of Nehru and Zhou Enlai,[7] is as revolutionary a status symbol as can be found in recent history.

On 27 September 1955, Abdel Nasser announced his "Czech" (in reality Soviet) arms deal. It is difficult today to relive the shock at this bold declaration of independence from the West. Abdel Nasser had long hesitated. All through the summer, he continued to negotiate for Western armaments, with few results. Then he announced his decision, and it hit a political jackpot. The Western powers grumbled and acquiesced in evident respect. A new epoch had begun for the Arab East: the stranglehold of Western imperialism was broken, by the one power that the West feared and that, by breaking this stranglehold, had shown itself the friend of the Arabs.[8] The Arab public was delirious. The Jordanian Chamber of Deputies, elected the year before with all the safeguards that Chief of the

General Staff John B. Glubb's Arab Legion could provide, sent Abdel
Nasser its enthusiastic approval.[9]

The progression was orderly: from the mortification of Israel's Gaza
raid; through the challenge of the Baghdad Pact; then on to Bandung, a
triumph but "political" and hence still lacking the satisfaction of implied
violence; to, finally, the achievement of the Soviet arms deal, combining
the magic of weaponry with the humiliation of yesterday's masters and
the prospect of having the best of both worlds.

The first fruits of the arms deal in the Arab official sphere were mutual
defense pacts signed between Egypt and Syria on 20 October 1955 and
between Egypt and Saudi Arabia on 27 October.[10] These pacts, worthless
in retrospect as instruments for war, were in their time formidable as a
challenge. They created Egyptian–Syrian and Egyptian–Saudi Arabian
supreme councils, war councils, and joint commands, each with a commander in chief, which might prove operational for all anybody could
guess. They emphasized, even more than did the constituent bodies of
the Arab League, the centrality of Egypt on the Arab scene (the Egyptian
minister of war, Major General ʿAbd al-Hakim ʿAmir, Abdel Nasser's
intimate, was promptly selected as commander in chief of the Egyptian
and Syrian Joint Command). These pacts created the interdependence of
Egypt and Syria, which was to remain a determinant of the Middle East
until 1967. And lastly, Hussein must have noted the potential significance
of the alliance that hugged Jordan from then on: not immediately hostile,
but a fearful threat should he deviate from the line laid down by Abdel
Nasser.

At the end of 1954, the world at large, and the Arab public in particular, still saw Abdel Nasser as a Little Egyptian, a not particularly significant leader. He was a competent technician and an ambitious and un-
scrupulous intriguer; his victorious struggle with Neguib had demonstrated
that. But Abdel Nasser lacked the common touch, or so it seemed, and
in the Arab world his credentials were less than inspiring, if not downright bad: in regard to Islam, this could be seen in his bloody confrontation with the Muslim Brothers; and in regard to anti-Westernism, his
recent agreement with Britain was no doubt a solid achievement, but its
luster was dimmed somewhat by its consideration of British imperial interests too. Abdel Nasser's will to fight Israel was diminished in the Western
press by stories that an accommodation was taking shape. His social commitment was tarnished by the Kafr Duwayr killings of August 1952, and
his agrarian reform was settling into bureaucratic routine. As for *qawmiyya ʿarabiyya*, there was as yet no reason to regard Abdel Nasser's
devotion as more than the required lip service.

A year later, Abdel Nasser's image, and especially his self-image, had changed beyond recognition. He had become the answer to a dream, a messiah to the masses yearning to be free. And into this exhilaration broke the news that Hussein of Jordan might lead his kingdom—piffling, patched together, and downright illegitimate in the eyes of many—into another military alliance with the West.

On 12 January 1955, Prime Ministers Adnan Menderes of Turkey and Nuri al-Sa'id of Iraq announced at Baghdad that their countries were about to conclude a military alliance that other Middle Eastern countries were invited to join (except Israel, by means of an escape clause.) Britain's adherence was already a foregone conclusion. The three partners early on considered Jordan a desirable acquisition.[11] The reasons were the need for more Arab members to bolster Iraq; the patron–client tie between Britain and Jordan that made Jordan seem an easy target (in addition to the dynastic tie between Jordan and Iraq and the traditional friendship between Jordan and Turkey); the high reputation of the Arab Legion[12] and the supposed imperviousness of its beduin soldiers to seditious propaganda; and the inducements that Britain might offer to Jordan—the revision, perhaps the abrogation, of the 1948 Anglo-Jordanian treaty, military hardware, an increased subsidy, and aircraft for Jordan's embryonic air force (Hussein's pet project).

From the start, Hussein was of two minds. The inducements attracted him, apart from the compliment paid to his country's importance. He certainly was not "soft" on Communism or the Soviet Union. But Hussein had a lively premonition of Egyptian hostility, should Jordan join Iraq in a new regional alliance, and of the unpopularity with Jordan's Palestinian majority of such alliance. Hussein also knew that under existing arrangements, Jordan had all it needed for its security and that joining the Baghdad Pact offered little that was of real national significance. Tawfiq Abu'l Huda, Jordan's prime minister, opposed accession. He was a staunch believer in the Hashemite Entity. But ever since the Iraqi intrigues in the wake of Abdallah's death, when he had steered Jordan through the worst crisis it had yet experienced, he thought Iraq more dangerous to Jordan's independence than Saudi Arabia or Egypt was. It was a position that after the death of Ibn Saud in 1953, and with Abdel Nasser's profile still being shaped, was not as absurd as it came to look within the year. But although Abu'l Huda must be counted as one of the few statesmen that Transjordan and Jordan have produced, it was Hussein who had the last word in policy making, and on 28 May 1955 Abu'l Huda resigned, never again to hold office.[13]

The result was that until the autumn of 1955, Jordan's position regarding the Baghdad Pact was reserved. The British Foreign Office certainly favored an early accession, or at least a decision on principle, but it would not exert pressure; it also had no wish needlessly to provoke Abdel Nasser. The unsympathetic attitude of the U.S. Secretary of State John Foster Dulles, who feared, with good reason, that the accession of Jordan would accelerate Jewish demands in the United States for guarantees to Israel, left its mark, too. But all this changed with the news of the "Czech" arms deal in late September 1955.

The Turkish government went wild with apprehension. Abdel Nasser clearly was about to sell out to the Soviet Union and so had to be confronted by a solid Arab bloc to his northeast: Lebanon, whose President Camille Chamoun was a friend of the West; Syria, whose government was known to favor a military pact with Egypt and must be turned out, by fair means or foul; and Jordan. Turkish diplomacy was not then known for its subtlety, and Turkey's leaders started to warn any Briton likely to have a say in the matter that the time had come to twist Hussein's arm. It took some time, but it appears that Turkey's Foreign Minister Fatin Rustu Zorlu convinced Britain's Foreign Secretary Harold Macmillan when they met at Baghdad for a Baghdad Pact Council meeting on 21 November.[14] Macmillan, in turn, convinced Prime Minister Anthony Eden, who disliked antagonizing Abdel Nasser at a time when Anglo-Egyptian relations seemed to be improving. But when Eden was convinced, he got into a state of mind that foreshadows that during the Suez Canal nationalization crisis of the following year, and the heat was on. It was symptomatic of the mood in London in those days that the "chiefs-of-staff were instructed to prepare plans for military action against Israel—including sea-borne invasion—if Israel attacked Jordan."[15]

In Jordan, the Circassian notable Saʿid al-Mufti, by then active only in his resistance to changes, had replaced Abu'l Huda. His timidity (and his precarious health) might have been compensated by Hussein's choice for minister of the interior, Hazzaʿ al-Majali of the loyal Kerak clan, who was known as a partisan of Iraq and who did not object to improving Jordan's military, financial, and international standing by trading what was, after all, only one British tie for another. Hussein was won over by promises of gain and prestige, as well as by a Turkish state visit to Amman in early November. But he still had a nagging doubt about the wisdom of joining the pact, and when it became known in London that Egyptian Major General ʿAmir was about to descend on Jordan, the Foreign Office decided on a spectacular gesture.

At Macmillan's suggestion, Eden sent to Amman General Sir Gerald Templer, chief of the imperial general staff—who was known for having ruthlessly suppressed Communist guerrillas in Malaya—in order to "push Jordan over the brink."[16] It was believed that Templer—his personality and his status—would flatter Hussein, who "fancied himself a soldier."[17] However Hussein might have felt—and as he had been so recently at the Royal Military Academy at Sandhurst, it may have been true—the choice was a mistake. Templer was very much the bluff soldier, with no innate respect for native potentates and politicians, and from the first, he felt his position in Amman to be somewhat undignified.[18] Publicity in Britain was handled ineptly.[19] The Soviet *New Times* scored a telling point when it spoke of Templer's "brazenness" (12 December 1955). In any case, by 6 December, when Templer arrived in Amman, nothing could have changed the excitement of the Egyptian and Syrian media and hence the mood of the public. Yet the presence of a British general presuming to dictate policy to an Arab state supposedly sovereign but in fact in British bondage worked wonders to demonstrate the character of the British connection.

The appearance at Amman at that time of two very important Egyptians magnified the imprudence of Templer's visit. ʿAmir and Colonel Anwar al-Sadat—a minister of state, editor of the free officers' daily *al-Gumhuriyya*, and secretary general of the Islamic Conference[20]—visited Jordan from 30 November to 3 December, and from 11 to 14 December, respectively. Their timing could not have been better. Here appeared authentic fighters for Arabdom and Islam, while imperialism had sent out its delegate to subvert a member of the Arab and Muslim *umma*. Their message was clear, even though they did not blatantly rail against what still seemed to be the policy of their official hosts.[21] The "press" they had in Jordan was all they could hope for, and their visits did more than a little to condition Jordan for the sixteen months that followed.[22]

In the meantime, Templer in Amman brought out all the inducements that he had been empowered to make, chiefly military hardware and the necessary financial props plus the abrogation of the 1948 treaty. He stressed that Jordan's joining the pact imposed on it no terms respecting Israel. He refrained, after some soul-searching, from invoking Britain's "ultimate threat" of withdrawing its support from Jordan, which he was authorized to make. (He also knew that Hussein was to be awarded the honorary rank of air vice-marshal after the accession agreement, but Hussein was not told.) Prime Minister al-Mufti expressed his consent on principle but was afraid of the repercussions at home and abroad, which seems in retrospect not as "weak" a position as the irate Templer thought at the time.

Finally, on 13 December, Templer was handed an informal counter-proposal drafted by a Jordanian cabinet committee: Jordan would join the pact, but its accession would not impose any obligations outside Jordan's own frontiers, and in the future the Arab Legion subsidies were to be paid into the Jordanian Treasury, instead of into the British-controlled Arab Legion bank account in London.[23] These proposals were not rejected out of hand as a basis for discussion, although the British Treasury would clearly have fought the second demand tooth and nail. But the counter-proposal was outdated by the time Templer had the leisure to consider it: that same day, the four West Bank ministers in the Jordanian government tendered their resignations, but Saʿid al-Mufti resigned instead. On 15 December, the king appointed to the premiership the minister of the interior, Hazzaʿ al-Majali, who was determined to procure Jordan's accession on the terms proffered by Templer, possibly with some embellishments.[24] On 14 December, Templer had left Jordan with a sense of personal failure but certain that the objective would be obtained after all.

The composition of the new Jordanian government, and of Majali's chief objective, was known by 15 December. On the following day, riots broke out. Glubb was at first doubtful about their seriousness. The king was more apprehensive, but he too was not prepared for what followed. By 17 December, the country shook as it had never done before, and was never to do until after the Six-Day War. Even the conservative south of the West Bank and Transjordan was not spared, and in faraway Aqaba, a mob sacked the American Point Four depot. The refugee camps erupted, a rare and ominous occurrence, as they were easy to control and tightly guarded as a matter of routine. In Jerusalem, consulates were attacked, and the French and Turkish consuls were wounded.[25] A general strike was declared in Amman; it may not have been "general," but it certainly impressed the authorities. The opposition climbed on what appeared to be the bandwagon and convened a "national congress," with "constitutional" demands that were outrageous in the Jordanian context. The police halfheartedly contained the riots—some observers thought them sympathetic—and there is no doubt that they were caught unprepared. So was Glubb. Charles Duke, the British ambassador, and Thomas Wikeley, the British consul general in Jerusalem, believed that if the army had been brought in to shoot at the crowds, the riots would not have got out of hand.[26] Whether or not they were right, it was not a traditionally British attitude, and it shows their sense of shock. However, by the evening of 19 December, when Hussein summoned Duke to inform him that an immediate accession to the Baghdad Pact had become impossible,[27] the British adjusted with remarkable ease, as though they were glad to have an excuse for abandoning a course in which they no longer had faith. Majali resigned on the following morning, 20 December.

Hussein dissolved parliament and called for elections, officially in order to decide on the Baghdad Pact. It was a risky decision to announce in the accelerating crisis. He then appointed a caretaker government headed by the elderly Ibrahim Hashim, who by birth was a Palestinian from Nablus but who had lived in Amman since the early days of the amirate, a lawyer not known as an activist, although he had served in Abdallah's inner circle for decades. This quick succession of events all within one week was viewed as a dramatic defeat of the regime, and an uneasy quiet ensued. Then, it seems, Hussein realized the danger in which he had put himself: the pact indeed might be beyond redemption, and good riddance, but a showy victory by all the enemies of the Entity, domestic and foreign, had to be reversed. Both Glubb and Samir al-Rifa'i, Hashim's deputy prime minister, may have had a part in convincing him, but most likely Hussein's gut reaction played the decisive role.

On 5 January 1956, a decision of the Diwan Khass, the Supreme Council for the Interpretation of the Law, declared the dissolution of parliament invalid on a technicality, and hence it canceled the elections.[28] A court decision setting aside a royal decree was unprecedented, and there are indications that the Diwan Khass acted on a hint from Hussein, advised perhaps by Ibrahim Hashim, who had much experience in Jordanian constitutional law, such as it was. The reversal of the decision to dissolve parliament was understood as stemming from the government's fear of elections. The riots broke out with redoubled violence, but now the regime was ready. Hussein demonstrated for the first time his brutal determination after earlier indecision had brought him to the brink of disaster.[29] Glubb brought in the army, and the soldiers cleared the streets and sealed off the camps, quite easily although with considerable bloodshed, which was not entirely one-sided. One British officer, Lieutenant Colonel Patrick Lloyd, was killed at Zerqa. Hashim resigned, gladly by all accounts, and Rifa'i succeeded to the premiership on 8 January 1956, immediately declaring that Jordan would not join "a new pact." The onus for the violence with which order was restored fell on Glubb rather than on the king, although this may not have been Machiavellian premeditation on the king's part.

When the second bout of riots was at its height, the British government decided to build up its strategic reserve in the Middle East. On 10 January, the War Office announced that paratroopers would be flown to Cyprus on 12 January "as a precautionary measure to increase the number of troops at the disposal of the commander-in-chief [Middle East Forces] for the protection of British subjects in the area, should the need arise." *The Times* surmised that the cause for the decision was the situation in Jordan and the possibility that Israel might use the preoccupation of the Arab Legion for its own purposes.[30] But by then, the crisis was over. No British reinforcements were flown in from Cyprus, although the defense of the Mafraq airfield in northern Jordan was strengthened by a contingent from a Royal Air Force Regiment in Iraq.

No doubt the Egyptian media and Saudi money abetted the riots. It is difficult today to realize how great the influence was of the Cairene broadcasting station of the "Voice of the Arabs" (Sawt al-ʿArab), with its star commentator Ahmad Saʿid, on the Arab East, from its inception in 1954 until the breakup of the Egyptian–Syrian union in 1961. Suffice it to state that in Jordan during those years, the Voice of the Arabs, followed at a distance by the Egyptian press, was a factor with which the authorities always had to reckon and which in a crisis could always act as the proverbial match in a powder keg. The Templer riots were the first occasion when they did so.

In addition, until Saudi Arabia and Jordan became political allies in 1957, some people claimed to know how much Saudi money had been channeled to Jordanian manipulators, street thugs, politicians, journalists, and the population at large.[31] Still, besides these two external factors, the rage, fear, and disappointment at the perceived diversion of the state's resources away from Israel to the Soviet Union, by means of another tie with the hated West, were genuine. On a less rational plane, the pact was seen as a trick to achieve a settlement with Israel, if not an alliance. One important aspect of the episode is that a major policy decision was influenced by popular action. But in the longer view, Hussein's surviving the crisis is even more noteworthy.

On 2 February 1956, Glubb sent a top secret memorandum to General Templer in which he spelled out the lessons of recent events.[32] What would have been rank heresy to Glubb before, he now pondered: whether the Arab officers of the Arab Legion should turn to politics as a means of safeguarding the Hashemite monarchy. In that case, the British commanding officers, including Glubb himself, would have to leave first, and Arab officers would have to be appointed to their posts, although professionally the Arab officers were by no means ready as yet. Glubb mentioned that this contingency was "extremely remote," but he was clearly attracted by the idea. A copy of the memorandum went to the British ambassador in Amman, but not to King Hussein.

2

Glubb's Ouster and Its Aftermath

On 1 March 1956, King Hussein dismissed Lieutenant General John Bagot Glubb, chief of the general staff of the Arab Legion.[1] With him were dismissed Glubb's closest assistants, Colonel W. M. Hutton, his chief of staff, and Colonel Sir Patrick Coghill, director of General Intelligence. Also, eight British commanding officers were suspended, apparently those who had been most active in suppressing the riots in January. The British government ordered all the remaining British officers in executive positions to relinquish their commands immediately. Glubb was escorted out of Jordan by air the following day; it was a royal favor that the original few hours' notice was extended even that much. Because Glubb had served in Jordan on the basis of a personal understanding—not a formal contract[2] or on loan from the British army—neither he nor the British government had legal redress.

The dismissal came like a thunderbolt for Glubb, for British Ambassador Charles Duke, and for the British government.[3] They should have been prepared. Reports from the British embassy at Amman during 1954 and 1955, based on direct observations by the ambassador and Glubb himself as well as rumor, repeatedly mention the king's outbursts against his British mentor, half-reconciliations, speculations concerning Glubb's possible supersession, and Glubb's own doubts whether he could go on for long.[4] The reports were regarded soberly enough at Whitehall, but it is clear that they were just not recognized as anything more than speculation. But when they did materalize, Eden, beside himself with rage,[5] and Selwyn Lloyd, who had succeeded Macmillan as foreign secretary at the end of 1955, assumed that Abdel Nasser had instigated Glubb's ouster and that he had probably known in advance of the dismissal—even orchestrated the occasion to coincide with Lloyd's stay in Cairo, as an additional twist of the lion's tail.

It is certain that Abdel Nasser did not persuade Hussein to dismiss Glubb, and he may have been as surprised as everybody else.[6] But the dismissal delighted him and seemed to him as yet another proof of his ascending star. (The parallel to the Iraqi coup d'état of 14 July 1958 is close. Then, also, Abdel Nasser was widely assumed to have engineered the event, whereas in fact he had little, if any, advance knowledge of the plot, and certainly not of its timing. But in Iraq, as in Jordan two years before, it was Abdel Nasser who by precept and example set the scene.)

Hussein himself later made much of a plan to defend the West Bank that Glubb proposed and Hussein rejected. This plan would have concentrated the Arab Legion in the mountainous heartland, a concept that was sound strategically but dangerous politically. (Both men remembered the evacuation of Lydda and Ramla by the Arab Legion in July 1948 but had learned different lessons.) Hussein also resented Glubb's foot-dragging over the "Arabization" of the Arab Legion: the commands of most regiments and all higher formations, as well as all sensitive staff appointments, were still in British hands, which could be defended on professional grounds but which certainly made for much bad blood among the army officers (except the beduin). Glubb himself stressed the inevitable friction caused by the generation gap—he was almost old enough to be Hussein's grandfather—and Hussein's jealousy of Glubb as the "uncrowned king of Jordan," as named by some Western media.

Another cause for resentment was the procedure by which the British annual subsidy for the Arab Legion, then about £12 million, was paid into a special Arab Legion account at the Ottoman Bank in London. For years, the Jordanian government had been trying to have the subsidy paid into its own Treasury. Officials at the Foreign Office had some sympathy for the request, "since it is understandable that the Jordanian Government feel that it rubs in their 'client status.'" But prudence prevailed: Jordanian accounting was deficient; there would be delays in arms procurement; and, above all, Glubb was strenuously opposed.[7]

But something else was at work. After the visit of General Sir Gerald Templer and the suppression of the riots that had erupted in the wake of that visit, the latent distaste in Jordan for Glubb burst into a hate campaign orchestrated from Cairo. (Again, this campaign did not extend to the beduin. However, in the mounting tide of anti-British excitement, the beduin counted for less than at any other time.) Image and reality, ideological pretense and political logic, coincided. The British "commander" of an Arab army was slaughtering the people in order to chain another Arab state to the imperialist chariot. The image made sense, and Cairo used it relentlessly.

Hussein hardly figured in this buildup, for here, too, rationality and expediency coincided. It seemed so obvious he was being managed that it served no purpose to blow him up beyond his natural size. But as far as Hussein did figure in the Egyptian and Egyptian-inspired media (and in a minor way he did figure), he was cast in a role that endangered his survival, just as it endangered his self-respect: the boy king strutting about in his gaudy uniform by the grace of British ministers and their local agents, that is, a nonperson. Once the role had been determined, it might be difficult to change. In regard to Glubb and the British connection, it was not easy for Hussein to break away from what the tradition of his house, material advantages, and his own upbringing indicated; nor was Hussein by nature insensitive or ungrateful. But the danger of remaining identified with Glubb in the public mind grew from week to week, together with the jeering and the goading from Cairo and Damascus; the insinuations of his aide-de-camp, ʿAli Abu Nuwar, were a mere concomitant. It needed a tactless step by Glubb—asking Hussein to sign the discharge of officers considered unreliable, without having bothered to ascertain Hussein's pleasure beforehand—and Hussein took the plunge.[8] He acted with all the determination he later demonstrated in crises of his own timing. Hussein knew the risk; that is, he could not know how Glubb, the British officers in Jordan, the British government, or the beduin soldiers would respond. It is only in hindsight that he appeared to overreact to the situation. Hussein also knew that if he wavered after taking the plunge, he would be lost. It is certain now, however (and it was accepted by the British authorities within a week of Glubb's ouster), that Hussein had seen Glubb's dismissal as not affecting Jordan's relationship with Britain, and so he was understandably shocked by the first furious reactions from London.

An outburst of popular enthusiasm unprecedented in the annals of the Hashemite monarchy followed, together with the wholehearted approval of Egypt, Syria, and Saudi Arabia.[9] In Britain—in both the cabinet and the media—the first expressions of resentment were equally unrestrained. Glubb may have changed history in that he immediately set out to dampen the indignation.[10] It is frightening to imagine, in the light of Britain's moves during the next year, what Eden might have done and the British public might have condoned if Glubb had demanded retribution. But he did not, and Sir Alec Kirkbride, the retired British minister in Amman and second not even to Glubb as a recognized authority on the Jordanian scene, added his voice in favor of restraint.

After the first furor had passed, the cabinet sent Kirkbride on a secret mission to Amman to sound out Hussein. Kirkbride returned and reported to Eden what he had been convinced of even before he left London, that Hussein was anxious to maintain the British alliance.[11] Eden acquiesced. The Anglo-Jordanian treaty remained intact, and the British subsidy continued uncurtailed. But the remaining contingent of British officers in the Arab Legion indeed could not stay and so departed within three months with as much dignity and show of goodwill as the circumstances permitted. (A few British officers stayed on as instructors and experts; they left during the Suez war.) Thus the resulting *ta'rib*, Arabization, did not lead to a breakdown.

One aspect of Glubb's ouster, in retrospect the most incisive, has generally received too little attention. It is that his departure changed Jordan's place in people's minds. So far nobody, enemies or friends (and indeed friends above all), had regarded Jordan as anything but a British dependency. But after 1 March 1956, this had changed. Jordan would soon again be identified as a Western ally, and rightly so. But no observer could ever again ignore Jordan's essential emancipation from British tutelage. Alongside many vital continuities, the drama of 1 March 1956 is the deepest cut in the history of the Hashemite state between 1948 and 1967.

Hussein tried hard to sustain the admiration he had gained among Arab nationalists, without cutting his lifeline to Britain. Before he became certain how the British government would respond, Hussein sounded out the United States as an alternative supplier of armaments. His argument was that if the United States did not agree to his proposal, he would have to turn to Czechoslovakia. This was his first attempt at playing the Soviet card. Hussein seems to have hinted that his survival depended on a prestigious arms source, no matter where that was.[12] But he did not get far with the United States, and the normalization of Jordan's relations with Britain soon after proved that an American alignment was yet unnecessary for either side.

The British side reached within a few days of Glubb's exit the conclusion that "resentment at the ignoble manner of his dismissal [had] led us to take a more tragic view than is justified, of the significance of this episode of Anglo-Jordanian relations generally."[13] That is, the Anglo-Jordanian treaty, together with an institutionalized British foothold in the Arab Legion, was to be saved if at all possible, and the summer and autumn of 1956 saw prolonged and exhausting negotiations in Amman toward this aim. The Jordanian government proved amenable, although hard bargaining. However, the army proved obstructive, and with the advent of the Nabulsi government in late October, the British gave up. Hussein kept in the background throughout, wisely.

Hussein's actions during the following months show that he was aware of the dangers of Abdel Nasser and *qawmiyya*. But he also loved his new popularity. He made lavish gestures calculated to enhance the Jordanian army's newly established Arabism: formations were given names stressing the Hashemite connection, and ranks were adapted to the Egyptian and Syrian pattern. The Arab Legion, with its imperialist connotations, was changed to the Jordan Arab Army. The police—the core of the Arab Legion for many years—was separated from the army command and put under the general security administration, accountable to the minister of the interior. This obeisance to constitutionalism seemed innocuous when, in July 1956, the prime minister was Ibrahim Hashim and the minister of the interior was another trusty war-horse, the Transjordanian 'Umar Matar from Ma'an in the south. (Hussein had been toying for over a year with the idea of "demilitarizing" the security services. The British—in Amman and Whitehall—were apprehensive but did not go beyond uttering doubts about the wisdom of the step.) In a different alignment, this change would expose the keystone of the Entity to dangerous forces. But Hussein rarely preferred a hypothetical tomorrow to a certain today.

The promotions that swept through the army were unavoidable, and for a time they buoyed up the most volatile element of the political public: the young officers of urban origin, who by virtue of their British superiors stood first in line to take over the vacated appointments. 'Ali Abu Nuwar became a major general and, in May 1956, the chief of the general staff, upon the retirement of Radi 'Innab. Abu Nuwar's fellow Salti 'Ali al-Hiyyari—in contrast to Abu Nuwar, an experienced regimental officer—became his deputy as head of the general staff branch. Ma'n Abu Nuwar, a cousin of the new chief of the general staff, was appointed to command a brigade group, the operational formation that was the backbone of the army on the British model.

For the opposite reasons, the beduin officers were slower to reap the fruits of *ta'rib:* as a group, they had had respect for their British commanders, and for some time they were uncertain of their qualifications to replace them, until prompted by the example of the young urban officers. The dangers inherent in the new situation—the progression from those expectations that Hussein could satisfy without undue risk to those he could not, and the tension building up between the beduin and the young urban officers—took time to develop.[14]

To his Arab colleagues, Hussein followed up Glubb's exit with protestations of brotherhood and cooperation that were no less politic for emanating from the euphoria that he genuinely felt (to judge by the sense of his pronouncements at the time). He met President Shukri al-Quwatli

of Syria and King Faysal of Iraq; he exchanged messages with Abdel
Nasser and King Saud. But Hussein made a point of not favoring one
Arab camp over another, as he was chary of offers that might make him
dependent on another set of masters, possibly less dependable and more
exacting than those from whom he had just become emancipated. He
declined a joint offer from Egypt, Syria, and Saudi Arabia to replace the
British subsidy, arguing that it was foolish to release Britain from its chief
treaty obligation, an argument as well turned as it was specious. Hussein
did, however, sign in the following months—with Egypt, Syria, Lebanon, Saudi Arabia, and Iraq—a series of bilateral agreements on defense
cooperation that looked good and left Jordan unfettered. He specifically
refused an invitation from Abdel Nasser, Quwatli, and Saud, made immediately after Glubb's departure, to join their entente, because it was
"a stand to be limited to the four of us only."[15] It is an oversimplification,
however, to dismiss this insistence on pan-Arab coordination, including
Hashemite Iraq and Chamoun's Lebanon, as mere lip service to an ideal.
Although this contention served Hussein tactically and was congenial to
the intellectual atmosphere of the time, it represented his honest conviction.

Hussein may well have been satisfied with his control of affairs when
Abdel Nasser's nationalization of the Suez Canal threw the Middle East,
and other parts of the world as well, into another frenzy on 26 July
1956.

On 26 June 1956, Hussein had dissolved the Chamber of Deputies
"because of the loss of cooperation between [the Chamber] and the Executive."[16] It was an ironic end for an assembly handpicked by Abu'l
Huda less than two years before, but ever since the Bandung conference
the deputies had shown an unhealthy enthusiasm for Abdel Nasser and
his own system of alliances that Hussein just then was having some trouble evading. It was also ironic that Prime Minister Saʿid al-Mufti, the
head of the executive supposedly denied cooperation by the legislative,
followed it into limbo on that very day. But the executive was really
Hussein, and Mufti had tended to be unreliable ever since he had been
secretary to the National Congress opposition in the late 1920s. (This,
Mufti's fourth cabinet, was his last, although he continued to serve for
years in responsible ministerial posts.) Mufti's successor was Ibrahim
Hashim, who presided over an impeccably loyalist cabinet entrusted with
organizing the general elections that had become necessary. It is doubtful
whether Hussein would have called the elections if he had envisioned the
political intoxication engendered by the Suez Canal nationalization ex-
actly one month later.

As elsewhere in the Arab world, Abdel Nasser's resounding insult to the West—for that was the import of his nationalization speech—received resounding acclaim throughout Jordan.[17] Hussein himself voiced his approval; he may have shared some of the pride.[18] As before, political excitement engendered political action on secondary fronts. While Britain and France were moving toward cutting down Abdel Nasser—Eden yearned for the fighting days of his pre-Munich youth, and the French government attributed to Abdel Nasser a key role in its Algerian troubles—Jordan's armistice line with Israel erupted in bloody raids and counterraids.[19]

Public pressure in the West Bank, in conjunction with the prevailing election fever, forced Hussein to join the military pact of Egypt and Syria, which he had up until then avoided doing without too much embarrassment. The agreement was signed on 24 October 1956, after the election results were known but with the caretaker cabinet of Ibrahim Hashim still in office. It was a serious setback for Hussein, especially as he could not risk offsetting it by a simultaneous deployment of Iraqi troops in the East Bank, as he had originally intended. A British warning to Israel delivered on 12 October that Britain would honor its treaty commitments to Jordan undoubtedly relieved Hussein of his immediate fear. But he knew, what the Israelis cannot have known, that throughout 1956 the British commitment was progressively reduced, hastened by Glubb's ouster and Nasser's canal nationalization.

By mid-October, when Britain had decided on military action against Egypt but before Eden had actually agreed to France's proposal to cooperate with Israel, the following limitations were made clear to Hussein and Abu Nuwar: the *casus belli* would be determined in London and not Amman; no British ground forces would be involved, except possibly to cover the northwest of Transjordan and Aqaba, with its British garrison, by seizing Elath; and the British commitment was to protect Jordan from "invasion" but not "raids."[20]

Inevitably, it has been suggested since that the British démarche at Tel Aviv was a feint to draw attention away from its impending collusion with Israel. This is not so. On 12 October 1956, the secret Sèvres meeting, which sealed the three-party understanding, was still nine days away. Even then, the partnership was distasteful to both the British and the Israeli sides and was brought about only by a temporary need and by French persuasion. There is no doubt that the threatening note of 12 October represented a real feeling in London during those days, perhaps with a vague idea of conscience tribute paid to the Arab cause. If this sounds irrational, it is because British policies were not entirely rational at this time.

It has been often said that the elections for the fifth Chamber of Deputies, held on 21 October 1956, were the freest that Jordan had ever experienced and would ever experience.[21] It certainly was Hussein's will that they should be so; he believed, in his continuing sense of well-being, that "[no] more than two or three extremists [would be] returned." A detailed amendment at that time to the Elections Law ensured that the elections would be safe from improper interference.[22] When the elections were held, three months later and in a changed atmosphere, Hussein's intent was still accepted as genuine, with a vengeance.

Of many examples, an editorial in *Gumhuriyya*, the organ of the Egyptian free officers, stated: "Elections nowadays [in Jordan] are held with no orders from the British ambassador, and thus they will always be held [in future]."[23] But the analysis and the implied directive were wrong inasmuch as it was not the ambassador who commonly directed elections, and Sadat, the editor of *Gumhuriyya*, failed as a prophet. But the complacency is still remarkable for its own sake, even though the elections were not all that free. First, the authorities did make their expectations known. Second, those politicians found objectionable—candidates and others—were removed from the scene, usually by being called up for National Guard training; most seem to have been Communist sympathizers. But there was certainly less interference at every stage than was common, and it is fairly certain that voting and scrutiny as such were not impeded. More important, the public at large felt free and voted as they wished, unless the prevailing atmosphere is seen as itself discouraging freedom of choice. There is irrefutable evidence of Saudi financing and Egyptian-inspired agitation. But in contrast with the customary interference by the Hashemite authorities—straightforward and bureaucratic—the Saudi–Egyptian factor in the elections was not, by its nature, measurable.

Even so, the question of why Hussein permitted the elections to go forward still remains. On later occasions, he showed less concern for "popular feeling" even when there was less danger to all he stood for than in the autumn of 1956. His own explanation—"[It was a] period of experiment . . . I had decided, therefore, that younger and promising politicians and Army officers should have a chance to show their mettle . . . and I wanted to see how they would react to responsibility"—smacks of retrospective rationalizing.[24] The better, and more complex, answer seems to be that he was basking in the afterglow of popularity engineered by the ouster of Glubb; that he hesitated, as was his nature, to take up a challenge unless crisis overtook him; and that, unexperienced as he still was, he did not forsee the election results and their significance.

3

The Nabulsi Interlude

A prime principle of the Hashemite Entity was that it was the cabinet's function to carry out the policy determined by the Hashemite ruler. The Nabulsi cabinet denied the validity of this principle in accordance with a widespread wish to adopt a new approach, presumably better suited to the spirit of the times and in the expectation that Hussein would acquiesce. Also, the cabinet had a new political orientation: pro-Nasser, pan-Arab nationalist, "radical."

The general elections of 21 October 1956 were governed by several election laws based on the 1952 constitution that gave the vote to every Jordanian male citizen of twenty and over. The candidates could, and usually did, act within limits of the Political Parties Law of 1955, which regulated the licensing of parties at the cabinet's unrefutable discretion.

The "opposition," a loose term for those candidates known to be critical of the Hashemite Entity, obtained an absolute majority in the Chamber of Deputies, by returning twenty-two deputies out of forty (including those of the Muslim Brothers, not nominally a party). To these must be added two "independents": Dr. Da'ud al-Husayni, a relative of the former Mufti Hajj Amin al-Husayni, who was still outside the pale of toleration, and the maverick chief of the Banu Sakhr, 'Akif al-Fa'iz, representing the northern beduin. In reality, the weight of the opposition was not what its numbers implied, although this is partly a historian's hindsight. First, it lacked cohesion. The Muslim Brothers, which with four deputies was the second largest group, hated Abdel Nasser more than they did Hussein. The National Socialist party occupied the largest place in the new chamber, with twelve deputies. The two Ba'thist party candidates were returned in the elections, and the three Communists, camouflaged as a National (*wataniyya*) Front, were indeed radicals in the accepted sense. But

their personalities soon proved them unfit to be leaders in a popular rising. The stigma of atheism that clung to the Communists also cannot have
been helpful. The most convincing opposition candidate (in retrospect,
at any rate) who was returned, the Tahrir party member Ahmad al-Da'ur,
was the deputy for Tulkarm in the West Bank, but his ideological credentials were ill suited to day-to-day cooperation with secular "revolutionaries." The Qawmiyeen, or Arab Nationalists, like the Muslim Brothers, were not registered as a political party. They did not participate in
the elections because they were the organized nucleus of Palestinians who
saw the Hashemites as archtraitors to the Cause, and at that time they
were all-out Nasserites. But when necessary, they stood, of course, with
the opposition.

Considering the atmosphere and the prevailing stresses, the loyalists
made a respectable showing in the elections. Their number—sixteen, ignoring the Muslim Brothers—and their geographical distribution gave them
a measure of credibility as a loyal Rump, should the day of reckoning
arrive. However, it is too much to attribute to the young king the far-
sightedness of considering this possibility when on 27 October he invited
the chairman of the National Socialists, Sulayman al-Nabulsi, to form
the new government.

Two days earlier, parliament had convened, and the Chamber had elected
as its speaker Hikmat al-Masri, another National Socialist. At the elections, Nabulsi had been a candidate for Amman and had been narrowly
defeated by his "Entity" and Muslim Brothers rivals. (The Jordanian constitution did not preclude nonmembers of parliament from serving in the
cabinet.) Hussein's invitation, although naturally understood as addressed
to the leader of the winning political party, carefully avoided spelling out
such revolutionary innovation. Rather, it was Hussein's trust in Nabulsi's
"loyalty, sincerity and willingness to serve the country" (*al-balad*) alone
that made him offer Nabulsi the premiership. The importance of this
phrasing cannot be over-stated: it was the king, and not the electorate,
who had chosen the prime minister. Nabulsi obviously saw his mission
differently, and his interpretation might yet be accepted. But as far as
Hussein was concerned, Nabulsi's source of authority—the king—was
clear and was stated as being so. Otherwise, the royal invitation was full
of platitudes. *Qawmiyya*, the issue that had brought Nabulsi and his allies
into office, is not mentioned. But Nabulsi, in his letter of acceptance,
referred to the "Nationalist [*qawmiyya*] ministry" he would establish.[1]
The cabinet, as proposed by Nabulsi and appointed by Hussein included
six National Socialists and one Communist ("National Front")—the min-

ister of agriculture, 'Abd al-Qadir al-Salih. The most conspicuous member proved to be the West Banker 'Abdallah al-Rimawi, secretary of the regional (i.e., Jordanian) command of the Ba'th party, who was appointed minister of state for foreign affairs. (Nabulsi himself doubled as foreign minister.)

The cabinet was hardly formed when the Sinai war broke out on 29 October 1956. Hussein's immediate solidarity with Abdel Nasser was undoubtedly sincere. Hussein also demanded to declare war on Israel, which Nabulsi refused.[2] The contretemps gave Hussein an argument for both his nationalist ardor and his opponents' cowardice, for years to come. We shall never know whether Hussein expected to be held back, and it is as intriguing as it is profitless to speculate on what might have happened if he had had his way: Britain would certainly not have come to his aid.

Otherwise, official Jordan combined zeal with circumspection. Syrian, Saudi, and Iraqi army contingents were invited into Jordan on the strength of the various existing defense agreements. (The Iraqis were summoned on Hussein's insistence. Nabulsi demurred but later relented.)[3] The allied troops arrived from 3 November onward—when any apprehension regarding Israel's invasion plans was past—and were deployed in the East Bank only. Jordan servered its relations with France but preserved those with Britain; in any case, there was no effective ambassador at Amman. Sir Charles Duke (recently knighted) had just concluded his term and was about to leave. His successor, (later Sir) Charles Johnston had not yet arrived. The Jordanian government announced that it would not permit British installations in Jordan to be used against Egypt—these included the air bases at Amman and Mafraq, naval installations at Aqaba, armored detachments at Aqaba and Ma'an, and ordnance depots at Zerqa. The population was less reserved. There was looting at the Zerqa base and a strike at Mafraq that caused discomfort to the garrison. On 13 November, the Iraq Petroleum Company (IPC) pipeline leading to Haifa was blown up near Irbid, in obvious imitation of the much more serious sabotage of the pipeline crossing Syria. (No oil had flowed through the southern Jordanian branch of the pipeline since 1948. But a trickle of oil from the torn pipe gave rise to a rumor that the British had secretly been supplying Israel with oil with the connivance of the Jordanian government; the rumor had to be officially denied.) The British showed extraordinary forbearance, culminating in an assurance from the British government to Jordan on 2 November that the Royal Air Force at Mafraq would not be used against Egypt.[4] Because at that time the British and French military action against the Suez Canal was still building up, this assurance demonstrated a lack of determination that could hardly fail to be noticed elsewhere.

The political history of Jordan from the cessation of hostilities in the Canal Zone on 7 November 1956 until Nabulsi's dismissal on 10 April 1957 revolves around two hubs, a situation unique in the experience of Hashemite Jordan.

Nabulsi and his politically active colleagues envisaged, and worked for, a state that was integrated into the Arab East, then gaining its freedom from the Western yoke under the inspired guidance of Abdel Nasser. They were conscious that this integration might lead to the surrender of Jordanian sovereignty. But until that happened, they stood for a regime with the king as a decorative convenience, as long as he behaved; cooperation with Egypt and Syria; suspicion of Iraq, and overt sympathy with the Soviet Union, to spite the West as much as for any other reason. It was a somewhat ambiguous position for the majority group in the government, the National Socialists, and it did not give them strength for the troubles ahead.

Hussein stood for a state that not merely was independent as a nonnegotiable principle, but also, under the stresses of the Cairo–Baghdad polarization, had struck out on its own. Optimally, this meant a nation-state based on the native people of Transjordan, both the settled and the beduin. The king, who was the origination of all policy, might be persuaded to compromise to some extent for the time being but would certainly retain his position as the arbiter in difficult or controversial questions.

The Western connection, at any rate, was necessary, with Jordan as ally rather than client, and it would have to be nursed back to its former vigor, after the crises of 1956. But because the British tie had been compromised politically, probably without redemption, the United States was the obvious alternative. The Soviet Union was the patron of Communism, and thus objectionable on that ground as much as on the purely political consideration of Jordan's need to resolve its disagreement with the West.

In the Arab world, Egypt and Syria should be kept on good terms within these limits; otherwise their goodwill was expendable. Hashemite Iraq was a natural ally, but no patron. Saudi Arabia shared many principles with Jordan: the dynastic enmity was a thing of the past as far as Hussein was concerned. King Saud's alignment with radical Egypt and Syria was a momentary aberration caused by the Buraymi dispute and jealousy of Iraq, which would disappear once the Saudi king and his advisers realized their own true interests. Thus Hussein.

The first major business before the new government was the Anglo-Jordanian treaty. Until the Suez crisis, public opinion in Jordan had not unanimously desired the treaty's abrogation. All the opponents of the Entity did condemn the treaty, but others advocated merely its revision. Their chief spokesman was Samir al-Rifaʻi, who had the courage of his convictions to an extent uncommon among his contemporaries. The argument was that Jordan could not give up the British subsidy—£12 million a year—without a firm alternative. Admittedly, a "subsidy" had become unworthy of Jordan's sovereignty, but would not an equivalent sum suffice to pay for Britain's "lease" of its bases under the treaty?

In the wake of the Suez crisis, the case for total abrogation became overwhelming. In regard to the subsidy, an offer had come from Egypt, Syria, and Saudi Arabia after Glubb's dismissal and had then been politely declined. Now the proposal was renewed. On 27 November 1956, Nabulsi announced in the Chamber that the government would negotiate abrogation of the treaty, "having reached agreement with the Arab sisters who offered [financial] assistance."[5] The Chamber concurred, with thirty-nine votes out of forty. (The lone dissenter again was Ahmad al-Daʻur of the Tahrir party, who declared that he could not believe the government was in earnest.)

The British government had by then made up its mind that the treaty was an expensive bauble. But it was wise to refrain from gestures of disdain that might needlessly thrust Jordan deeper into Abdel Nasser's arms.[6] Nabulsi's declaration of 27 November cleared the way. December brought some sparring between Amman and London and the beginning of British and American contacts concerning an American "takeover" of Jordan. Arab capitals started to back up Nabulsi's announcement. Characteristically it was Syria, the poorest of the three would-be subsidizers, that led the way.

The promises were formalized in the Arab Solidarity Agreement, signed at Cairo on 19 January 1957.[7] Egypt, Syria, and Saudi Arabia bound themselves to "share the expenditure arising out of the obligations falling on the government of the Hashemite Kingdom of Jordan as a result of the policy of cooperation and solidarity for bolstering the Arab existence and independence. . . ." This expenditure was fixed as £E (Egyptian pounds) 12.5 million annually—roughly the British subsidy as it then stood—with Egypt and Saudi Arabia contributing £E 5 million each, and Syria £E 2.5 million. The agreement was for ten years, the unexpired portion of the British treaty. The two chambers of the National Assembly at Amman approved the agreement unanimously. At the same time,

American sources quoted "United States officials" as doubting the allies' ability to fulfill their obligations, explicitly including that of Saudi Arabia.[8]

At the same time, the Iraqi forces were maneuvered out of Jordan. They had never been welcomed by the Nabulsi government, and the technique it used to get rid of the troops is intriguing. In mid-November—the Suez war was over except for the shouting—Rimawi told the Egyptian Middle East News Agency that under the tripartite pact there could be no non-Jordanian forces in Jordan except those of Egypt (there were none) and Syria. A fortnight later, Nabulsi, always more cautious than his junior colleague was, broadcast his demand that the Iraqi troops be put under the command of General ʿAbd al-Hakim ʿAmir; if the demand was refused, they would have to leave.[9]

This was more than an injury to the king's policy of balancing his Arab commitments; it also was an insult. The Iraqi contingent in Jordan had been placed under the command of Major General ʿAli al-Hiyyari, who, under Glubb, had been the first local officer to command a British-paid regiment in the Arab Legion, as distinct from the "Hashemite Regiment," a sort of Household Guards, maintained out of the regular Jordanian budget. The Iraqi government indignantly rejected Nabulsi's demand, as no doubt it had been expected to, and thus was duly requested to withdraw its forces from Jordanian territory. The withdrawal was completed on 10 December 1956. At the same time, official and nonofficial Jordan joined the chorus, led from Cairo and Damascus and with echoes in Baghdad, and denounced Nuri al-Saʿid as a conspirator against Arabdom. If anything could indicate to anxious observers in the West the revolution ostensibly overtaking Hashemite Jordan, it was the passivity of the kingdom's traditional guardians in the face of this onslaught on the kindred regime at Baghdad. Hussein kept silent. He may have been waiting for the storm to blow over, but it is more likely that he did not know how to deal with an embarrassment that was not, after all, of immediate significance. He did not cut his personal line to Baghdad, and it is probable that Hazzaʿ al-Majali served at this time as Hussein's go-between for discreet communications.

On the home front, the government moved carefully at first. Since the last days of October 1956, many "Nationalist Guidance Committees" (lijan irshad qawmiyya) had been set up in the West Bank and a few in the East Bank. They were composed of representatives of the government coalition parties, yesterday's opposition. They gave "guidance" on the issues of the day but proved ineffective as catalysts for action. In the first half of December 1956, the government retired a few senior officials "who were not sincere nationalists" or were "corrupt" or "inefficient."[10] One of them was Saʿd Jumʿa, later the prime minister during the Six-Day War, and another was Ihsan Hashim, a relative of Nabulsi's predecessor. In late November, Anwar Nusayba, a former minister of defense, was detained for a few days on suspicion of hiding arms. But the real offense of those affected was their Hashemite orientation, particularly their reputed Iraqi sympathies.

All these events were put into context by an interview with Nabulsi by the *New York Times* on 15 December 1956.[11] "Jordan cannot live forever as Jordan," Nabulsi is quoted as stating. Jordan "must be connected militarily, economically and politically" with one or more Arab states. The "one Arab state" in Nabulsi's mind was believed to be Syria, although he did not say so explicitly.

It seems that Nabulsi, by thus wishing away his country's independence, first impressed on Hussein that parliamentary rule, with its attendant shift toward political parties, would be a mortal risk. Hussein thus began taking contingent precautions, but in public he still kept silent.[12]

On 18 January 1957, the day before Hussein and Nabulsi signed the Arab Solidarity Agreement in Cairo, American newspapers discussed a State Department release that Jordan had just "informally" asked the United States to step up its financial aid under the Point Four program from the 1956 ceiling of $8 million to $30 million in fiscal year 1957. This sum also generally equaled the British subsidy, which was about to end. "It was indicated that Jordan wanted the increased funds on a 'no strings attached' basis." This comment leaves no doubt that the request was politically rather than economically motivated and that the State Department regarded it with some sympathy.[13] This is the first overt indication of the new alignment that was to supplant Jordan's historic connection with Britain.

For years, the United States' interest in the survival of Jordan had been rather passive: Jordan, although clearly "of the West," was viewed by Washington as virtually a British protectorate. And even after Hussein had proved, by Glubb's dismissal, that he had a will of his own, he still had to prove first his will and then his capacity to keep Jordan in an alignment acceptable to the United States, in a Middle East hostile to such an alignment. On the other side, President Eisenhower and Secretary of State Dulles had acquired a distaste—which they never were to lose—for Abdel Nasser as a pacemaker of Soviet influence, and hence "as an evil influence."[14] This feeling persisted even during the Anglo-French Suez invasion when, in the eyes of official Washington, Anthony Eden

and Guy Mollet, the French prime minister, had done their best to make
Abdel Nasser a hero in the eyes of the Third World and much of the free
world.

Eisenhower's and Dulles's disappointment with their British and French
allies did not stem from fundamental differences. It was merely that in
this case, Britain and France had chosen "a bad time and incident on
which to launch corrective measures."[15] (Also, of course, they had de-
ceived the United States in a matter of major policy.) In the American
view, the European allies' misjudgment gave the Soviet Union a chance
to establish a military presence in the Middle East, whether directly as a
participant in the United Nations Emergency Force born out of the crisis
or indirectly through "volunteers."[16] An early result of this perceived military threat was the State Department's reiteration of support for the Baghdad
Pact, on 28 November 1956.[17] But this alone did not create the emergency; it was the greater ease with which Soviet influence might leap
across the barrier of the Northern Tier—Turkey, Iraq, and Iran—that
made the Suez crisis so dangerous.

The outcome was the Eisenhower Doctrine, which the president enunciated before a joint session of Congress on 5 January 1957. Its objective
was to procure "emergency measures . . . to fill the power vacuum left
by the sharp reduction in British and French influence" in the face of
Soviet and Communist infiltration or takeovers. It proposed to offer economic and military assistance, including American military forces, to any
nation in the Middle East that requested such aid in order to maintain its
independence in the face of "International Communism." It also authorized the discretionary executive use of $200 million for economic and
military assistance. Congress passed the Eisenhower Doctrine on 7 March
1957. As early as the second week of December 1956, "the Joint Middle
East Planning Committee [reporting to the U.S. Joint Chiefs of Staff]
was directed to develop plans for defense of the Middle East area under
conditions of general war, including the ear-marking of specific forces."
This directive led in the second week of January 1957 to intense staff
activity concerning the doctrine's eventual implementation.[18]

The question of which countries accepted the Eisenhower Doctrine is
one of the gaps in the history of the Middle East in 1957. A common
conjecture is that it was Lebanon (i.e., President Camille Chamoun) only,
or Lebanon and Saudi Arabia. Eisenhower himself officially included Libya
and Ethiopia as well, although his reasoning is not quite clear—all these,
apart from the Baghdad Pact countries, America's de facto allies.[19] In the
post-Suez atmosphere, however, the doctrine suggested a kind of bribery
attached to the offer of aid, which made even those eager to participate

hesitant to commit themselves. Hussein, at any rate, later that year boasted of having declined even to invite to Jordan Eisenhower's Special Representative for the Middle Eastern Area for the doctrine, Ambassador James P. Richards. By then, of course, relations between Jordan and the United States obviated the purpose for which Richards had been dispatched.

But even so, the Eisenhower Doctrine helped shape events in Jordan. It was instrumental in leading Hussein onto an anti-Communist track, which did much to "sell" him to the American public as a client in whose survival it was worthwhile to invest. Until this time, Hussein had been portrayed as a playboy-potentate to those American politicians who had a notion of his existence at all.[20] Not that Hussein's deprecations of Communism were false: He was a convinced Muslim, and to him, Communists were, above all, atheists, apart from their being enemies of the Hashemite Entity.

But Communism was not Hussein's main worry in January 1957. Instead, it was another instance of Hussein's ability to dress up a genuine, but not decisive, concern of his in order to fall in with the major concept of a major ally. The Beirut, Damascus, and Cairo presses assigned the first U.S.–Jordanian contacts to December 1956, when an American secret agent approached Brigadier Muhammad al-Muʿayta, the Jordanian military attaché in Beirut and Damascus, who indignantly refused him. The story may help explain Muʿayta's (who came from an impeccably conservative Keraki family) promotion to the directorship of public security by Nabulsi soon afterward (apart from Muʿayta's having been a personal friend of Abu Nuwar).

But what probably is true is the involvement, unpublicized and on occasion denied, of both the U.S. ambassador in Amman, Lester DeWitt Mallory, and particularly the military attaché, Lieutenant Colonel James L. Sweeney, in the intricacies of the evolving relationship with Bahjat al-Talhuni of Maʿan, chief of the royal cabinet, as a go-between for the king.[21] In the early weeks of 1957 were likely also the beginnings of the "CIA payments of millions of dollars," which made headlines twenty years later.[22] It is clear, at any rate, that at the same time, during December 1956, the matter was thrashed out at the highest level between Britain and the United States. Dulles was not at all convinced that the United States' replacement for Britain vis-à-vis Jordan was a worthwhile investment: "In his view the brutal fact was that Jordan had no justification as a state. This of course did not mean that this was the moment to liquidate it."[23]

The British government, by then determined to get rid of the financial burden that the treaty involved, without, if possible, causing the demise of the Entity because of bankruptcy or a Soviet–Egyptian takeover, and well versed in the pecularities of negotiating with Dulles, decided to hand to the United States a fait accompli. The British would tell the Americans "that as from such and such a date the subsidy from HMG will stop"— let the Americans then decide on their reaction.[24] To judge by the result, it was the correct step.

The "reduction of British influence" was translated into international law when the Anglo-Jordanian treaty of 1948 came to a premature end on 13 March 1957. Jordan agreed to make modest monetary payments in compensation for the transfer of British military property.[25] The negotiations had been smooth, despite the warlike noises uttered by the Jordanians in public.

Outwardly, the story of Hussein's break with Nabulsi is the story of their differences over Communism. It was Hussein who decreed that this should be so: the injured innocence that Nabulsi protested was real. Nabulsi was anything but a Communist sympathizer, and his overtures in that direction, never very significant, were partly a gesture toward his partners in the National Front and partly what was then considered obligatory in those Arab nationalist circles in which he wanted to be accepted. But Hussein chose this issue for two reasons: it supported his emerging relationship with the United States, and he could not—the spirit of the times being what it was—advertise that he was not willing to dance to the constitutionalist pipe.

Hussein began attacking Communism in public within a week of Eisenhower's address to Congress. The occasion was an unusually accommodating cable from two Communist (i.e., National Front) deputies. "As an Arab Qurayshi and a Hashemite," the king claimed in his reply of 10 January 1957, "I would sacrifice my blood for the sanctities of my nation . . . [I] will not allow in [the nation's] ranks a place for advocates of materialistic ideologies and principles contravening our religious teachings."[26] Here the pattern is set that recurred time after time in the six months that followed: there could be no coexistence between evil and godliness, between Communism and Islamic Arabism, of which Hussein, by virtue of his descent, was the protagonist appointed by fate. It is also worth noting that in this case Hussein sought out an adversary not quite ready for confrontation.

For the next three weeks, Hussein in his public pronouncements concentrated on godliness rather than evil; in brief, the Hashemite "Great Revolution" of the Arabs was of the Faith.[27]

On 2 February 1957, Hussein sent a message to his prime minister that was immediately broadcast.[28] In it he mentioned Communism by name,

although it was the infiltration of Communist doctrine rather than defin-
able policies that the king decried: he still did not want to provoke a clash,
although he did caution those who "feign loyalty to Arab nationalism
[and] indulge in hullabaloo." The occasion was evidently the appearance,
the day before, of *al-Jamahir* (*The Masses*), a weekly published by the
National Front, and thus the first Communist newspaper ever to appear
legally in Jordan.

In form, the message was no more than the exercise of a constitutional
monarch's right to warn his ministers against what he considered a national danger, Communism. Yet it received immediate and worldwide
attention as the first publicized instance of Hussein's distancing himself
from the Nabulsi government over a major matter. That his anti-Com-
munism was merely part of the truth, and the less significant part at that,
is corroborated—apart from the events themselves—in one brief sentence
tucked away among the pages of rambling about "Zionist Bolshevism":
"We believe in the right of this country . . . to exist."

The government was taken by surprise, as well it might, and it is credibly reported that Nabulsi first learned of the message over the radio. The
following weeks were replete with indignant assertions from him and Rimawi that they were being maligned: that they were not Communists;
that they were true Arab nationalists; and that they rejected alien creeds
from any quarter. For the first time in office they were on the defensive,
and against a charge all the more awkward for its lack of precision.

The same week, Hussein added clout to his admonition. On 5 February
1957, Jordanian security forces stopped the import of the Soviet agency
Tass's daily bulletin, printed in Damascus, and closed its Amman office.
On 6 February, the chief censor ordered the confiscation of all "Communist propaganda" (which included Soviet newspapers) from bookshops
and the removal of Soviet films from cinemas. On 8 February, that day's
issue of *al-Jamahir* was impounded. (The paper was finally closed down
on 25 February.) The domestic significance of these steps lay in their
supervision by Major General Bahjat Tabara, the inspector general of
police and the director of security. Tabara, a veteran Hashemite faithful,
was legally accountable to the minister of the interior, whose assent he
had, in this case, failed to secure. The interior minister, 'Abd al-Halim
al-Nimr, was a party colleague of the prime minister, and Tabara's defiance was duly noted for future action. However, the immediate result,
noticeable in utterances that made their way into the press and radio, was
the marked increase in the ministers' attention to the king. It looks like
a sudden realization that a dangerous contender had been overlooked so
far.

At this time, a process became noticeable that can be loosely described as a political polarization within the officer corps. It was a natural reaction to Glubb's ouster, accelerated by the trend that the Nabulsi government personified. Arabization—an institutional necessity, as the army needed commanders and staff officers to fill the place of the departed British—favored the *hadari* officers, the nonbeduin, as they had the better formal education. They were naturally impressed by the examples of Syria and Egypt, where their peers in age and background had so recently risen to dazzling heights. This was no "Communist infiltration," although it suited Hussein to regard it as such. From the start, there was no rejection of Hussein (in contrast with that of King Faruq in the case of Egypt), so long as affairs moved smoothly in what seemed to be the path of Arab liberation. But Hussein, superior as a politician to all of them, knew his adversaries as soon as he realized the risks he ran.[29]

While the king moved toward a new departure designed to safeguard the Entity, the cabinet pushed Arab unity. There was much overt and even more covert coming and going between Amman, Cairo, Damascus, and Beirut. Conversations were held regarding a customs union with Syria, which gave rise to optimistic prognostications. A statement made on 25 March by the Jordanian ambassador in Damascus, Sharif Hamid Sa'd al-Din, that Jordan "was looking forward to her return to her motherland, Syria"[30] was not perhaps meant to be taken literally. Yet coming when it did and from whom it did—a Hashemite prince making up to the upstart Rimawi—it must have raised eyebrows in Amman. The Egyptian government announced its decision to open an information center in Amman, with branches in Jerusalem and Nablus, "to take charge of Arab propaganda," and in the same vein the Egyptian cultural attaché in Amman "completed his talks with the ministry of education on the scheme to standardize the curricula in the schools."[31] Meanwhile, the military attaché, Major Fu'ad Hilal, cultivated his army acquaintances.

This all was very indirect and restrained, and in retrospect we sense no urgency. But then Abdel Nasser, the man who might have changed the history of Jordan at that time if he had acted on a master plan, had no master plan—as we now know.[32] His sympathizers received no firm direction, and they themselves were uncertain how far they wished to go and how fast.

Slowly, the real issue penetrated the public consciousness through the smokescreen of Communism. On 26 February 1957, Rimawi held a press conference at which he read out a cabinet resolution made three days before, defining Jordan's stand at yet another Arab conference to convene at Cairo.[33] Rimawi's message—upholding positive neutralism and rejecting the Eisenhower Doctrine—was less significant than was his introduction: "We hereby announce . . . the Government's policy. . . . On this basis the Government won the confidence of the Chamber of Deputies." The inference that Jordan was a parliamentary state does not contradict the text of the 1952 constitution (amended in 1954), even though the constitution did not state that policy-making devolved on the ministers rather than the king. But as everybody knew, this assumption negated all that Jordan had stood for as a body politic since its birth, and just as important, no officeholder had ever before dared to make it in public.

From then on, "informed sources" reported "a struggle" between the king and the government. It was usually described as between the pro-Western forces represented by the king and the anti-Western forces represented by the government, which, although not false, was merely one of its parts. Moreover, until Nabulsi's dismissal, the combat was not clear-cut. The very existence of a conflict was denied and admitted and again denied. Once, on 1 April 1957, the government decided at an emergency meeting to resign because of its "inability to stand any longer certain unconstitutional conduct"[34]—the king's of course, although that attribution was left unspoken.

The particular offense against constitutionality was the series of visits to Cairo, Damascus, and Riyadh on which Hussein had sent Bahjat al-Talhuni since February and about which he had not told the cabinet. But the government did not resign, apparently in response to urgent requests from Abdel Nasser.

Hussein's purpose had been to convince the tripartite partners that he would remain faithful to the letter and spirit of the recent agreements, no matter what his relations were with his government.[35] This step looks like common caution on Hussein's part rather than "plotting," although both interpretations are possible and indeed are not contradictory. Hussein's approach worked. Abdel Nasser and President Quwatli were more concerned with Jordan's place in the regional constellation than with Nabulsi's fortunes or Hussein's democratic credentials. King Saud was predictably gratified by the blow dealt to Communism. Abdel Nasser and Quwatli remained on the sidelines for two crucial months, until it became clear that Hussein's personal rule ran counter to their own objectives in decisive respects. And by then, King Saud had changed his alignment.

Nabulsi, again at Rimawi's prodding, announced at a public speech on 24 March 1957 that he intended to recognize the People's Republic of China and then, on 3 April, to establish full diplomatic relations with the Soviet Union.[36] As a vain and compulsive orator, Nabulsi[37] may have extemporized to some extent and said more than he intended to act on.

But whether Hussein was shocked by Nabulsi's intentions or infuriated by his verbal embroideries, here was the perfect way of impressing Hussein's grand new ally, on whom he depended for survival.

At the same time, the radicals in and around the cabinet, angered by the king's growing assertiveness, engineered another coup against "evil counselors." One victim whose dismissal deeply offended Hussein was Muhammad Amin al-Shanqiti, the chief *qadi,* who was disliked as a Hijazi and as an appointment by Abdallah in Transjordan. But this was not what convinced Hussein that time might be running out. Ever since Hussein began to take his own stand in February, it was on Bahjat Tabara, the director of security, on whom he relied in domestic matters. Tabara was an elderly man with about thirty-five years of service; so when the government retired him on 9 April 1957, it was easy to explain the step as nonpolitical, in a rather naive attempt to save the king's face. In fact it was—as everybody knew—an eminently political decision, the most momentous the Nabulsi government had ever taken. It mattered little that Tabara's successor was an old police officer himself, Brigadier Muhammad Muʻayta. With Tabara gone on the authority of a cabinet order, King Hussein had become "constitutional" indeed.

On the next day, 10 April 1957, Hussein dismissed the government. Despite all the weeks of simmering crisis, the step came as a surprise even to relative insiders.[38]

The constitutional pretensions of Nabulsi and his colleagues had roots in the recent past that are not so apparent now. In fact, the Nabulsi government was merely the nadir of the Hashemite kings' hold over their ministers. The process started in 1949 when the conquest of the West Bank placed among Abdallah's retinue Palestinians—lawyers, journalists, politicians—who had an independence of mind to which the king was not accustomed. This, in turn, provided the brake that Abu'l Huda, Rifaʻi, Saʻid al-Mufti, and Mulqi were able on occasion to apply to Abdallah's readiness to reach agreement with Israel. (Abdallah himself is known to have explained the phenomenon by his being "an old man."[39] Although there may be some truth in this explanation, he had never before been in need of a young man's stamina to impose his will on his ministers.) King Talal was weak and had to sustain a "nationalist" reputation, which was in keeping with the spirit of the times, in any case. Hussein, until the Nabulsi experience matured him, was unformed and eager to appear as a liberal, and so his mastery over the government had not been put to a serious test. When the test came, he met it squarely.

II

THE MAJOR TEST

4

The Crisis of April 1957

On the evening of 8 April 1957, the First Armored Car Regiment of the First—Amira 'Aliya[1]—Brigade Group left its camp at Zerqa and took up positions that controlled access to Amman.[2] The commanding officer of the regiment, Captain Nadhir Rashid, with his aide the only *hadari* in a beduin unit, told his men that they were to check the serviceability of their vehicles. Hussein, on finding Basman Palace under something close to siege, heard from Abu Nuwar that he had ordered a security check on traffic from and to the capital. Hussein angrily ordered the regiment back to base and was obeyed. The purpose of "Exercise Hashim" is not quite clear. It was later claimed at the Zerqa conspiracy trial that Rashid had called on Prime Minister Nabulsi to dismiss Bahjat Tabara. This is certainly what he told his officers when he returned to barracks the next morning and Tabara's dismissal became known. But it is just as likely that Rashid made up the story to save his face. The move may have lacked a clear objective. In those days of rumors, plots, and counterplots, Rashid may have intended no more than to flex his muscles and to set the avalanche rolling. The history of the crisis as it soon unfolded bears out this interpretation. If Hussein needed a final warning that a conspiracy was afoot, he had it delivered here with dramatic forcefulness.

By contrast, Nabulsi's dismissal was something of an anticlimax. At noon on 10 April, Talhuni called Nabulsi out of a cabinet meeting and asked him to hand in his resignation. Nabulsi returned to his colleagues and after two hours of discussion, in the presence of Abu Nuwar and Brigadier Mu'ayta, the newly appointed director of security, was empowered to do so. Both Nabulsi's letter of resignation and the king's letter of acceptance are courteously worded; the only deviation from the trivial is Nabulsi's reference to his resignation as coming "at the command of the king."[3] There can be little doubt that the stories that Nabulsi resigned expecting Hussein to be unable to find a successor are true; although to what extent this was a cover for Nabulsi's and his colleagues' own lack of resolution is anybody's guess.

The following three weeks are the most crucial period in the history of the Hashemite monarchy.[4] At the outset, the king—true to a pattern that was to be repeated—played down the crisis: it was "routine" and certainly unrelated to Jordan's brotherhood with the "liberated" Arab countries.[5] Needless to say, this did not impress anybody. Two observations are of special importance. One is the angry but evidently genuine optimism of Nabulsi's partisans abroad and, conversely, the faintheartedness of the Entity supporters.[6] This is not surprising, considering the prevailing trends during the preceding two years. The other observation is that Nabulsi's backers and well-wishers everywhere spared the king in their outbursts, then and for many weeks to come. Hussein's real part in the evolving crisis could not be understood as yet, and he was good at dissimulating.

During the next two weeks, Hussein experimented with cabinets that would be acceptable to "nationalist" and "progressive" opinion without challenging the traditional political order in Jordan. It is probably hindsight to see these cabinets, or the attempts at cabinet formation, as deliberately temporary until Hussein was ready for a radical advance. The support for Nabulsi was wide and deep, and it did not necessarily go hand in hand with disdain for the monarchy. It was not easy for a young king with a desire to be loved to adopt a policy predicated on repressing a popular mood.

In regard to the army, at first Abu Nuwar and his friends certainly provided Hussein with an argument for treading warily, and after they were gone, the reliability of the beduin units paradoxically allowed Hussein to reassure the political public that clamored for "progress."

Finally, there was no lack of candidates for the premiership who might possibly avoid an all-out clash. The three whom Hussein tried out all had proved in the past that they might achieve broad toleration, at least for a while, but under no circumstances could they prop up the king in a major struggle. The lightweight among the three proved to be Sa'id al-Mufti, who, as leader of the Circassian community, was at the same time tied to the regime in interest and gratitude and fearful of incurring the wrath of the yet unbeaten radicals. Mufti had been fairly successful during his past brief terms as prime minister when he had occasionally listened to complaints by the opposition without ever standing up to the king. But now he lost his nerve, apparently under threats from Abu Nuwar, after he had presented Hussein with a tentative list of cabinet members.

From the viewpoint of the previous Nabulsi cabinet, the most acceptable candidate was 'Abd al-Halim al-Nimr, Nabulsi's minister of defense and the interior and his unofficial vice-premier. Nimr was the representative National Socialist: he was a Salti notable—Salt and Irbid were the centers of urban opposition to the Hashemites, with traditionally close links with Syria and the West Bank—a member of parliament under Abdallah, a minister under Talal, a regent when Hussein was a minor, and a founding member of the National Socialist party. He got as far as presenting the king with a cabinet list, which was similar to Nabulsi's.[7] Its one significant difference—interesting for its own sake and as an indication that Hussein was negotiating in earnest—was the omission, at Hussein's request, of 'Abdallah al-Rimawi, who was replaced by another leading Ba'thi, Dr. Munif al-Razzaz, a Syrian by birth and arguably a more dangerous opponent of the Entity.[8]

Nonetheless, and probably gaining confidence from the "Zerqa plot," Hussein broke off and on 15 April 1957 returned to Dr. Husayn Fakhri al-Khalidi, whom he had already approached after Nabulsi's dismissal. Khalidi was an unexceptionable choice on many counts. A former mayor of Jerusalem, he would be the first true Palestinian prime minister.[9] His "nationalist" credentials were excellent. He had been exiled by the British in 1937 as a supporter of Hajj Amin al-Husayni, joined the Arab Higher Committee when it was reconstituted in 1945, and, like many adherents of Hajj Amin, went over to Abdallah in late 1948. All the same, the erstwhile government parties at first rejected him as prime minister— remember they were close to a majority in the Chamber, and other members could be expected to join them in a motion of no confidence. Here too the Zerqa plot seems to have had a sobering effect, and on 15 April 1957 Khalidi presented his cabinet to Hussein, with Nabulsi as foreign minister. The letter of appointment he received seemed to be much closer to the Egyptian–Syrian nationalist line than Nabulsi's had been six months before, and Khalidi responded in similar terms.[10] There is no evidence that in appointing the Khalidi government, Hussein acted in bad faith.

Whatever "Exercise Hashim" had intended to achieve, it alerted Hussein and the "free officers."

The free officers had appeared in Jordan, as in other Arab monarachies, soon after their prototypes in Egypt achieved power and glory in the coup of 23 July 1952. In one respect, their position in Jordan was peculiarly advantageous: nowhere was the "imperialist" hold over the army as visible. Also, no other country in the Middle East that aspired to modernity, from Libya to Iran, had as traditional a political culture. When Hussein assumed his regal responsibility in May 1953, his youth, his style, and his close friendship with Captain ʿAli Abu Nuwar, the free officers' representative, lent them a sense of royal favor, in itself remarkable. The ouster of Glubb and the departure of the British officers seemed to add to their importance and certainly propelled them, as individuals and as a group, into higher positions. It is clear now, as it could not possibly have been then, that this good fortune held the seeds of their downfall. It accentuated the rift between them and the beduin officers who were raised according to different standards. It denied the free officers the schooling of adversity. It obviated the need for their organization. It prevented the evolution of a genuine leadership. The obvious candidate, Abu Nuwar, lacked the gift of true authority, but at the same time his presumption stymied the emergence of better men. His official position as chief of the general staff kept him from the single-mindedness necessary for a task of such magnitude as the successful subversion of the Entity. And last, the very magnitude of this task was not known until the confrontation.

The idea of subversion may have taken root as late as the beginning of 1957 when it became clear to intelligent and politically motivated men that the king no longer was conforming to the ways and aims of the free officers in Jordan or elsewhere in the Arab East, whether above or under ground. The waning influence of the Nabulsi government and its demise on 10 April undoubtedly worried the free officers, and Hussein's apparent irresolution during the following days may have convinced them that they had an opportunity that they could not ignore.

An opportunity to achieve what? We shall never know for certain, as Hussein snatched it into his own hands. "[A] deeply laid, cleverly contrived plot to assassinate me, overthrow the throne and proclaim a republic"[11] is Hussein's later assessment. Was this true? Or was it merely a "plot situation" that Hussein managed to defuse in time, the assessment of most Western observers? Or was the "plot" all Hussein's, as Arab analysts, not merely the Egyptian and Syrian media at the time, even now tend to believe? The evidence is convincing that Abu Nuwar did actually conspire to overthrow the monarchy through the action of the free officers led by himself, although he may not have intended to assassinate Hussein, and one may discount Hussein's claim that the plot was "deeply laid" and "cleverly contrived."[12] And since it is the victor who usually writes history, the common description of the Zerqa affair is probably overdramatized in order to show Hussein as more heroic, and Abu Nuwar as more craven, than both really were.

In the evening of 13 April, Hussein received a visit from his uncle, Sharif Nasir bin Jamil, a Hashemite Entity hawk, accompanied by beduin officers who had just arrived from Zerqa. They brought sensational reports. At that very moment, *hadari* officers were inciting certain regiments to march on Amman and "save the country" by arresting or even assassinating the king, and the commander of the beduin Amira ʿAliya Brigade, Maʿn Abu Nuwar (ʿAli's cousin), was sending troops on a wild-goose chase into the desert, without ammunition. Hussein, suspicious after Saʿid al-Mufti's breakdown that day, confronted ʿAli Abu Nuwar, who professed amazement. Hussein then took Abu Nuwar with him to Zerqa, barely half an hour's car ride away, to investigate. In the meantime, excitement at Zerqa had risen to fever pitch. Bloody brawls broke out between beduin and *hadari* units. In some cases, beduin soldiers assaulted and locked up free officers. Other beduin soldiers poured out onto the Amman road, cheering al-Husayn and vowing death to Abu Nuwar. They met the king on the road. Hussein addressed them, embraced them, and swore brotherhood; and for all the histrionics, the emotion on both sides was genuine. Abu Nuwar, cowering in the staff car, feared for his life and asked to be returned to Amman. Later that night in an interview with the raging king, he begged for permission to go abroad. The next morning, he was escorted to the Syrian frontier with his family and went to Damascus.[13]

In Abu Nuwar's wake fled, or were arrested, the officers who supposedly were his co-conspirators. Prominent among those fleeing was the chief of military intelligence, Colonel Mahmud al-Musa. Abu Nuwar's deputy, the director of the general staff branch Major General ʿAli al-Hiyyari, was appointed chief of the general staff. Colonel Habis al-Majali, a distant cousin of Hazzaʿ, a hero of the 1948 war, and formerly the commander of Abdallah's own Hashemite Regiment, was promoted and made head of the general staff branch.[14] The Zerqa plot was over.

The Zerqa plot is important for two reasons. Hussein and the army's beduin contingent had recognized their mutual dependence. And Hussein emerged as the "plucky little king," an oversimplification that nonetheless was to serve him well.

Khalidi's cabinet lasted for nine days. It was in an impossible position from the outset, quite apart from the real difficulties of the situation and

Khalidi's unsuitability to take charge in a crisis. Khalidi saw himself politically and constitutionally in line with Nabulsi, with some damaging harshness eliminated, and so, evidently, he was seen by the king. But this view was not shared by the public that had supported Nabulsi. The public's contention of a few days earlier that Khalidi, despite all his credentials, had been chosen as a tool of the king and his traditional advisers, seemed to be confirmed by the Zerqa affair and Nimr's repudiation. The Ba'th and the Communist parties came out against the new government; the National Socialists—whose chairman, Nabulsi, was also foreign minister—wavered. The Qawmiyeen, who had kept their distance even from Nabulsi as lacking in Arab-nationalist decisiveness, were frantic. A new wave of unrest started to build up that, given the indeterminate character of Khalidi's government, threatened to surpass all that Jordan had known so far. That the Muslim Brothers—no mean force—made signs of joining the king, sharpened the specter of civil war. And that Abu Nuwar's successor, Hiyyari, should choose this moment, 20 April, to defect to Syria, where he alluded to "foreign military attachés'" (presumably the American, Lieutenant Colonel James L. Sweeney) taking over the country, merely underscored the general deterioration. (But it was clear even then that Hiyyari was a victim of nerves rather than an intriguer like Abu Nuwar.)

The declaration of martial law on 24/25 April 1957 was more than just another turning point; it was Hussein's return to those principles of governance that he never relinquished thereafter. No later crisis compares with those days in April 1957 in the abrupt change of direction.

It was not the Zerqa affair that brought "constitutionalism" to an end. Whether or not Hussein really considered it a full-fledged plot, he had taken it in his stride. Rather, it was the Patriotic Congress (al-mu'tamar al-watani), which convened in Nablus on 22 April 1957, that convinced Hussein that nothing but brute force applied at once—with minimal time allowed for preparation—could save him and the Hashemite state from disaster. The congress spanned the opposition that had identified with the Nabulsi administration: the government coalition of National Socialists, Ba'th, and Communists; Independents connected with Amin al-Husayni; and the Qawmiyeen. The Muslim Brothers and the Tahrir party were not represented. The former had thrown in their lot with Hussein for the time being, and the latter disliked identifying with secularists of any hue. Functionally, the congress was an extension of the Nationalist Guidance Committees. Its venue at Nablus was logical, too: Nablus had been the center of Palestinian nationalist sentiment even in mandate times.

The congress issued a "proclamation to the people" (*bayan*) over the signatures of seventy-seven participants; twenty-three were members of the Chamber of Deputies, and most of the remainder were doctors and lawyers. The proclamation was openly distributed; after all, Khalidi's government was still in office, with Nabulsi in a top post. The resolutions appended to the proclamation included a call for federation with Syria and Egypt; a call to "all authorities" (*sulatat*) to respect the constitution "in letter and in spirit"; a call to purge the administration of "all conspiratorial, traitorous, and corrupt elements"; a call for the repeal of "all measures and detentions taken against patriotic officers"; a call for unity between the people and the army; a call for a general strike and "general demonstrations" on 24 April 1957; and the formation of an executive committee composed of sixteen members.[15] The proclamation spelled out the dissolution of the Entity, the identity and the political alignment of its successors, and even the day of the crash. Hussein took in all points, and on the day he was ready.

By coauthoring these resolutions, the National Socialists as a body had crossed the divide. On 23 April, Nabulsi departed from the cabinet. On 24 April, Khalidi, after apparently having promised the congress's executive committee to implement the resolutions, tendered his resignation, the promise having been immediately disallowed by the king. He could not continue in office, Khalidi said in his letter to the king, because his government no longer represented a majority of the Chamber. This did not matter, as by then Hussein's mind was made up, except that it showed how public opinion, which swayed Khalidi, still regarded the balance of power. That day, the scheduled strikes and demonstrations took place in Amman and elsewhere, especially in the West Bank, although both were rather less than "general." More serious, and departing more from the accepted pattern of street politics, were the bloody battles between Muslim Brothers on one side and "leftists" and "nationalists" on the other, especially in Jericho and Nablus. But overall, they did not matter either, although they provided an ostensible reason for restoring order. At 1:30 A.M. on 25 April 1957, martial law (*idara 'urfiyya*) was declared throughout Jordan.[16]

Jordan's foreign relations during the three weeks after Nabulsi's dismissal on 10 April and until the consolidation of martial law demonstrate Hussein's skillful diplomacy in support of an overall policy. He made certain of the assistance of the two powers whose interests fundamentally matched his own, Saudi Arabia and the United States, by playing on their fear of Communism, even though this was not Hussein's principal concern, rather than by appealing to them for help in regaining effective rule—which was not their principal concern. Hussein neutralized the two powers whose interests fundamentally clashed with his own, Syria and Egypt, by convincing their rulers that what was afoot in Jordan was a genuine domestic affair that did not affect Jordan's place among the "liberated" Arab countries. He was brilliantly successful. Within days of Nabulsi's dismissal, statements were quoted from, or attributed to, official Washington that expressed encouragement of Hussein's struggle against aggression and discouraged the suspected aggressors, chiefly Syria.

The public effect in the United States was considerable: the media, which had already given up on Hussein, conceded that there was a fight ahead and that its outcome was not a foregone conclusion. This, in turn, created an atmosphere in which an American commitment to Jordan— political, military, and financial—became acceptable to the public. When Hussein struck, American opinion (as far as it cared) was prepared for declarations from the White House and the State Department that "the independence and integrity of Jordan [were] vital" to the United States[17] (even though Jordan had never accepted the Eisenhower Doctrine or even invited the president's ambassador-at-large to pay a visit to discuss it); for the hasty dispatch of units from the U.S. Sixth Fleet to the eastern Mediterranean; and for a special allocation of $10 million to Jordan with "considerable latitude" in spending it.[18]

Saudi Arabia's help consisted of declarations of support; an offer to put the Saudi contingent in southern Jordan under Hussein's command, an offer that in the hectic days of Abu Nuwar's and Hiyyari's defections might well have persuaded would-be mutineers to hedge their bets; and timely monetary support, reported to be $250,000,[19] independent of the subsidy due to Jordan under the recent four-party agreement. If Hussein indeed needed it to pay the debts of his beduin soldiers, as was reported at the time, then he may have made one of the great bargains known to history.[20] The semiannual Saudi portion of the subsidy, £2.5 million in hard currency, followed in days, on 22 April, and well before the American payment. Four days after the strike, Hussein flew to Saudi Arabia for a one-day visit, to give an account of his success to King Saud and cement the alliance.

Syria, with its brigade still stationed near Irbid—always a tense area— could have made trouble for Hussein during the April crisis. On the day of Zerqa, the brigade seemed restless but was restrained on orders from Damascus. Prime Minister Sabri al-ʿAsali paid tribute to Hussein's astuteness rather than his own when he asserted, after both the Zerqa affair and the imposition of martial law, that the king "had not departed from the liberal [i.e., liberated] policy pursued by Egypt, Saudi Arabia and

Syria."[21] And as for Syria's first half-yearly installment of the subsidy to Jordan, he said, the Chamber would ratify its payment in the framework of the 1957 budget when it convened at the beginning of May. (It was never ratified.)

Official Egypt, too, took care to disregard the signs that Hussein was about to depart from the group of "liberated" rulers, in what seemed to be a mixture of optimism, lingering disdain, bad intelligence, and concern with more pressing business. True to form, in the matter of the subsidy, Egypt was slightly more forthcoming than Syria, but not the point of actually paying it.[22] The media, among which the government-directed broadcasting station Sawt al-ʿArab was by far the most effective, certainly identified with the "progressive forces" in Jordan. But they did not vilify the king or even question his good faith, nor did they call on the people to rise up against him. Had they done so, the demonstrations of 24 April would have been worse, and resistance to martial law more fierce, as at the time of Templer's visit, when the Egyptian government had a clear interest in mobilizing its sympathizers inside Jordan.

The royal takeover came off smoothly. It was not, of course, the first time that the Arab Legion had gone into action to preserve the Entity; indeed, that had been its prime *raison d'être* since 1949. What is remarkable is that the *qawmi* period of Jordan—the Nabulsi government and the year that preceded it—had not affected the loyalty of the rank and file once the order for action was given; that staff work at all levels was meticulous—Glubb in his Sussex exile surely must have felt a glow of pride—and last, that the plans drawn up were carried out efficiently, ruthlessly as far as necessary, but essentially without bloodshed. The political and the military authorities acted together, a tribute to the king who directed both as their unquestioned master, but a tribute also to the potential the Hashemite monarchy could mobilize with proper leadership. It also was proof that the Entity's enemies did not monopolize the political will of the country, although undoubtedly they were much more vocal and more articulate than were its supporters.

Hussein had manipulated the exact hour of Khalidi's resignation in what was itself a minor feat of management. When Khalidi handed in his letter in the early evening of 24 April 1957, the successor government was literally waiting in the wings, in the royal palace. Its head again was Ibrahim Hashim, about whom nothing was remarkable by then except his unfailing readiness to serve as a respectable stand-in. The cabinet's power, which was considerable, lay with the deputy prime minister, again Samir al-Rifaʿi; the minister of the interior, Falah al-Madadaha; and the minister of defense, Sulayman Touqan. Rifaʿi was less given to independent concepts regarding the Entity than was Abu'l Huda, with whom he has been compared as a pillar of the regime. But Rifaʿi was Abu'l Huda's superior as an intelligent and practical adviser to the king, and he could be trusted to carry out his decisions once the ruler had made up his mind. Madadaha, a Keraki conservative of good family, was utterly reliable in the key Ministry of the Interior. Touqan was head of the Nablus family that in mandate times had been aligned with the Nashashibis against the Mufti, and he was also an old ally and collaborator of the Hashemites. Touqan's being a Palestinian in a more meaningful sense than Hashim and Rifaʿi was another point in his favor: it probably accounted for his appointment as the military governor general under the martial law, more than did his qualifications for the rather meaningless defense portfolio. (The minister of defense in Jordan normally does little more than sign budget appropriations and supervise military attachés abroad.) Also, for the first time in the nation's history, a beduin, ʿAkif al-Faʾiz, son of the paramount chief of the Banu Sakhr "northern" tribes, was appointed to a cabinet post, in recognition of the part that he, his tribesmen, and the beduin community had played in recent weeks. That he was given the portfolio of agriculture, not notably the hallmark of beduin civilization, was certainly not an intended irony. It was the presence of the man that counted.

Martial law, proclaimed under the provisions of the 1952 constitution, was applied widely. The chief potential centers of unrest—Amman, Irbid, Jerusalem, Ramallah, Nablus, and the largest refugee camps—were put under immediate curfew. Police and security forces were put back under army command. Political parties were declared dissolved; the Arab Students' Congress followed, together with the Nationalist Guidance Committees. Several hundred people were arrested, prominent among whom were Nabulsi and Nimr. Five weeklies were closed. Seven military governors were appointed to serve under the military governor general, one for each district. (Loyal Hebron saved the regime one military governor by being thrown in with Jerusalem.) Two military courts were set up to deal with any problems in the military government, one in Amman and one in Jerusalem; later their number was increased to four.[23] During the following weeks, most of the town councils in the West Bank were disbanded, and three in the East Bank—Amman and Zerqa, which were heavily "Palestinianized," and Madaba, the center of Communism in the East Bank.

The consolidated "instructions for martial law administration" were published in the local press.[24] In their combination of breadth and detail, the twenty articles justify the comment of the U.S. military attaché that they "provide complete coverage of everything that the Jordanians could think of and . . . many things they haven't."[25]

The media everywhere—outside Egypt and Syria—made a big issue of Hussein's charging "openly for the first time that the conspiracy [which he alleged had compelled him to impose martial law] was getting its support from Egypt."[26] Although this was not false, the king's statement was plaintive rather than accusatory, let alone polemical. He did not cast aspersions on his brother rulers, although he stated: "I had hoped the Voice of the Arabs [from Cairo] would cease this conspiracy. . . . I certainly hope the pricking pins and wagging tongues will be stopped."[27] This distinction gave Abdel Nasser and Quwatli, in conference for hours at Cairo, where Quwatli had flown before noon on 25 April, the rational underpinning for their hope that nothing terrible had occurred after all at Amman and that business with Hussein could proceed as usual for the time being, with options open for a future settling of accounts.

By the end of April 1957, the Hashemite Entity was reestablished, with the ruler in his appointed place. Who can take credit for this? Iraq had remained in the background. Although its goodwill was assured, Iraq's rulers preferred public discretion. But when a Syrian invasion backed by Egypt was a distinct possibility in the second half of April 1957, King Saud proved to be an effective friend. His public support not only demonstrated that Hashemite Jordan had at least one determined ally on the Arab side, but also showed that Hussein was not completely isolated from the *qawmi* camp in which Saud still—just—kept his place. Saud's backing was all the more impressive, as the world had not as yet grown accustomed to see the two royal houses in harmony.

The American government had from the first accepted Hussein's claim to be an aggressive fighter against Communism, and it had encouraged him to shore up his stand. The United States also came out at the crucial moment with a near-guarantee against Soviet intervention, unlikely as this contingency looked even then.[28] Monetary aid may have been given in secret as early as January 1957. The publicized payment of $10 million immediately after the royal "coup"[29] was, beyond its financial significance, an American underwriting of the Entity. It was a dramatic gesture that the United States had taken the place of Britain, with an important difference. The American government responded swiftly and forcefully to the needs of Hussein as he himself perceived them. Unlike Britain, it did not presume to suggest his policy for him, aside from the general assumption that the objectives of both countries tallied. (That the American government took for years, albeit secretly, a doubtful view of Hus-

sein's chances of survival is a different matter.) The waiver of Hussein's
formal adherence to the Eisenhower Doctrine by so doctrinaire a politician as John Foster Dulles is in itself a portent.[30]

Here we should try to assess to what extent "the menace of international
Communism" accounted for the United States' strategic decision—which
became operative in the second half of April 1957—to stand behind Hussein. "Overt armed aggression from any nation controlled by International
Communism" was, after all, a key expression in the Eisenhower Doctrine
as enunciated by the president. Historians disagree. On one end is the
view that the "White House, seeing the trouble as instigated by Communists, invoked the doctrine."[31] On the other is that "the United States
in January 1957 improvised the so-called Eisenhower Doctrine, by which,
in the guise of resisting communism, it sought to rally and stiffen the
timid Arab governments and to roll back Nasser's influence where it was
already established."[32] There is truth in either view. The fixation of both
Eisenhower and Dulles on Communism is a matter of record. But by then
they had also come to hate and fear Abdel Nasser. They believed that he
offered an opportunity for Soviet penetration, but they did not equate him
with the Soviet puppets of Eastern Europe. During the critical days of 23
to 25 April, there seems to have been something like collusion between
the administration—the White House and the State Department—and
Hussein to stress the "Communist" aspect of the emergency.[33]

Britain's part in the royal coup was passively supportive. Ambassador
Charles Johnston conveyed to Hussein that Britain bore no grudge and
would do nothing to make things difficult. This was a role for which
Johnston's predecessor, Charles Duke—chief British witness to the Glubb
crisis—would have been less suitable.

The friends at home who stood by Hussein's side when he took the
decisive step continued as stalwarts of the Hashemite monarchy: Queen
Mother Zayn; her brother, Sharif Nasir bin Jamil; Bahjat al-Talhuni, chief
of the royal cabinet; Hazza' al-Majali in the background, as a link to
Baghdad; Bahjat Tabara, a pillar of the police from the time when the
police was the Arab Legion, Major John Glubb was a special service
officer among the tribes of southern Iraq, and Hussein had not yet been
born; and, above all, Samir al-Rifa'i. Most of them, especially the king's
family, had reportedly suggested to Hussein during the early months of
the year a safe and reasonably opulent exile. But they had stuck by him,
faithfully and actively, once they knew that his mind had been made up.

For there is one hero in the drama. At the opening of 1957, the scales
were weighted against Hussein: "The current of history," as it seemed to

observers, was about to sweep him away. It is true that his adversaries proved to be second-rate, but it was Hussein who proved them to be so. And it is true that Hussein found backers who proved indispensable, but it was he who rallied them, rather than the reverse. (The events that fifteen months later destroyed Hussein's kinsmen in Baghdad made this point. In the early hours of 14 July 1958, some common courage might have sent the assailants of Rihab Palace scuttling over the Syrian frontier. But instead, Crown Prince Abdul Ilah and King Faysal begged for mercy and were lost.)

We should also say something about the predictions made during the two weeks from Nabulsi's dismissal to the imposition of martial law. All contingencies and combinations were closely examined: Hussein had rashly challenged irresistible forces, and a leftist-nationalist republic would rise out of his ruin. Or perhaps Iraq, Saudi Arabia, Syria, and Israel would divide up Jordan. Or American troops would occupy Jordan and turn it into a protectorate, as under the British, but more crudely so. Or Hussein and Nabulsi would yet work out a compromise that might even lead to a new equilibrium. Or maybe all the uproar would prove to be a deception by the traditionalists to mislead the leftists, or vice versa—much ado about very little, and nothing of consequence to follow. And one conclusion popular in Britain was that the East was, as ever, inscrutable, and it was futile to look for explanations acceptable to Western rationality. All variants were presented, all plausibly argued, except one: that Hussein would emerge within days as the sole effective ruler of the country and stay so indefinitely.

5

The Military Government

A brief description of Hussein's rule in the nine months from his coup of 24 and 25 April 1957 until the proclamation of the United Arab Republic on 1 February 1958 is as follows: he forced his authority on the country by way of military government and threatened back those who threatened him from outside. He himself delivered the key to "the events of the recent weeks" at a press conference on 30 April, "the largest ever."[1] He had dismissed the Nabulsi government, he said, because it had disobeyed his instructions. It was almost an aside amid the nationalist, Islamic, and anti-Communist rhetoric, but his very nonchalance underlines the gist of what had occurred: it was the king's to instruct and the government's to obey; if the government disobeyed, it would be dismissed.

One big task was clearing up the debris of those recent weeks. The trial of the Zerqa plotters charged with "conspiring to assassinate the king and establish a republic" started on 27 July 1957 before a special military court presided over by Colonel 'Akkash al-Zabin, a beduin. The prosecutor delivered his summation on 11 September:

> Officers and men of the army had become much more interested in politics since the crisis in Egypt last year. The king was criticized and the Nabulsi regime praised. Some officers said in lectures to their men that it had been decided to press the king to dismiss his uncle, Sharif Nasir bin Jamil, and the chief of the royal cabinet, Bahjat al-Talhuni. Officers discussed a plan to besiege the royal palace and force the king to abdicate, and to kill him if he refused. A ministerial crisis was brought about artificially by extremists and leftists.[2]

Major General Muhammad al-Mu'ayta petitioned the king to release the arrested officers "as the Zerqa affair had passed off peacefully and they were 'only boys, while the king is broad-minded.'"[3] It is as good a plea for the defense as can be put into one sentence—overstating its case but making points that made sense. At the opening of the trial, the prosecutor had demanded the death penalty for all the twenty-two accused except one. On 25 September 1957, the court acquitted five of the men and sentenced the remaining seventeen to ten to fifteen years' imprisonment, with nine of them being sentenced in absentia.[4] This indicated more than leniency and an appreciation that the situation had stabilized. It was the first instance of what was to become a pattern in Hussein's political code: not to perpetuate enmities but to regard a defeated opponent as a potential client rather than as a potential avenger. A case can be made for this approach as much as for its opposite, that in the Middle Eastern power game the only safe enemy is a dead enemy. Both approaches have been proved and disproved time and again. In the end, we are left with Hussein's personality as the main key to his behavior, wedded to the needs of the hour. Also, he survived.

But a relatively lenient view of the past did not mean relaxing the grip. A beduin Royal Guards regiment (later expanded to brigade strength) was formed from handpicked men and put under the command of Sharif Nasir bin Jamil, who had proved his mettle during the Zerqa crisis. The military regime was strengthened by replacing Sulayman Touqan as the military governor general in July 1957 by Falah al-Madadaha, the minister of the interior who had stiffened Touqan's resolution from the outset. In October, this task went to Major General Habis al-Majali, recently confirmed as chief of the general staff, who thus expressed the army's primary role as the mainstay of the regime. (In February 1958, Majali was promoted to lieutenant general, Glubb's old rank.) Also, at the time of Hussein's coup, the army regained from the Ministry of the Interior the command of the police and the security service, and so the circle was complete in this respect too.[5]

The political parties remained outside the law. (Cadres continued to exist underground, but as organizations—apart from whatever feeling of discontent they may have stood for—they had lost their significance.)[6] The vigilance over groups traditionally prone to subversion was systematized and consistently translated into follow-up action. Particularly pertinent and, as it turned out, effective was the appointment of a committee at the Ministry of Education to screen schoolteachers. Political censorship of the press was a matter of course. In the atmosphere that had prevailed since the imposition of military government, it was not too cumbersome a task.[7] An interesting concomitant was an order by the military governor general punishing with long imprisonment any "writing or drawing with the intent of portraying the king as a comical figure."[8] The governor general issued the order just when the Egyptian press was beginning to apply to Hussein its talent for political caricature, although it took another month to attain its peak. Hussein, although not thin-skinned in many respects, was sensitive to being portrayed as a dwarf king.[9]

The National Assembly reconvened on 1 October 1957, and the Chamber elected as its speaker Dr. Mustafa Khalifa, a Muslim deputy from Amman, who had stood up to the majority under Nabulsi's administration. (Khalifa and his two deputies, Tharwat al-Talhuni, deputy for Ma'an, and Kamil 'Ariqat, from Jericho, all had come out months earlier in favor of suspending the constitution for a lengthy period. This seems to have been their qualification for parliamentary promotion.) Hussein himself read the speech from the throne. Of his thirty-minute oration, one sentence matters: "We shall fight to keep our independence." The rest is tactics and detail, mostly a spirited defense of martial law, which had saved "land" and "people" (*balad* and *sha'b*, that is, Jordan) from "the tools of Communism" that served to "make the Holy Places easy prey [presumably for Israel] and destroy Arab nationalism."[10]

For all the lessons of the past six months, the absence of eight members (out of forty) who were under arrest or had fled,[11] Hussein's imperiousness, and Rifa'i's close watch over the proceedings, the chamber was not entirely without a spirit of its own. The seven members who abstained from approving the speech from the throne—the followers of Nabulsi's government who by then were neither in exile nor under arrest—are of less interest in this respect than are the twenty-five who did approve, the majority being old-time loyalists from the East Bank. Their endorsement expressed the hope that now with peace restored, martial law might be lifted and parliamentary life fully restored. The endorsement also surpassed Hussein in singling out those issues that Hussein had mentioned as being demanded by protocol: the need to combat imperialism, to avoid foreign alliances, and to ward off attempts at solving from the outside the Palestine problem, including the fate of the refugees. This response merely reflected the spirit of the times. But it must have underscored for Hussein the lesson that an elected chamber was an enemy at worst, a sycophant at best, but no ally in the fight for existence.[12]

One of the compelling arguments favoring financial aid to Jordan had been the need to humor the army. Evidently this objective was attained, as the pay of all ranks was substantially increased in July.[13]

If Hussein's domestic dealing during these nine months gives the impression of masterful self-confidence, in foreign affairs he showed signs of tenseness. This is easy to understand. Whereas the basic problem was simple—survival with American support in the face of Egyptian and Syrian ill will—the tactical situation was not clear-cut. The friendship of the United States indeed was visible, and Hussein did not bother to apologize for it so long as he could stress his abstention from endorsing the Eisenhower Doctrine, which meant that the aid he did receive was without strings attached. What seemed to be a pose maintained with the connivance of both partners was in a deeper sense true. There indeed were no strings attached to the American support: the conviction first gained in Washington in January 1957 and confirmed by the events of April—that Hussein was determined to defend Jordan under all circumstances and thus serve American interests in the Middle East—was all the collateral needed. (A White House staff note of the time contains a striking confirmation that the "no strings" principle applied: when yet another $10 million was appropriated to Hussein toward the end of May 1957, the State Department instructed the Amman embassy that it could release the sum "substantially without condiitons" in view of representations by the Jordanian ministers that "the usual conditions" were politically unacceptable.)[14]

The understanding with the United States worked without a hitch from the first days of this period. President Eisenhower's reference to Jordan in his broadcast to the nation on 21 May 1957, devoted to mutual security programs, is as good an example of the current U.S. perception as can be found:

> The Kingdom of Jordan came under the sway of a succession of cabinets, each one seemingly more tolerant of Communist infiltration and subversion. King Hussein has acted swiftly and resolutely to forestall disaster, and the peril now seems checked. Yet this victory would surely be lost without economic aid from outside Jordan. Jordan's armed forces must be paid. The nation's utilities must function. And, above all, the people must have hope. Some necessary aid can come from neighboring countries, such as Saudi Arabia, but some also must come from the United States. For the security of Jordan means strength for all the forces of freedom in the Middle East.[15]

In public, this policy materialized in the payment of another $30 million in the early summer of 1957, and in a modest airlift of military hardware early in the autumn. The finanrcial aid came under the provisions of the Mutual Security Act (Point Four program) of 1954, and not under the funding appropriated by Congress for the Eisenhower Doctrine, to which Jordan had not agreed, an additional fig leaf to cover the nakedness of the relationship. Secretary Dulles explained the allocation as made necessary by the default of Egypt and Syria to fulfill their obligations under the Four-Power Treaty of 19 January 1957.[16] The airlift—on 9 September

1957, officially in response to aggressive noises from Syria, which was veering to the left under its new would-be rulers Khalid al-ʿAzm and ʿAfif al-Bizri—was well publicized. Hussein himself was abroad, but members of the government, the army, and the diplomatic corps and multitudes of spectators watched the U.S. Air Force transports at the Amman airport. The British ambassador, who was present, thought, perhaps with a bit of envy, that the publicity was a mistake.[17] But subsequent developments do not vindicate his view.

As a complement to the American connection, the remaining British bases were evacuated by July 1957, in accordance with the agreement of 13 March 1957 that terminated the Anglo-Jordanian treaty of 1948. The attendant ceremony was somewhat overdone; the British ambassador's description in particular, with its inimitable mixture of wry humor, nostalgia, and self-congratulation, is a testimonial to the spirit in which British historiography likes to view the last days of the Empire.[18] But the ceremony here served a purpose: it emphasized that Britain and Jordan had rediscovered their mutual usefulness on a new level adapted to the post-Suez reality, and Hussein, for one, exploited its inherent anti-imperialist credentials to the fullest.

As Hussein's political personality took shape, he developed an eye for the essential. He knew, of course, that his own world view did not tally with Abdel Nasser's and the compound mirage of political Syria: His nationalism was not theirs, nor his religiosity, nor his sense of what constituted progress, nor his aversions and phobias. He knew indeed that they had no interest in the survival of the Hashemite monarchy; Hussein had many advisers who kept reminding him of this. But they merely confirmed what his intelligence—not brilliant but always sound—had told him in any case by the end of 1956.

The Syrian and Egyptian media had competed ever since April 1957 in vilifying what he himself stood for. Their differences in style did not impress him as making a distinction: the Egyptian and Syrian media were tools of their regimes,[19] and if the spoken media—more dangerous by far than the printed—tended to be more restrained during the first half of 1957, this was at best a ruse and more important for that reason. Hussein had known all along that the Egyptians were actively involved in whatever subversion went on in the body politic and in the officer corps especially, ever since Major General ʿAmir's visit at the Zerqa officers' club just before Templer's visit. And although ʿAmir was a temporary guest, at least three Egyptians of great visibility, army officers but "politicals" all, stayed on in Jordan to guide and strengthen, as Hussein saw it, the assault on himself and the Entity: the consul general in Jerusalem, Brigadier Muhammad ʿAbd al-ʿAziz; the representative of the Joint Arab Military Command in Amman, Colonel Yusri Kansawa; and the military attaché in Amman, Major Fuʾad Hilal.

For some six weeks after the royal coup and the establishment of the military government, both sides adopted a measure of restraint. Hussein first had to set his house in order. It was in his interest to leave his perceived enemies at Cairo and Damascus in some doubt about his aims and, above all, his fitness to survive domestic opposition. The Egyptian and Syrian regimes, however, underestimated Hussein and overestimated the opposition, their resources in both matter and spirit.

In this, Egypt and Syria were victims of their own post-Suez euphoria, which made them reluctant to evaluate realistically the evidence collected by their various intelligence organs, which always had been good. In addition, both had more important considerations. Abdel Nasser was having trouble deciding how best to harvest the fruits of his political Suez victory snatched from military defeat—indeed, as amazing a turn of fortune as can be found in contemporary history. Syria was tottering toward another domestic upheaval. Thus as long as Hussein reiterated his faith in the principles of liberated Arabdom and refrained from too brazenly challenging their prestige with their own publics and the Arab world, Egypt and Syria were inclined to ignore him, or perhaps to give him rope to hang himself. Hence there remained for a time a measure of official restraint, and even a pretense of friendship and sympathy for the head of state, although not for his mentors and seducers. Hussein's frequent speeches on the merits of his house as the true progenitor of the Arab national movement were an irritant. But it could be said that Hussein merely intended to prove his membership as a right in the *qawmi* club alongside liberated Egypt and Syria, and as long as Abdel Nasser and Quwatli wished to preserve the peace for other reasons, this was hardly a *casus belli*. (Once their enmity was openly declared, this particular argument of Hussein became a club with which to beat the "fake nationalists" of Cairo and Damascus.)

The same dilemma obtained at Cairo and Damascus in the face of Jordan's demands, reiterated throughout May, that Egypt and Syria pay the first half of their annual subsidy, as Saudi Arabia had already done. Obviously the assumptions under which the financial aid had been agreed on in January 1957 had radically changed, but because Jordan had taken the precaution to ratify the agreement, Egypt and Syria needed a reason to give to the Arab public for the breach.

We do not know how close Hussein came to provide that reason when he asked Syria at the end of May 1957 to withdraw its army brigade, which had been stationed on Jordanian soil since the Suez war. The request was courteously styled and the grounds given were inoffensive, and so Syria had no real choice but to comply, which it did with little grace. The demand was probably not caused by Hussein's desire to provoke Syria. But the presence of Syrian troops in the strategic Mafraq region, straddling the Damascus–Amman route, had created apprehension during the crisis of April, and by now Hussein and his advisers obviously felt that in this matter at least, they no longer had to consider Syria's feelings.

It was in regard to Egypt that Hussein at last strained relations beyond the breaking point. The influence of the Cairo media on the Jordanian public cannot be gauged. Hussein probably overrated their efficacy in the face of his own means of coercion, but this would be hindsight. The three Egyptian functionaries mentioned earlier were in a different category of concern to Hussein. Their diplomatic immunity and the aura of grandeur borrowed from their master posed an additional danger, and also, they were on the spot. There can be no doubt that they violated the rules imposed by their official status, in that they consorted with groups and individuals they knew to be enemies of the regime that hosted them. And there can be no doubt that they listened to wild and treasonable talk and that they gave comfort and advice, although this does not indicate that their advice was not occasionally for restraint. There is no conclusive evidence that they were guilty of "plotting" before April 1957.

Regarding the Zerqa affair, Hussein's claim may be accepted that Egyptian officials in Jordan with diplomatic status were actively involved in whatever Abu Nuwar was up to. For two months, Hussein bided his time, but then the moment arrived when he felt compelled to strike. On 9 June 1957, the government expelled Major Hilal and Brigadier ʿAbd al-ʿAziz. Colonel Kansawa was immediately withdrawn by his government. Cloak-and-dagger stories were produced, buttressed by clandestine tape recordings, and similarly rebutted by the other side. Hilal was said to have engaged a Jordanian soldier to assassinate "members of the royal family and prominent members of government" and to have provided that soldier with a revolver and money; Sharif Nasir bin Jamil, Samir al-Rifaʿi, and Bahjat al-Talhuni come to mind as intended victims. The soldier felt remorse and reported to General Majali, chief of the general staff. According to Hilal, the soldier was an agent provocateur whom he had arrested and handed over to the Jordanian authorities. The truth seems to lie somewhere in between, with the Jordanians not entirely innocent of putting Hilal to the test and Hilal not quite as outraged by the proposal as he pretended to be. Hussein would naturally tend to accept the harshest interpretation of Hilal's behavior.[20]

The importance of this demifarce is that it finally removed the pretense that Hussein had not recrossed the line between the opposing camps in the Arab world. The withdrawal of ambassadors from Cairo and Amman and the cancellation of the Egyptian and Syrian promises to pay Jordan's monetary subsidies followed.

From then on, Hussein considered that the time to preserve appearances was past, although he evidently preferred to have verbal assaults on Abdel Nasser be carried out by Rifaʻi, who did so with gusto.[21] The guiding principle throughout was that attack is the best defense. And it clearly was a case of defense, for Hussein cannot have believed that a mutual contest for existence on anything like equal terms was involved.

The gist of Hussein's argument—the essentials of which were to appear and reappear until the very eve of the Six-Day War—was that Abdel Nasser was a fake. He cared only for his survival in power, but not for Arab nationalism or for the struggle against Israel. Nor was Egypt's role as a whole illustrious. An example of Nasser's indifference to anything but himself is the semiofficial settlement of the recent Sinai campaign, which is seen as proving that Abdel Nasser secured vital advantages to Israel: allowing the passage of cargoes for Israel through the Suez Canal, opening the Gulf of Aqaba to Israeli shipping, and creating and subsequently stationing the United Nations Emergency Forces (UNEF) on the Egyptian shore—and the Egyptian shore only—of that gulf. And, according to official Jordan, Egypt had never been at the core of Arab nationalism. In World War I, while Arab nationalism was growing in the Hijaz, Syria, and Iraq, the Egyptian public "was writing poems praising the Turkish caliph and opening [the] gates for the British occupation,"[22] this last a deft touch in letting Egypt have the worst of both worlds, with a touch of credibility. As for the Palestine war of 1948, the Egyptian army did not cover itself with glory: its heroism at Faluja was a fabrication; Egypt had sabotaged King Abdallah's war effort; and Egypt was the first to sign an armistice with Israel. (The Faluja thrust should be explained: it is difficult to describe the stand of the Egyptian brigade there as anything but honorable, and Captain Gamal Abdel Nasser was a combatant.) The Hashemite princes, and under their leadership the Arab peoples of the Fertile Crescent, had given all that Egypt, with or without Abdel Nasser, had not given, even though Abdel Nasser and his minions in Egypt and elsewhere did all they could to rewrite history.

In response, by the end of June the relative restraint exercised with respect to Hussein personally was withdrawn: the prime mover of the Jordanian trouble—from the Egyptian viewpoint—was at last recognized beyond a doubt. The press and the various broadcasting services maintained distinct levels of expression, although of course not of essential disapproval: *Al-Sha'b* was the most scurrilous; the French- and English-language papers, catering to a presumably more fastidious clientele, were the most restrained; and *al-Ahram* was ponderous and magisterial. Among the broadcasting stations, Sawt al-'Arab was naturally the most vindictive. Abdel Nasser himself stayed out of the melee. The aim of this propaganda was the alleged propensity of Hussein and his government to make peace with Israel at the behest of the imperialists and thereby to resolve the refugee problem. It was an explosive charge, more so than discussing the relative merits of Egypt and the Hashemites in the history of Arab nationalism.

Occasionally a particularly detailed, or sensational, claim led to outbreaks of rage and rioting in the Palestinian refugee camps that had to be put down by force. It is probable that in these cases, agitators, directed from Cairo, played their part, but it is certain that the rage was genuine. Attempts at rationalizing the charges—often made in Israel and the West, although never by the Jordanian authorities—that resolving the refugee problem through resettlement and rehabilitation was after all the best that could happen to the refugees, do not touch the heart of the matter. Physically, restoring order in the camps was never a difficulty, as the power was there, and so was the will to use it.

When compared with Egypt, Syria was perceived as the lesser threat to the Hashemite Entity, despite the vigilance necessitated by the proximity and length of the frontier. There was nobody in Syria remotely approaching Abdel Nasser in charisma, and the interminable squabbling among the Syrian factions, clans, and individuals was unappealing. There were in Syria prominent politicians with impeccable nationalist credentials, such as the Ba'thi founding father and foreign minister Salah al-Bitar, who seem to have disliked the demonization of Hussein and so tried to achieve a détente. But they had only temporary success: their standing was insufficient, and the tide ran against them in both camps.

The Jordanian propaganda was that Syria was a "Communist menace," rapidly growing. In this case, the Communist menace was a more convincing argument than at any other time or place. The conviction that Syria might actually come under Communist domination was shared during the last half of 1957 by observers who were more experienced than Hussein, including, as it turned out, the political elite in Syria itself. Nothing shows that Hussein and his advisers were aware of the approaching merger between Syria and Egypt, until it was announced. (Actually, Abdel Nasser was somewhat surprised himself.) This lapse of foresight is puzzling, considering that the process of unification, whether aiming at a federation or a unified state, had been in full public view since November 1957 at the latest.

6

The Arab Federation

Abdel Nasser was dragged into the union with Syria by the momentum created by Ba'thi jitters in reaction to Ba'thi rhetoric. Based on his rational convictions, he would have preferred a Syria whose Arab and global affairs he could control, without also having to manage Syria's domestic politics. However, once Abdel Nasser had allowed himself to be involved, his self-view or his vanity and lust for power were introduced, and so he committed to his role as president of the United Arab Republic (UAR) all the resources of his position, prestige, and person. This propensity to let himself be swept to the head of the current is a recurring pattern in Abdel Nasser's career. It is also the heaviest indictment against his being remembered as a great statesman.

Hussein probably did not realize the misgivings that Abdel Nasser had to overcome before he signed the document of union on 1 February 1958. But in any case, it was not Abdel Nasser's earlier misgivings that mattered. Nor was Hussein concerned with the obvious difficulties, indeed the obstacles, that lay ahead of the unified state in every field. The Lebanese press of the first half of February 1958 offered sophisticated analyses of the advantages and disadvantages of union. Hussein's sense of the essential told him what mattered: it was the clarion call, the Republic, "the first step towards the realization of complete Arab unity,"[1] the sensational uplift of every hope and ambition hostile to the Hashemite Entity. Hussein was too circumspect, perhaps too honest, to quarrel outright with what was, after all, a hallowed concept that he himself acknowledged as much as anybody.[2] But he could pit "unity" against "unity," and this is what he set out to do.

Hussein's first thoughts centered on a community of wider political, rather than narrowly dynastic, interests.[3] But King Saud, estranged as he had become from Egypt and Syria, and frightened as he was of a union between the two under Abdel Nasser, would not consider a constitutional tie with Iraq so long as Iraq was a member of the Baghdad Pact[4] and its Arab representative. Then Hussein took the easier approach.

The Iraqis were not particularly enthusiastic about the union. King Faysal and his prime minister of the hour, the ineffectual Shi'i 'Abd al-Wahhab Mirjan, did not count for much. But Nuri al-Sa'id, who had returned hastily from leave in Europe, and Crown Prince Abdul Ilah realized that a federation with Jordan in competition with Abdel Nasser's United Arab Republic posed problems. Yet they had proposed Hashemite union schemes more than once in the past, and their vague doubts gave way to Hussein's urgency. Moreover, the bait he offered—the presidency of the union to go permanently to the king of Iraq—was hard to refuse, the more so, as Hussein evidently offered it with a heavy heart. (His first suggestion was for the presidency to be rotated.) And so after three days of talks at Amman, the Arab Federation (*ittihad*) agreement was signed on 14 February 1958. The preamble of the agreement is here given in full. It is as complete a statement of Hussein's doctrine of Arab nationalism as was ever published in an official document, and it demonstrates Hussein's lack of sensitivity at the time to what swayed the public that he addressed.

Whereas: the great Arab Revolt led by His Majesty the Great Saviour Al-Hussein Ibn Ali was a proclamation of a new dawn for the Arab nation advanced by the sacrifices of martyrs for the liberation of the Great Arab Nation and unification of its peoples; an attempt to regain the prestige of Arabs among the nations of the world; and a contribution to the progress of human civilization.

Whereas: the mission of the Arab Revolt, for which its leader had striven, passed to the sons and grandsons and was inherited by generation after generation to remain always as a flame illuminating the path of the Arab nation toward the realization of its hopes and aspirations for the complete unity which integrates all the elements leading to liberty, happiness and strength; the regaining of the glories and preservation of its heritage, and its sacred aims; and the assurance of a happy future under the auspices of this blessed unity.

Therefore: the two Hashemite states decide to form a federation between themselves based upon these sublime aims.[5]

In one respect, however, Hussein was clear-sighted: the federation agreement expressly kept Jordan out of the Baghdad Pact, although obviously it did not affect the position of Iraq.[6] Hussein had not forgotten the lesson of December 1955.

The federal constitution, although officially dated 14 February 1958, the date of the federation agreement, was published five weeks later, with the guiding hand on the Jordanian side having been Samir al-Rifaʻi.[7] The constitution provided for federal bodies at the legislative, executive, and judicial levels; it assigned defense and foreign affairs to the federation; and charged "the kingdom of Iraq" with 80 percent of the expenditure of the federal budget "of the first year." Otherwise, it left the identity of the two constituent kingdoms intact with the proviso, already mentioned, that the king of Iraq be the "head" of the federation, with the king of Jordan deputizing in his absence "for any reason," a turn of phrase that proved prophetic for a brief time.

Such as it was, the constitution foresaw no shadow union, provided that it could be realized. It is also proof of Hussein's, its progenitor's, belief in Arab unity as he understood it, of his readiness to compromise his ego if necessary, of his shock at the UAR that had made these sacrifices necessary, and perhaps of his conviction that he could manage his cousin in Baghdad.

The implementation of the federation as constitutionally envisaged was deliberate and, to outer appearances, fairly smooth. The federal government, with Nuri al-Saʻid as prime minister, Ibrahim Hashim as deputy prime minister, and Sulayman Touqan as minister of defense, was established on 18 May 1958. It enabled Rifaʻi to assume formally the leadership of the government in Amman, which had been his in effect ever since the coup of 25 April 1957. Because Madadaha remained Jordan's minister of the interior, the cabinet was actually strengthened: the Ministry of Defense, made redundant under the federal constitution, had never been significant opposite the army command, and foreign affairs were managed by Rifaʻi as before, as far as was necessary, even though that ministry was abolished as well. On 1 July 1958, the federal Defense and Foreign ministries officially took over, with their seat in Baghdad, and ambassadors began to present their credentials to King Faysal II as head of the union. (The British and American ambassadors at Baghdad stayed on, and their colleagues at Amman temporarily lost their status.)

However, at the operating level, there is evidence of difficulties. It seems that Iraqi and Jordanian officials in their few working contacts began bickering and yearning for prefederation days. The people in both countries had reason to find the federal authorities sluggish, gruff, and not inspiring a sense of nascent nationhood. There is no way of knowing whether these difficulties were mere birth pangs or whether confusion and irritation would have become cumulative and self-perpetuating, as the UAR case was to prove.

In the mood of those days, no "union" set up in contraposition to the

UAR could have pleased the Jordanian (or the Iraqi) public, but the dynastic banner under which the Arab Federation marched made its detractors' task easier.

Indeed, Abdel Nasser's immediate response was all that protocol and belief in the common aim of Arab unity required. His cabled congratulations to "His Majesty King Faysal II, King of Iraq" were dignified and cordial, without apparent reservation. That "the depth of the Arab conscience" was substituted for "the Great Saviour al-Hussein ibn Ali" as mainspring of the federation was only reasonable under the circumstances.[8] (The comment of an obviously embarrassed Cairo daily was that now it was incumbent on Iraq to respond by withdrawing from the Baghdad Pact.)[9] That the king of Jordan was not given a similar message can be explained away: it was the king of Iraq who was the designated head of the federation, although without a doubt Abdel Nasser gagged at the thought of rehabilitating Hussein for having deliberately added injury to the insults already inflicted. It has been speculated that Abdel Nasser hoped to wean the new federation away from the Baghdad Pact.[10] His own explanation, given six weeks later when the mutual antagonism had already become apparent, makes more sense, without, of course, directly contradicting the other interpretation: "to create cooperation and block the way for imperialist intrigues," in other words, doing what was proper.[11]

Neither the Egyptian nor the Syrian media responded to Abdel Nasser's early generosity. Muhammad Hasanayn Haykal, the editor of Egypt's *al-Ahram,* after a skeptical analysis of the background of the federation and its chances for the future, concluded with formal good wishes for "the union of these two crowns."[12] The Damascus press was hostile from the beginning. At the official level, Sabri al-ʿAsali, for Syria, at first repeated Abdel Nasser's welcome, without any of Abdel Nasser's show of spontaneity. However, within two days, he was sure that "the federation did not express the Arab wish for liberated union. Therefore it is fated to disappear. And finally the Arab peoples of Iraq and Jordan will join the United Arab Republic."[13] This remained the UAR's position, official and unofficial, from that day until the bloody demise of the Arab Federation five months later.

The Iraqi and Jordanian responses also remained true to form: they complained, they explained, they demonstrated pained surprise; they appeared noticeably less assertive than before the federation; and, of course, they seem as unconvincing now as they did then. Neither union ever accorded the other diplomatic recognition.

A case can be made that of the four sides involved, Jordan was the most aggressive, in a manner that was annoying rather than injurious.

Thus Jordan unilaterally made passports again compulsory for Syrians seeking to enter its territory, a rule that had been waived under Nabulsi. The incidents of mutual harassment along the common frontier at that time were usually at Jordan's initiative. And the expulsion from Jordan of yet another Egyptian consul, from Jerusalem, in March 1958 on the charge of "stirring up discontent against the government"[14] was undoubtedly legitimate by any international judgment. Still, it conformed to the pattern not so much of Egypt's lack of rectitude—Sayyid Muhib al-Samra seems not to have been direct—as of Jordan's truculence. And as a last example, on a different level of public policy: when King Saud stood arraigned before the Arab world as having tried to contract for Abdel Nasser's assassination, failing other ways of preventing the union between Egypt and Syria, Hussein identified with Saud in a glare of publicity.[15]

The UAR's counterpropaganda centered on the dynastic—that is, non-populist (*sha'bi*)—character of the federation. The treason of its leaders in attacking the UAR came second, and its imperialist connection, worn thin by now, third.

The media war had its scurrilous occasions too. The Jordanian Ministry of Communications, in a widely publicized communiqué, "apologized to the National Bank [of Egypt] and the UAR for being unable to pass on the letter to the Jewish bank in the occupied area, as Jordan does not recognize Israel. . . ."[16] The offending document was a financial statement sent, probably by an oversight, to the Japhet Bank in the Israeli sector of Jerusalem but delivered to the Jordanian sector. And a Cairo magazine expressed doubts that the Hashemites were genuine descendants of the Prophet.[17] (The purpose in both cases was to hit the enemy where he was supposed to be strongest: the UAR as the unrelenting nemesis of Israel, Hussein's unique merit within the *umma*.)

Domestically, the Jordanian regime built up the image of Iraqi resources as serving, if not actually solving, Jordan's specific problems. The Zionist military menace might be frustrated, perhaps extirpated, by the Iraqi army; had not the Iraqi army saved Jenin in June 1948?[18] Iraqi wealth would alleviate Jordanian poverty and provide an outlet for unemployment, and a consignment of Iraqi oil products sold in Jordan at not too great a rebate was prominently advertised.[19] In all, it sounds contrived and uninspiring. In politics, the nascent federal bureaucracy and diplomacy attracted the interested favor of Jordanian politicians, hardly a group to generate enthusiasm.

Generally the government in Amman, like that in Baghdad, took a cautiously optimistic view of domestic security. Military law continued in force, defended by Rifaʻi as being necessitated by the regional situation—as in Lebanon.[20] This was an honest argument as far as it went, although it did not explain its application to Jordan. That was done by a new wave of arrests of prominent figures of the Nabulsi era whose dissatisfaction with the federation had been incautiously eloquent. But they were soon set free, as it was not in the regime's habit to keep persons like Maʻzuz and Hikmat al-Masri, Faʼiq al-ʻAnabtawi, or Naʻim ʻAbd al-Hadi detained in desert camps, or even exiled to remote towns like Maʻan or Shobak, for any length of time. But Ahmad al-Daʻur of the Tahrir party, a different type of opposition figure, was finally expelled from parliament and sentenced to two years' imprisonment by court-martial "for spreading reports causing confusion."[21] The real reason, of course, was nothing of the sort. Rather, it was Daʻur's fundamentalist and uncorruptible rejection of all the Entity stood for, with which the regime had despaired of coming to terms.

In view of the events in the second half of July 1958, we shall now return to the Suez crisis and its aftermath.

Military staff work to implement the Eisenhower Doctrine had started within days of its presentation to the U.S. Congress on 5 January 1957 and many weeks before Congress finally passed it on 7 March as House Joint Resolution 117 "to promote peace and stability in the Middle East."[22] The main planning body was the Joint Middle East Planning Committee reporting to the Joint Chiefs of Staff, who were in this matter directed by the assistant defense secretary for international security affairs. Their overall concern was to protect the Middle East (defined to include Pakistan and India) from Soviet aggression in all its manifestations. A single Middle East command was strongly recommended, even for the planning stage, although it was never actually established. Nor were "specific forces . . . allocated" or "a headquarters responsible for implementation of a plan . . . established in the area." But analytical work and contingency planning proceeded apace.

The place of Jordan within this framework gained significance when the planners recognized that Hussein was determined to save his rule and that he stood, through his beduin army, a fair chance of doing so. Conversely, Hussein's overthrow as a result of Egyptian and Syrian subversion might bring Jordan under Communist control. And in view of Jordan's strategic situation, this would be an enormous setback to American interests: hence the applicability and cost-effectiveness to Jordan of the "American Doctrine."

Because the Jordanian army, despite its presumed loyalty, was small and incapable of substantial growth without endangering its quality,[23] American aid under the doctrine would have to be direct military help in a crisis, and financial help at other times. The probable attacker was thought to be Syria, but it did not seem much of a peril. Israel, whose independence of mind was regarded in the United States with some suspicion since the Suez war (if not before), might also have to be dissuaded, although by nonmilitary means. Egypt was geographically in no position to invade Jordan. Iraq was Hashemite. Saudi Arabia was committed not to take any aggressive action that would injure major American interests. The danger to Jordan from the outside was therefore not great.

But in regard to domestic subversion, it was best not to take things for granted. And so by the end of 1957, papers had been submitted to the Joint Chiefs of Staff to "provide the basis for U.S. operational planning to assist the present governments [of Jordan and Lebanon], if required, in event of a coup d'état within the country." (Lebanon was included, as President Chamoun's declared pro-Western stand invited domestic "subversion," although the constitutional clash that led to the civil war of 1958 was as yet in the future.) Moreover, American ill feeling toward Britain over divergent Middle Eastern perceptions had been overcome in the interest of higher concerns, and joint U.S.-British planning "for military action in Jordan and/or Lebanon . . . in event of a *coup d'état*" had been initiated, with preliminary "guidance" completed "as a matter of urgency." The decision makers of both countries—the Eisenhower administration and the Macmillan government—had by then decided that "in the case of direst need" they would translate the military plans into action, and when "the need was about as dire as one could imagine," they did.[24] In the result, the military planners had served their national leadership in a concrete contingency with a balanced sense of realities, and in good time. The "division of labor" that eventually materialized—American troops to Lebanon, British to Jordan—was apparently envisaged from the first.[25]

It is unlikely that Hussein knew what was being worked out by the general staffs of the two Western powers. Aside from considerations of secrecy, Jordan was not a member of the Baghdad Pact and was decidedly the junior partner in the Arab Federation. Moreover, during the spring and early summer of 1958, things went rather well for Hussein, after the previous year, and so apocalyptic measures such as providing for Western military intervention seemed remote. But as the spring of 1958 turned into summer, a group of British officers, some with Arab Legion experience, again turned up in Jordan—not as commanders and general-staff functionaries, to be sure, but as instructors and advisers. This turn of the wheel was aided by the close relationship between the British and the Iraqi armies. The British guests were accorded affection and respect by King Hussein and their erstwhile colleagues and subordinates.

7

The Crisis of July 1958

The crisis through which Hussein, and the Entity with him, passed in July 1958 lacks the public drama of that of April 1957 or, for that matter, of Black September 1970. However, it was unique in two respects: it was the one emergency in Hussein's perilous career in whose timing he had no part, and as far as we know, it was the one that brought him to the brink of giving up.

As far as Hussein was concerned, the crisis did not begin with the coup in Baghdad on 14 July.[1] Rather, it had begun almost two weeks earlier, on the receipt of urgent information from the U.S. diplomatic mission at Amman (just demoted from the status of embassy because of the birth of the Arab Federation, with embassies placed at Baghdad) that a military putsch was about to take place in Jordan. The alert had come from Western intelligence, and it conceivably originated in Israel. The date of 14, 16, or 17 July, later mentioned at Amman as intended as the coup day, may have been guesses inspired by what happened at Baghdad or else may have represented shifting resolutions soon superseded and elicited during the investigation. It does not matter.

What does matter is that the plot had substance. Its central figure was Lieutenant Colonel Mahmud Rusan, just returned from Washington, where he had served as minister (that is, deputy chief of mission) at the Jordanian embassy and as military attaché during an earlier stay there. Rusan was from Irbid in northern Transjordan, like most of his fellow conspirators. Both his appointments at Washington—the first in 1952, apparently at Glubb's instigation—had come to remove a subversive officer against whom nothing could yet be proved. His chief collaborators now were his brother Muhammad Rusan and the brothers Sadiq and Salah Shara', all serving senior officers. In Damascus, Colonel Mahmud al-

Musa provided the link with ʿAbd al-Hamid Sarraj, a Syrian army officer who was then interior minister of the Northern Region of the UAR. Unlike his fumbling predecessors, Rusan planned carefully. Hussein was to be killed in the palace. A republic would be proclaimed. It seems that accession to the UAR had not yet been decided, although there was a predisposition in its favor—on both counts, similar to the line taken by the Iraqi officer plotters at the same time; it was the sensible line to take. There was, however, no coordination with the Iraqi top team around ʿAbd al-Karim Qasim, although there may have been contacts with sympathetic Iraqi officers.[2]

It is certain that the coup was supported by Damascus, including the necessary financing. There is no clear evidence that Abdel Nasser himself knew in advance about it. Sarraj was quite capable of acting independently in such matters. (The involvement of the UAR embassy in Washington, which apparently kept in constant touch with Rusan during the planning period, proves nothing in this respect.) It is ironic that the UAR intelligence establishment was certainly implicated in the Rusan plot, which failed, but was ignorant of the Qasim plot (except that there was a coup in the offing), which was successful. It is also ironic, but on a different level, that the discovery of the plot had a delayed effect that might have enabled it to succeed after its demise: Hussein was particularly shaken by plausible charges that Major Radi ʿAbdallah al-Khasuna, his senior aide-de-camp and personal friend, was one of the plotters. The charges were probably planted by UAR intelligence.[3] Radi ʿAbdallah was ultimately cleared of having taken part in Rusan's or any other plot. But his alleged treachery helped bring Hussein close to despair.[4]

It is another of the ironies of the Rusan plot that a measure taken for Hussein's preservation became the means of destroying his would-be preservers. On 1 July 1958 or shortly afterward, Nuri al-Saʿid decided in response to an appeal from Hussein to send a brigade to Jordan in addition to that stationed in the east of the kingdom since May, when the Lebanese situation had deteriorated. It is not yet clear what caused Hussein to make his request just then. Probably it was the shock of the first news of the Rusan conspiracy and the need for additional protection against Syria.[5] In any case, the Iraqi Twentieth Brigade Group stationed at Jalaula, east of Baghdad, was chosen for the task, and after some delays it set out on 13 July. In the morning hours of 14 July on its way through Baghdad, it overturned the monarchy.

While the Rusan plot and its implications were still being unraveled in Amman, the news from Baghdad burst like a thunderclap in the morning hours of 14 July. At first, Hussein overrated the price in blood, high as it was: Nuri al-Saʿid was not butchered together with the king and the crown prince; he was discovered the next day while fleeing in disguise toward the Iranian frontier. Fadil al-Jamali, a former prime minister and more highly respected abroad than most of his colleagues were, was not harmed despite the initial news announcing his murder. Two of the three Jordanian members of the federation cabinet (Deputy Prime Minister Ibrahim Hashim and Minister of Defense Sulayman Touqan) were indeed killed, but Khulusi Khayri, minister of state for foreign affairs, escaped with minor injuries and was returned to Jordan soon afterward. The general slaughter in Baghdad, at first pictured as immense, was in fact kept in control, considering the circumstances, thanks to the energetic measures taken by the revolutionary military governor, Brigadier Ahmad Salih al-ʿAbdi. But Hussein believed for days that the coup was virtually limited to Baghdad, whereas in reality the insurgents had taken over the whole country within hours with hardly a hitch.

It is this combination of misinformation, on top of the succession of shocks—a treacherous friend, his own fortuitous survival at home thanks to the vigilance of foreigners, and the murder of his gentle and beloved cousin—that determined Hussein's reactions during the first week after the Baghdad coup.

Hussein at first was in a state of fury. He immediately and with a flourish assumed the presidency of the federation, which had been vacated by Faysal's death. He considered marching on Baghdad and actually had advance columns of his army under his uncle and commander of the Royal Guards regiment, Sharif Nasir bin Jamil, crossing the desert frontier. It appears that he had persuaded himself that the Iraqi brigade, which had been on Jordanian soil since earlier in 1958, was ready to join. But this was pure fantasy; the Iraqi formation, on orders from Baghdad, at once retreated to beyond its frontier—unmolested by Jordanian forces—and remained in the vicinity of the oil-pumping station H3 on Iraqi soil. There is no reason to believe that they would have helped the Jordanian army mount an attack on the newly proclaimed republic, not even passively by moving out of its path.

Hussein at once contacted the British and American representatives in Amman. He struck the right note: come what may, he would fight it out; he would try to crush the Iraqi coup; and he was taking vigorous measures to secure his home base. He was counting on Britain and the United States "to stand by Jordan as [a] 'good and trusted friend.' "[6] He did not—unlike Lebanon's President Camille Chamoun—as yet ask for troops to come to his aid. Hurried consultations between London and Washington—Macmillan and Eisenhower conferred by telephone time and again—led to a consensus for immediate action without delving too deeply into lasting solutions: Hussein's violent deposition seemed imminent and would mean a deadly blow to what remained of Western prestige in the Middle East. This at any rate had to be averted, and so any day gained was a gain indeed.

The United States, having already landed marines on the beaches of Beirut, would restrict itself to moral, logistic, and financial support to be given with great publicity—this last point was essential. Britain, however, would dispatch to Amman forces from its imperial strategic reserve stationed in Cyprus.[7] To do this, Hussein would have to make a specific request in accordance with international law: as head of a sovereign state asking for aid in an emergency that threatened national independence. He did so by cable in the late evening of 16 July, and the orders went out from London at once.[8]

As with the Americans in Lebanon, the planning had long been ready. However, when Lebanon was drawn into civil war, with Jordan remaining quiet so far, the assumption in Washington and London was "that if it were necessary to go into Lebanon we [i.e., the United States] and the United Kingdom would go in with approximately equal numbers of troops, we going in first." But with the crisis of 14 July hitting Jordan with equal strength, "General Twining [the U.S. chairman of the Joint Chiefs of Staff] now thought that it might be desirable if the United Kingdom held back, and formed a reserve for possible use in Jordan and Iraq."[9] And thus the two governments reverted to what seems to have been their original line of thinking.

A snag that might have become a catastrophe developed when somebody on the British staff forgot to get clearance to fly over Israeli airspace. The omission was repaired and apologies were tendered, after the first batch of aircraft had already crossed Israel. The compliance of the Israeli government was not as automatic as the British authorities seem to have assumed. Pertinent questions of national prestige and territorial inviolability apart, there were then, as later, weighty voices in Israeli politics who advised leaving Hussein to his fate. Prime Minister Ben-Gurion did not belong to this school, but even so he asked for American advice before he gave the Israeli government's assent. By the evening of 17 July, two battalions of the British Sixteenth Independent Parachute Brigade, together with supporting units and fighter aircraft, were deployed at Amman airport.

As a corollary to the summoning of foreign troops, Baha al-Din Touqan, Jordan's permanent representative at the United Nations, also on 17 July 1958, complained to the Security Council "of interference in its [i.e.,

Jordan's] domestic affairs by the United Arab Republic"[10] (which, in turn, led to the breaking of relations with the UAR three days later). The complaint represented the facts of the situation as understood at the time by the international community, whether approving or disapproving of the British intervention.

Public opinion in the United States rallied overwhelmingly behind Western military intervention. Eisenhower's prestige as a soldier made its mark, and besides, he "communicated" well. The Americans also hated Abdel Nasser, in much the same way as the British public had hated him two years before. The British public was divided but generally inclined to give the government the benefit of the doubt. Strong opponents of the involvement, such as Aneuran Bevan of the British Labour party's left wing, had less of a following than might have been expected so shortly after the Suez debacle. Indeed, this was not Suez, as Anthony Nutting explained: the United States was on Britain's side at the "specific requests [of the] victims of aggression"; also, happily, France and Israel were out.[11] The Soviet Union predictably objected, but even then British and American observers believed that they detected an unwillingness to translate censure into military action.[12] They were right.[13]

But the hub of events was in Amman. The universal reaction to the news from Baghdad was the assumption that Hussein's end—his death or his flight—would come in a matter of days, if not hours. The hatred found in the refugee camps and among high-school students had been taken for granted all along, and so its upsurge now was no more than a predictable emergency calling for predetermined action. What was different was the new freedom that pervaded circles that until then had been guarded in their contacts with outsiders: the middle-class coffeehouse crowd, professionals of every kind, government officials, diplomats, and *hadari* army officers. It seemed to be an attempt to curry favor with tomorrow's masters, by kicking at a beaten dog.[14] But the expected masters did not turn up: those who had prepared for the role had been arrested only days before, too short a time for a new command group to evolve.

In retrospect, this spectacular breakdown of prestige was not in itself dangerous, as it was based on the expectation that others would act, but it was impressive, and it might have created its own momentum. But the "march of the Palestinians on Amman" predicted by some foreign observers did not materialize. Apart from stringent countermeasures, the Palestinians as a body capable of such a move did not exist. Nablus, the usual trouble center of the West Bank, was shut down by the army, after a day's hesitation. It was an additional advantage that the area commander was the elderly Brigadier ʿIzzat Hasan, who as a Circassian was considered impervious to treachery and thus given a free hand. In Basman Palace, Hussein moved amid a throng of beduin elders and army officers. Hussein did not waver. On the afternoon of 16 July, he announced to a joint session of the National Assembly and then to the army and "the people" (*sha'b*) what may have been the most humiliating decision of his public career: his appeal for the return of Western troops. The reasons that Hussein gave were entirely honest according to his lights: to have the military cover of friendly countries, in accordance with paragraph 51 of the United Nations Charter; and to protect Jordan's frontiers from its surrounding enemies so that the country might gain the breathing space needed to stabilize the domestic front, build up its army, strengthen its economy, and thus save itself and indeed the Middle East from international Communism and *fitna*, such as had been visited upon Iraq.[15] (*Fitna*, unsatisfactorily translated by the BBC monitoring service as "sedition," is the key to understanding much of Hussein's thinking. It is a fundamental Islamic concept, at once religious, political, and deeply conservative, and in Western languages it can only be paraphrased.)[16] Even so, the justification for the return of Western troops was hardly inspiring. According to the local press, "every [foreign] soldier who lands in Jordan under the UN charter is a UN representative, and no longer a national of his state."[17] However, the National Assembly unanimously approved Hussein's call for military aid. Ahmad al-Da'ur, the one delegate in the Chamber who might have been able to dissent in the prevailing circumstances, had been expelled half a year before.

The arrival and stay of the British troops in Amman were uneventful. Their presence at the airport, in radio communication with Basman Palace and in a state of alert, discouraged any attempt to storm the palace. Hussein's call and Britain's response proved to friend and foe alike that public opinion would not keep Hussein from doing what he considered necessary for his survival. It was an attitude that served as a source of strength, despite all the embarrassment it involved.

Hussein descended into his personal crisis only after the first threat was over. About a week after the "Rihab slaughter"[18] at Baghdad, he virtually locked himself up in his palace, tightly surrounded by his bodyguards and inaccessible to the visitors who normally paid their respects. It was the low point, to this day, of his image as a ruler, of his morale, and of his resilience.[19] There are reports of Hussein's fear of assassination bordering on panic during those days. And it is said that he spoke of going into exile abroad: no such stories are credibly connected with any other emergency through which he has passed.[20]

The foreign reports were certainly not likely to cheer Hussein. The ghastly details of the Baghdad killings became known (a photograph of Abdul Ilah's naked body strung up a lamppost is etched into the mind of whoever saw it). Abdel Nasser came as near as he ever did in calling for Hussein's death.[21] (His favorite formula was equating Hussein with Hussein's grandfather, the implication being obvious. It was a particularly cruel reminder: sixteen-year old Hussein was standing by the side of his grandfather when he was shot to death.)

When the Baghdad crisis began, King Saud had frantically implored the American government to crush the insurrection while there was still time.[22] But Saud by then took second place behind his brother Amir Faysal, the prime minister, who wanted to mend Saudi Arabia's relations with Egypt. Thus to illustrate his intentions, Faysal prohibited American transport planes from crossing Saudi airspace with cargoes of vitally needed oil for Jordan from the Persian Gulf. (Hussein never seems to have blamed Faysal in later times. He came to appreciate Faysal's political personality, so different from that of his older brother, and he apparently dismissed the episode as an understandable piece of realpolitik.)

The outlook toward the west was a little more comforting. Britain and the United States gave Hussein the material support that he considered indispensable. British ambassador Charles Johnston, American chargé d'affaires Thomas Wright, and the coordinator of the Mutual Security Program, Robert G. Barnes (later to return to Jordan as American ambassador), did their best to keep up his spirits, and Hussein can hardly have known that in the inner circles of the American administration, many doubted that he would survive. But he did know that from the first, neither Britain nor the United States would upset the new government in Iraq, nor would they permit him, Hussein, to do so. Moreover, by the fourth week of July, it was all too clear that British and American recognition of the Qasim regime would come in a matter of days.

Sometime toward the end of July, Hussein emerged from his depression and his self-imposed isolation. Internal security was holding. The officer corps was undergoing yet another purge, directed by Sharif Nasir bin Jamil. Neither Abdel Nasser nor Qasim had made a materially aggressive move. The fuel crisis passed when American transport planes flew in oil over Israel first and then from Aqaba as port facilities there were improved under American management. (Britain sent an additional battalion to protect Aqaba, this time from Bahrain.) Although the media of the free world continued to deplore the imminent demise of "brave little King Hussein," the United Nations headquarters in New York gave signs that a calm was ahead. But it must have been mainly a natural process that restored Hussein to his accustomed posture of leadership and thereby helped restore his position of leadership, too. It was both a symbol and a token of his return to reality that Hussein, as constitutional head of the Arab Federation succeeding his murdered cousin, on 2 August 1958 declared ihe federation to be dissolved.

The proceedings at the U.N. headquarters in New York during the late summer of 1958 are an example of its usefulness in a complex and dangerous situation, when the main actors are interested in de-escalation but have difficulty in achieving it without stepping down or failing their home audiences.

By the last week of July 1958, when the first furor had abated, the positions taken regarding the crisis were as follows: the Baghdad Pact countries, including the United States, had finally written off Iraq and were inclined to believe Qasim's assertions that he did not intend to use oil for blackmail and that his interests were confined to Iraq. (This was to prove justified, by and large.) In Lebanon, where the United States was the principal Western power involved, a sensible solution beckoned, with President Chamoun waiving his desire to amend the constitution and have himself reelected for a second consecutive term, in favor of the army commander General Fouad Chehab, energetic, conservative, and a proven evader of political controversy.

The Eisenhower administration, "recognizing that the indefinite continuance of Jordan's present political status has been rendered unrealistic by recent developments," generally believed that in the face of the irresistible forces of nationalism, antimonarchism, and anticolonialism, the most that could be hoped for was an orderly devolution leading to Hussein's dignified withdrawal and an agreed absorption of Jordan by its Arab neighbors with the "peaceful acquiescence" of Israel.[23] But the United States also listened to the British assessment, which with greater knowledge of the Jordanian situation saw no reason that with some luck and support from the West, Hussein could not survive.[24] The British Foreign Office, the American State Department, and their representatives in Amman sought an arrangement that might preserve Jordan for the West in the event of Hussein's death or retirement. A regency was envisaged on which the army chief of staff (soon to be titled commander in chief,) Lieutenant General Habis al-Majali, was to figure prominently, together with Hussein's uncle Sharif Nasir bin Jamil—the latter, if the situation warranted, as a means of preserving the Hashimite monarchy.[25] The legal crown prince, Hussein's younger brother Muhammad, who was considered unbalanced, had no place in the scheme.[26] (The plan lost its relevance by the mid-1960s when Hussein's youngest brother Hasan came of age; by then, the Hashemite skies had brightened in any case.)

However, the key to the future was understood to lie elsewhere. As Anthony Nutting, who had close contacts with American as well as British officials, put it, "Everyone is awaiting the next move which . . . it is felt will come from UAR President Abdel Nasser."[27] It did not, at any rate not in a way that conformed to the West's image of Abdel Nasser since 1955 as "great . . . wickedly great." Abdel Nasser until the Six-Day War believed in the inevitability of his final victory over the forces that stood in his way and hence in the foolishness of taking risks, although opportunities had to be exploited. Because this was also the philosophy of the Soviet leadership, the main actors opposing the West in the Middle East were prepared to consolidate peacefully the stupendous advantages that had accrued to them. The diplomacy of Dag Hammarskjöld, the United Nations secretary general, arranged a phased de-escalation of the situation.

A special delegation from Jordan headed by ʿAbd al-Munʿim al-Rifaʿi,[28] the prime minister's younger brother and an experienced diplomat, vigorously attacked Abdel Nasser in the U.N. General Assembly on 14 August 1958 as the source of trouble in Jordan and throughout the Middle East. The attack is of interest in that it proved Hussein's willingness to ignore Arab inhibitions when he was aroused: no Arab government had ever before denounced Abdel Nasser by name before a comparable international forum. Otherwise, Jordan weighed too little to influence the prevailing trend.

President Eisenhower, addressing the assembly the day before, had scrupulously refrained from identifying the "aggressors."[29] Although he denounced "aggression, direct or indirect" and defended the U.S. action in Lebanon, his program was circumspect and, particularly, not suited to give comfort to Hussein. Among its "six elements . . . [to] be viewed as a whole," the need for development and the avoidance of a new arms race were linked with "United Nations measures to preserve peace in Jordan." Hussein must have realized that preserving peace in Jordan was not the same as eradicating subversion, especially when the pronouncement came from as vital (and as honest) a supporter as President Eisenhower. Nor did the abjuration of an arms race, which would hardly bind the Soviet Union and its allies, bode well when Jordan was looking increasingly to American armaments.[30]

It was just as well that Hussein had by then recovered his poise and optimism. British Foreign Secretary Selwyn Lloyd, in office since Jordan's Baghdad Pact crisis, was much more outspoken in defending the right of the Jordanian regime to survive, with help of outside friends if it so chose. This was to be expected, but in the changed situation, the support of a British minister, however senior, could not make up for deficiencies in the attitude of the United States president. In all, it was more than Jordan had a right to expect when on 21 August 1958 the U.N. General Assembly unanimously adopted a resolution in the name of all Arab League member states, calling in accordance with Article 8 of the Arab League Pact, "to respect the system of government established in other [Arab League] member states and regard them as the exclusive concerns of these states" as well as "to abstain from any action calculated to change established systems of government."[31] The resolution also called on the U.N. secretary general to make in intention, although not by definition, a fact-finding tour of the Arab countries in regard to the political situation there. Hammarskjöld left the following day.

III

THE VETERAN

8

Relaxation

In the political history of Jordan, the period between the crisis of summer 1958 and the call for the first Arab summit in December 1963 lacks the dramatic unity that characterized the preceding three years. There are common denominators: *qawmiyya* was still the dominant ideology of the Arab world, and it still considered the Jordanian Entity to lack legitimacy. Abdel Nasser remained the embodiment of *qawmiyya,* and thus Hussein continued to regard him as the major threat to his existence. But the drama had been diminished in the denouement of 1958.

In July of that year, Abdel Nasser, so it seemed, might have made good his threat. But he did not do so, and what he may have gained in dignity in the West, he decidedly lost in clout, in the fear that he had been capable of inspiring throughout the Arab world and beyond. But Abdel Nasser's challenge survived. In Jordan, at any rate, it was always discernible, sometimes bursting into crises as frightening as any in the past. Yet at the same time, certain issues and events stand out during these five years that were not related, or only indirectly related, to Abdel Nasser and *qawmiyya,* and it is these that tended to ease the situation, although they still pertained to the survival of Hussein and the Hashemite Kingdom.

It was during this period that Jordan's economy advanced to an extent unforeseen at any previous time, even though Hussein's part was principally one of benevolent indifference.[1] Nothing fundamental changed. Jordan remained poor in mineral wealth. There were no improvements in the field of banking and related services like those made in Jordan because of the Lebanese civil war in the late 1970s. But on a modest scale, there was a steady development of what resources Jordan did have: the phosphate deposits of Rusayfa and the waters of the Yarmuk River harnessed for the East Ghor project. A refinery was opened near Zerqa in 1961. The communications infrastructure was greatly strengthened. The mounting prosperity of the industrial West encouraged tourism and was intelligently nurtured by the Jordanian authorities (except when overriding considerations of policy dictated restrictions like the exclusion of Jews). The growing number of Jordanian citizens, most of them Palestinians, who worked in the Persian Gulf countries or in Western Europe meant a stream of remittances to their families back home.

But Jordan's dependence on direct financial aid remained—in addition to CIA funds, American aid amounted to $50 million a year. Even so, poverty was everywhere in the refugee camps and among the beduin and the unemployed of the major cities. But such as it was, Jordan's economic advance was good for its collective self-respect and its image of viability abroad. To this extent, it was another political factor in Hussein's favor. That halfway through this period a witness could write, "For the first time . . . optimistic observers have begun to think that . . . an adequate national consciousness may be developing to hold [Jordan] together . . . "[2] is in itself no mean piece of evidence.

Dag Hammarskjöld returned from his journey through the Middle East on 13 September 1958. A first round of meetings with Hussein and Rifaʻi at Amman on 27 to 29 August had not been entirely successful. Hammarskjöld, ideologically and politically committed to a speedy departure of Western troops from the region, found Hussein stubbornly determined to decide for himself what was good for Jordan and disinclined to see a United Nations presence as a substitute for British paratroopers.[3] However, Hussein and Hammarskjöld did agree that a United Nations special delegation in the Middle East based in Amman had a role to play in upholding the uneasy equilibrium in existence after the frenzy of those July days. The delegation was not seen as a panacea. Rather, it was a token of world concern with preventing chaos, an objective that had ostensibly received the assent of all governments in the Middle East, including those that refused to agree publicly lest their image as revolutionaries be compromised.

The agreement between the two leaders—formally between the secretary general and the government of Jordan—called for

> the stationing in the Hashemite Kingdom of Jordan of a subsidiary organ of the United Nations under the charge of a Special Representative of the Secretary-General [with ambassadorial status], as a "practical arrangement" within the purview of the resolution of the General Assembly of 21 August 1958, with the task of helping to uphold the principles and purposes

of the Charter in relation to Jordan in present circumstances, including the development of a good-neighbour policy towards Jordan.[4]

Hammarskjöld appointed as his special representative the Italian diplomat Pier P. Spinelli, formerly the U.N. undersecretary in charge of the European office of the United Nations in Geneva, who arrived in Amman on 27 September 1958. Spinelli lost no time in setting up his mission, which enjoyed full diplomatic privileges. In the main, it got on well with the Jordanian authorities, thanks largely to the personal qualities of Spinelli and his chief of staff, the Canadian professor Taylor C. Shore. Spinelli stayed in Jordan until the civil war in Yemen four years later handed him another challenge on behalf of the United Nations. Although it is difficult to specify what benefit the Spinelli mission brought to Jordan, or to Middle Eastern stability in general, Spinelli and his colleagues became a well-known and well-respected part of the diplomatic community in Amman. And presumably the mission's prestige, and that of its head in particular, added some badly needed legitimacy to the Hasemite kingdom in United Nations circles in New York.

The General Assembly received Hammarskjöld's report on 30 September 1958 and accepted it with some skepticism, but without utterances of outrage.

The passing of the crisis meant a decrease of attacks on Hussein and Rifaʿi in the UAR media, which was noticed with relief by Middle East watchers in the West. Inside Jordan, the excited hopes of those who hated the Entity subsided into the accustomed state of sullen acquiescence interspersed with discreet mutterings and the occasional explosion of bombs in public places, noisy but doing little damage. It is significant that this faintheartedness did not apply to the Muslim Brothers, whose members, like the Tahrir activists, had a faith that sustained their civil courage in adversity. The prevailing tactical situation—the Western presence all too visible, Abdel Nasser for the moment in a subdued mood—made the Brothers forgo their strategic cooperation with Hussein. Their leader in Jordan, ʿAbd al-Rahman Khalifa, was arrested on 16 August "to protect the security of the country."[5] (He was soon released: there was a case for mutual toleration as long as Abdel Nasser regarded the Brothers as his most dangerous enemies at home, more so even than the Communists.)

In the meantime, fears that the British military presence would be counterproductive to security proved groundless. Week after week passed without incident, until the withdrawal of the British from Jordan was completed on 2 November 1958, together with that of their American allies from Lebanon. The Amman contingent—that at Aqaba was evacuated by sea—

was flown to Cyprus over Syria, permission having been duly received from the UAR authorities. Among the few instructors and technical experts who stayed behind at the request of the king and his government was Major (soon promoted to lieutenant colonel) Walker P. Gardiner of the Royal Engineers, who brought over his wife and his teenage daughter Antoinette Avril, "Toni"—Hussein's future wife.

The détente between Jordan and the UAR was interrupted by the bizarre incident of Hussein's intercepted flight over Syria. The king was in the habit of seeking relief from the strains of his existence by going on trips abroad. At the beginning of November 1958, he judged that he could leave Jordan to go on a vacation in Switzerland without undue political risk at home. The date was set for the morning of 10 November 1958. The king intended to pilot his own plane, an ancient twin-engined Dove, to Beirut, with his friend and trainer, Wing Commander John Dalgleish, as the copilot. Also on the plane was Sharif Nasir bin Jamil. Soon after the plane crossed from Jordan into Syrian airspace, it was ordered by Damascus air control to touch down at Damascus, as the flight had not been properly cleared. Hussein and his uncle, fearing for their fate in Syrian hands, disregarded the order, and Hussein handed over the controls to Dalgleish. Two Syrian MIG-17 interceptors tried to force down the Dove—they did not open fire—but Dalgleish succeeded in bringing the plane to the safety of the Amman airport, where a hero's welcome was arranged.

Hussein claimed, and apparently believed, that the Syrians had deliberately tried to lure him to his death or at least into captivity. What might have happened to Hussein (and—no small consideration—to Sharif Nasir) at Damascus must remain a guess. Perhaps nothing at all except, of course, for an inconvenience damaging to Hussein's prestige. But observers at the time thought that pressure would have been exerted on the king to abdicate the crown and leave the Middle East. As it was, Hussein's attempt to create an international scandal, including a complaint to the United Nations Security Council, fell flat when the Jordanian authorities admitted on 13 November that because of an "administrative slip," Hussein's plane indeed had not received clearance to fly over Syria. (The Jordanian authorities had satisfied themselves with a general assurance from Beirut airport that all was settled. It is possible that Hussein, to protect his dignity, had purposely avoided direct contact with Damascus.) On the advice of Rifaʻi and Spinelli, Hussein announced on 17 November that he had "forgiven" the Syrians, and on the face of it, the unenthusiastic state of "nonbelligerency" between Jordan and the UAR was resumed. The net result was to prove once more how fragile any coexistence between the regimes was bound to be, given the facts of political life in the Middle East then and, on a lower level, how eager Hussein was to take up arms when he felt provoked. The incident also added one more item to the legend of the young intrepid king.

On 19 November 1958, Hussein announced that martial law would end on 1 December. On that day, both houses of the National Assembly unanimously passed the requisite government bill. Martial law had been in effect for nineteen months, and it had served the king well. Its abolition was to serve notice that the times of trouble were past, and that the Entity had triumphed over its assailants. Although this did not prove to be the whole truth—and surely neither Hussein nor Rifaʻi saw it as such—it contained enough truth to boost the regime's prestige, especially with the United States, official and nonofficial. The law itself made sure that nothing untoward could occur for lack of government powers, with the minister of the interior resuming his traditional role as guardian of (political) law and (political) order, assisted and complemented by the chief of the general staff. The minister of the interior was the experienced Falah al-Madadaha, and the chief of the general staff, a fellow Keraki, was General Habis al-Majali, who was rewarded on 4 January 1959 with the newly created appointment of commander in chief. (The king, of course, remained supreme commander.) Political parties remained banned.

An event of major significance for the Middle East had an indirect effect on the official postures of the Jordanian regime: toward the end of 1958, the common front of Abdel Nasser, as the embodiment of *qawmiyya*, and the Soviet Union came apart. As so often in the region with respect to destabilizing developments, the catalyst was Syria. Abdel Nasser had not found it difficult to deal with the Egyptian Communists through brutal suppression. But the Syrian Communist Party was more difficult. For local reasons—Syria's political society, as Abdel Nasser knew, was much more fractious than that of Egypt—the Syrian Communists had ever since independence played a more active role than had their comrades in Egypt. In January 1958, the Syrian Communists had opposed "union" with Egypt, as compared with "federation." Their discomfiture then had not improved their attitude toward the accomplished fact, especially when the new rulers soon made their worst fears come true. Although the Syrian Communists were not a real danger to the UAR, their dissatisfaction and, so far as feasible, their subversive activity were intolerable to Abdel Nasser's vanity.

On 23 December 1958 in a public speech, Abdel Nasser denounced the Syrian Communists as enemies of Arab nationalism and unity, and so the die was cast. A chain reaction followed: Al-Azhar ʿulamaʾ, political tools of the government, attacked Communism as the negation of Islam, and Nikita Khruschchev attacked Abdel Nasser. The break was not complete. The sides were too closely tied to each other, more because of what both detested than because of what both fought for. But it was a major reshuffling all the same.

Hussein was not pleased. The danger to himself from Abdel Nasser was the same, as it was not their respective attitudes toward Communism that separated them. Abdel Nasser's dramatic turnabout would improve his standing in Washington, and Hussein did not believe that Washington could give aid and support to Abdel Nasser without reducing its commitment to himself, a point that became even more important during the Kennedy administration. "Never quarrel with success" was not part of Hussein's philosophy. So he set out to deny the virtue in Abdel Nasser's conversion: it was not moral abhorrence combined with political insight—as it had been in his own case—that had swayed Abdel Nasser; it was merely Abdel Nasser's rage at finding his ambitions stymied, in Syria and, a few months later, in Qasim's Iraq.

But in the longer view, it was advantageous for Hussein to have Abdel Nasser ensconced on another front, which might make him more amenable to American wishes. In historical perspective, the ill will that broke into the open between Moscow and Cairo did Abdel Nasser's standing in Arab eyes no good. Whatever Western observers might believe regarding Abdel Nasser's newfound independence, it was not they who were the backbone of his power. And to Arab nationalists, and even to the Arab public at large, the dissonance, however convincingly Abdel Nasser expressed it, did impair his image as the ever-triumphant pioneer of anti-Western forces throughout the world. But this additional benefit may not have been obvious to Hussein.

Hussein was conscious that Israeli political thinking saw Hashemite Jordan as the lesser evil when compared with radical Arab nationalism both before and since Abdel Nasser. There was a tradition of mutual sufferance—something less than mutual toleration—on both sides. Militarily, Israel was no enemy any realist would take on without a compelling reason, and Hussein was a realist, however great his pride in his army. But he also knew that his perceived "softness" on Israel, or Zionism, was a telling reproach, especially so with his Palestinian subjects. He tried to square the circle by combining coexistence along the meandering armistice line with a noisily anti-Israeli policy on details. Between the spring of 1957 and the end of 1964, the overall security along the Jordan–Israel lines was better than at any other time after 1949 and until long after the Six-Day War. (The same was true for Israel's borders with its other neighbors, although largely for different reasons.) Also, there was an un-written agreement between the two governments to share the Jordan basin waters, along the lines of the Johnston proposals of 1953, thereby en-abling Jordan to carry out its East Ghor project.

At the same time, the Jordanian government sought occasions to dem-onstrate Jordan's ideological purity and political concern in fields that carried a minimal risk, such as the censorship of writings suspected of advancing Zionist ideas; savage penalties meted out to those convicted of spying for Israel, with maximal publicity and including capital pun-ishment; a trumpeted refusal to reconsider implementing certain obliga-tions Jordan had once accepted, such as Israeli access to the Western ("Wailing") Wall; anti-Israel resolutions regularly presented at Arab League meetings or other suitable forums; and the search for heresy among other Arab states, chiefly the UAR. Of greater significance, at least spiritually, was an anti-Jewish, anti-Zionist, anti-Israel hate campaign disseminated throughout Jordan's schools, especially the elementary schools in the West Bank.[6]

On 8 March 1959, Hussein set out on a seven-week world tour via Tai-wan, the United States, and Britain on which his mind had been set since his aborted flight to Switzerland in November 1958. The first stop at Taipei was particularly satisfactory, as Hussein had for some time stressed his friendship for Nationalist China as another token for his disdain for global Communism.

But of greater importance to Hussein was his visit to the United States, his first. As early as September 1958, he and Rifa'i had angled for an official invitation.[7] The State Department was unenthusiastic. But be-cause the king had decided to come to the United States "anyway on his own initiative," and "in view of [his] . . . courageous and praiseworthy manner," Secretary of State Dulles suggested to the president that Hus-sein be invited to Washington "on an informal basis" for a visit of three to four days.[8]

On 25 March 1959, Hussein, accompanied by Prime Minister Rifa'i and Ambassador Midhat Jum'a, met President Eisenhower at the White House.[9] The president, in keeping with the "background memorandum" submitted to him, mostly stuck to pleasant generalities. He asked about ways to reconcile Abdel Nasser with Qasim of Iraq, as relations between these two radical rulers were then at their worst in the wake of the aborted Shawwaf mutiny at Mosul two weeks earlier. Considering Hussein's total lack of influence with either, and his interest in keeping them at each other's throat, it seems a strange subject to be brought up, but the president was mainly interested in the real danger of Iraq's being drawn into the Soviet orbit, and Hussein's situation probably did not mean much to him. Hussein and Rifaʿi were evasive. Hussein asked the president about deliveries of tanks for Jordan's incipient armored regiments, and the president was evasive in turn. One point of more than transient interest was Rifaʿi's reply to the president's hope that Jordan's "present preoccupation with Israel would not be permitted to disrupt [the] defense against communism. Prime Minister Rifaʿi agreed and said that the smaller evils should be sacrificed if necessary to cope with larger ones." It was a rare Arab politician of high rank then who would refer to Israel as the smaller evil in any context. Hussein kept quiet.[10] In all, the meeting must be rated a success for Hussein. The American attitude toward him showed a distinct advance over the tenor of the National Security Council Statement of 4 November 1958, which was unknown to Hussein. On 2 May 1959, the king was back in Amman.

Hussein's trip was connected with the last recorded attempt of a military coup in Amman. It is said[11] that a few days before his departure, Hussein's intelligence service informed him of a takeover to be carried out in his absence by Major General Sadiq Sharaʿ, the assistant commander in chief of the army and the chief of the general staff; his foremost accomplice was to be his brother, Colonel Salah Sharaʿ, then the military attaché in Bonn. Hussein kept silent but took the hapless Sharaʿ with him on his journey, to be arrested and court-martialed after their return. The brothers were sentenced to death, but Sadiq was reprieved, and Salah escaped to the UAR. Both were later pardoned. However, it seems more likely that the Sharaʿs were implicated in the Rusan conspiracy of July 1958 but that sufficient evidence was not found until later. Their trial became the political staging area of the prosecutor, Captain Muhammad Rasul al-Kaylani, who soon became a pillar of the monarchy.

On 5 May 1959, Samir al-Rifaʿi resigned, and, as the constitution stipulated, the government resigned with him. In public, Rifaʿi's resignation was attributed to his health and age (he was sixty). Rifaʿi's performance during his future, and last, cabinet in 1963 makes this explanation plausible. However, it may not be the whole truth. At a time when it suited Hussein to mend his fences with the Arab world, Rifaʿi's open scorn for the Arab League as an Egyptian tool was a liability. Also, Rifaʿi had for a long time been politically allied to the powerful Banu Sakhr tribes, and he was personally friendly with their representatives in the army command and in the government—especially with ʿAkif al-Faʾiz, son of the paramount chief. This friendship was objectionable to the Majali, second—if second—in consequence to the Banu Sakhr.[12] The balance of power between the major tribal confederations was undoubtedly swinging to the Banu Sakhr, and Hussein, whose sensitivity in such matters was one of his assets, may have thought a redress appropriate.

Hussein appointed as Rifaʿi's successor Hazzaʿ al-Majali, formerly his "minister of court," mainly a liaison official with the cabinet but not a member of it. In loyalty to the Hashemite Entity, Hazzaʿ al-Majali equaled Rifaʿi; otherwise he was a lesser personality, so that his family ties with the commander in chief Habis al-Majali could improve the situation without threatening to become a danger. The newly constituted government was largely identical with the last. The Circassian Wasfi Mirza took Madadaha's place as minister of the interior, and like the prime minister, he was his predecessor's equal in loyalty, if inferior in strength. (He also was, as rumor had it, his superior in financial integrity.) The gossip of the time that Majali's accession signified the return to a British instead of Rifaʿi's American alignment, can be discounted. Jordan's American alignment was by then a fact of life; the rumor probably stemmed from Majali's association with the Baghdad Pact project in 1955 and his discreet liaison assignments at Baghdad during the Nabulsi period.

The change of prime minister paid off when Jordan and the UAR agreed on 15 August 1959 to renew diplomatic relations. It is clear that both sides aimed to please Dag Hammarskjöld, who had tirelessly worked for a reconciliation. But there was no real breakthrough, and the bickerings in the media continued, with recurrent highs and lows depending on relatively insignificant provocations from both sides. The uneasy equilibrium did not last.

9

Fresh Storms and Tense Interludes

The end of 1959 saw the beginning of two processes that, in retrospect, were milestones on the road to the Six-Day War. On 18 November 1959, the Israeli government announced that it would give top priority to the diversion of Jordan water from Lake Tiberias to the Negev—that is, the National Water Carrier project, on which Israel's development was to depend in decades to come, with all that this implied for the absorption of mass immigration, advance toward economic independence, and pride in the Zionist achievement. Because the carrier project was to originate in Lake Tiberias, Syrian (and Lebanese) water reserves would not be affected. Jordan, which might claim concern, was at the time at the second stage of its Eastern Ghor project, only slightly less important to Jordan than the National Water Carrier was to Israel.

But it was not the immediate—and, in Western eyes, rational—aspects that were decisive: Israel was on its way to scoring another success of immense value. Yet for the time being, the danger to the precarious balance of nonmilitancy between Israel and its neighbors was not great. The ruler of the UAR was unlikely to change from rhetorics to actual warfare. Hussein would restrain himself from taunting Abdel Nasser as a paper hero when he himself was involved in a somewhat similar project that depended for success on Israeli toleration. Thus it was only after 1961 when an independent government at Damascus was once more initiating its own foreign moves that the Arab one-upmanship was set into motion.

The other development was the emergence of the "Palestine entity." Since the official dissolution of the Gaza "Government of All Palestine" at the hands of the Arab League in 1953, the Arabs of the former mandated country of Palestine had been without a recognizable national representation, although Ahmad Hilmi, the prime minister of that government, continued formally to represent "Palestine" on the Council of the League. The Higher Arab Committee for Palestine (al-hay'a al-'arabiyya al-'ulya), reconstituted in 1945, had long lost any claim on the Palestinians' loyalty, although it continued to vegetate in Beirut, where its president, the ex-mufti Amin al-Husayni, had withdrawn after a spiteful break with Abdel Nasser in the summer of 1959. (The mufti continued at the same time to style himself as president of the extinct Gaza government.) In hindsight, it seems obvious that sooner or later the Palestinians would have to create a meaningful organization, although it is difficult to perceive what part those Palestinians living in Jordan and Israel would be permitted to perform.

It was significant that when it came, the public breakthrough was at the instigation of Iraq, an Arab government that was not directly concerned with Palestine. Toward the end of 1959, 'Abd al-Karim Qasim, prime minister and "Sole Leader" of the Iraqi Republic, an erratic character with remarkable tactical gifts and at odds with both the UAR and Jordan, discovered a convincing way to score on his opponents: in 1948, they all had divided up Palestine among themselves. Accordingly, this wrong could be righted only by creating a Palestinian sovereign state, ultimately to include the whole territory of the British mandate but, to start with, the West Bank and Gaza Strip, the West Bank being currently under Jordanian control and the Gaza Strip under Egyptian control. Qasim's rationale for leaving out Israel for the time being was the greater difficulty in persuading Israel to commit suicide than in convincing the Arab states to repair their injustice. Apart from the injury intended, the insult to Abdel Nasser and Hussein could not have been greater. It did not draw them together, however. It was not a common case against a common enemy: Abdel Nasser had no conceptual objection to a Palestinian state, provided that the state accepted his guidance on his terms. (In fact, Qasim had been upstaging an earlier UAR initiative at an Arab League Council meeting in March 1959 for the establishment of a Palestine entity.) Hussein, however, had from the first regarded his rule over the West Bank as an inseparable part of his inheritance.[1] Thus the Palestine entity was from the first bound to become another strain on Hussein's coexistence, precarious at best, with Abdel Nasser. The trend of relations between Jordan and the UAR hence was reversed from the hesitant improvement initiated by the resolution of the U.N. General Assembly in August 1958. The deterioration lasted throughout 1960, until the election of President John F. Kennedy introduced a new factor into the Middle East.

The Palestine issue heated up at the session of the Arab League Council in Cairo in February 1960. The absence of an Iraqi delegation served to remove a possible buffer—a common enemy—between the UAR and Jordan. Shortly before the session, the UAR government established the Palestine National (more properly, "Nationalist" [*qawmi*]) Union, like the domestic National Union set up in Egypt after the Suez war. The Jordanian government responded with a resolution to facilitate the grant of Jordanian citizenship to every Arab Palestinian abroad who desired it. Both steps were mainly gestures, but as gestures they left nothing to be desired in the way of provocation.[2] At the anguished request of the Arab League secretary general, ʿAbd al-Khaliq Hasuna, the council stalled in its concluding resolutions in regard to the implementation of the Palestine entity, although it expressly conceded the "right of self-determination." Hussein, in reply, announced that he was willing to have a plebiscite held, "if necessary" under the auspices of neutral observers from the Arab League, to "clarify the true position."[3] In contrast with many such expressions after the Six-Day War, when the West Bank was no longer in his possession, Hussein's declaration must not be accorded more than debating significance.

By March 1960, relations between the UAR and Jordan had again sunk to their lowest. The ensuing campaign was marked by attempts on the lives of the supporters of the Jordanian Entity: the king, Sharif Nasir bin Jamil, and Prime Minister Majali. It was as though Hussein's enemies had lost faith in either army coups or popular action. However that may be, the facts are that the attempts on Hussein's life, which make such lurid reading in his memoirs,[4] took place in 1960, and his escapes read like good luck bordering on the miraculous. In other cases, but of lesser media value, Hussein's survival may be credited to the vigilance and efficiency of his security services. And although this could hardly have been foreseen in May 1959, by the beginning of 1960 Hazzaʿ al-Majali was an object of hate second only to Hussein himself. In part, this was natural for a prime minister who was loyal to his king and followed his political cues and who, moreover, was particularly identified with the king as his recent minister of court. In part, Majali's past was implicated as the "man of the Baghdad Pact" and as the suspected Jordanian confidant of Nuri al-Saʿid. That Majali was a renegade National Socialist, a founding member of Nabulsi's party, was no help either. But what determined his image and, ultimately, his fate was the recklessness of his verbal attacks on the UAR and its president, which were beyond what even Rifaʿi had considered wise.

In March 1960, and again in July, the Jordanian authorities announced the uncovering of two conspiracies to assassinate Sharif Nasir bin Jamil and the prime minister. The third attempt was successful on the morning of 29 August 1960 when a time bomb exploded in the private office of Hazza' al-Majali and buried him, together with scores of officials and chance visitors, under the wreckage of the building. Eleven people were killed, including the prime minister and his uncle Jamal, chief of the Majali clan. (Hussein maintained afterward that the plan was to kill him, too, and that he was saved through an accidental delay on his way to the prime minister's office. Hazza''s secretary Zayd al-Rifa'i—Samir's son and a future prime minister—had left the building minutes before the explosion.

There is no doubt that the three attempts—the two that failed and the one that succeeded—involved mainly Palestinians at the operational level. Prominent were members of the Zahir family, originally from Nablus, who had built up a flourishing transport business at Amman, an important asset when frontier crossings played a crucial role. Also, there is no doubt that Rimawi and Abu Nuwar, heads of a "revolutionary council" of Jordan in Damascus, were active as planners, recruiters, and operators, abetted in turn by Sarraj, then chairman of the executive council of the UAR Northern Region. What the connection was from Damascus to Cairo is again not clear. Hussein predictably charged the UAR with complicity and, less unequivocally, Abdel Nasser in person. The Egyptian media denied complicity, but their joy over Majali's end, as well as their predictions of a similar end for Hussein soon, were undisguised.

Within Jordan, the act of terror caused no visible rise of expectations among that part of the population that was innately hostile to the Hashemite Entity. Rather, the strict curfew immediately proclaimed in Amman after the murder was a precautionary measure to prevent beduin soldiers from running berserk in the streets. This did not mean that Hussein would be content with political retaliation, or even with countersabotage. (The Jordanian military attaché in Beirut, Major Ghazi al-Khatib, had to be recalled at the discreet insistence of the Lebanese government for having organized rather unimpressive actions in Syria; Hussein promptly appointed him his aide-de-camp.) In the first half of September 1960, Hussein evidently considered military measures against Syria short of all-out war, perhaps a major raid in the direction of Damascus. He had a right to consider his army as much superior to anything that the Northern Region of the UAR could put in the field, although the UAR's air superiority would have to be considered. Jordanian concentrations along the Syrian frontier caused apprehension in Damascus and Cairo, as well as in Western capitals.

In the end, Hussein listened to advice; we have no way of knowing whether he had expected from the outset to be restrained.[5] He adopted a more congenial mien before the U.N. General Assembly in New York. In his address there on 3 October 1960, he attacked the UAR for "seeking to dominate our part of the world"; it "encouraged, or at least permitted," subversion; and underlying both, it followed the Soviet line.[6] Although Hussein's words were comparatively temperate and he did not name Abd-el Nasser, it was the first outright attack on the UAR before this or a comparable international forum by an Arab head of state, and Abdel Nasser had a point when he alluded to this blot in the public record of "an Arab king, even though a traitorous one".[7] (Abdel Nasser, on his part, had just conversed in New York with President Eisenhower, the two heads of state meeting on neutral ground as it were, attended by their chief aides—an environment that undoubtedly improved Abdel Nasser's mood.)[8]

Thereafter the immediate consequences of Majali's assassination petered out, except for the sentencing and public hanging in Amman on 31 December 1960 of four of the plotters, who had been unable to escape to Syria. Hussein never believed in the efficacy of executions, but that particular crime was particularly horrible in its success. Also, the Majali thirst for vengeance demanded a sop. (At least one murder was committed in open daylight by a Majali for blood revenge; later the king engineered a formal settlement between the clans involved.)

Majali's murder provided the background, and Hussein's stay at the United Nations the opportunity, for a political act already overdue: the reconciliation between Jordan and republican Iraq. Qasim had never borne Hussein any ill will beyond what tactical exigencies demanded. Hussein indeed hated the murderers of his cousin, apart from the dangers inherent in a radical neighbor to the east that had replaced a dynastic ally. But by the summer of 1960, Qasim had given ample proof that his peculiar republicanism was not meant for export, and Qasim was threatened by Abdel Nasser as much as Hussein was.

Preliminary talks in New York between Hussein and the Iraqi foreign minister, Hashim Jawad, were followed by Jordan's official recognition of the Iraqi regime on 1 October 1960. Hussein explained in a speech from the throne in a mixture of cant and plain honesty, that he "was putting [his] duty toward the country [*balad*, i.e., Jordan] above personal sentiments, in the interest of the Arab nation [*qawm*]."[9] To ease Hussein's personal sentiments, Qasim was understood to have assured Hussein that he condemned King Faysal's murder as having been carried out against his order. (But Qasim later denied by implication, in a manner characteristic of his convoluted mode of expression, that he regretted Faysal's death.)[10] Iraq did not particularly welcome the Jordanian step: Hussein was at the time neither a useful nor a reputable ally for an Arab government supposedly "liberated." But it did not, or could not, reject it either, and on 19 December 1960 Wasfi al-Tall submitted his credentials in Baghdad as the first Jordanian ambassador to the Iraqi Republic. The choice of someone already known as one of Hussein's most-trusted aides shows the importance that Hussein attached to the relationship. Qasim, however, hesitated for many more weeks before he appointed his ambassador to Amman, and then he was an ordinary brigadier shunted into the diplomatic service. The reaction at Cairo was predictably scornful. The renewed connection between Amman and Baghdad never amounted to much.

The reconstruction of the Jordanian government after Majali's death—constitutionally the formation of a new government—presented no problems and wrought no significant change. Bahjat al-Talhuni's six years of loyalty as chief of the royal cabinet were rewarded with the premiership. His roots—Ma'an in the Transjordanian south—were an asset. Madadaha returned to the Ministry of the Interior, where a strongman had again become necessary. The displaced Wasfi Mirza, whom as a Circassian it would be foolish to alienate, went to the Ministry of Agriculture and Social Affairs, to free 'Akif al-Fa'iz for the Ministry of Defense, a prestigious appointment conferring no power. A sign of the times was the inclusion in the cabinet for the first time of a Husayni, a cousin of the ex-mufti of Jerusalem, in Rafiq al-Husayni, who became economic minister. Hajj Amin's break with Abdel Nasser had made this move not merely innocuous, but also a clever shift.

After this, the Palestinian entity again receded into near-invisibility for another three years, for reasons unconnected with the plight and aspirations of the Palestinians.

The advent of the Kennedy administration was a cause of worry to Hussein. It never assigned a high priority to the Middle East.[11] This alone should have been a reason for concern, although Hussein probably did not reason deductively in this fashion. What did worry him was his observation that the new president, with his advisers, believed in the possibility of taming, or even harnessing, Abdel Nasser by assuring him of his legitimacy in American eyes and by playing to his ego. A tendency to make the best of Abdel Nasser had not been absent in the later years of the Eisenhower administration. But what was new was the doctrinaire faith that postulated a harmony between America's "new frontiers" with the interests of a nationalistic Third World, and the view of the UAR accordingly as "progressive."[12] Hussein was disdainful of the idea that

Abdel Nasser might be appeased by aid and gestures. Worse, Hussein refused to believe that all these would not lessen the American commitment to Jordan, despite Ambassador William B. Macomber's efforts to reassure him.[13]

The Kennedy administration did not, of course, change Hussein's outlook. He remained apprehensive of Abdel Nasser as the prime enemy of Jordan, who kept his subordinates at Damascus on a long leash to do their worst, and of the Palestinian intellectuals and the refugee camp population—by no means the Palestinians of Jordan as a whole but those Palestinians who mattered politically—as the latent enemy within. Hussein did occasionally make gestures of conciliation. But these were never more than gestures, and they disappeared when opportunities arose to do Abdel Nasser real harm.

In general, Hussein's legitimacy profited from the absence of any sustained challenges during these three years. The United States' financial aid to Jordan and, on a less significant level, the supply of American military hardware continued, as under Eisenhower. There are signs that Kennedy was prepared to engage American forces to help Hussein had the need arisen, but in the only overt crisis of the regime while Kennedy was president, Hussein managed without appealing for outside help.

Jordan's relations with the UAR during the first nine months of 1961 were determined by the correspondence between Hussein and Abdel Nasser from 23 February, the date of Hussein's first letter, to 7 May, Abdel Nasser's second reply.

The contents of the four letters—two in each direction—need no more than brief summaries.[14] They were based on Hussein's initial assertion that the common interests of the Arab nation surpassed differences that should be mutually tolerated in the cause of "solidarity"—this last was a code word that denied Abdel Nasser's call for "unity." Abdel Nasser, in a reply much longer than Hussein's letter, objected to the playing down of differences among the Arab states and described the instances in which the UAR (and not, by implication, Jordan) had combated imperialism. Indeed, Abdel Nasser asserted that it was "full Arab unity" (rather than "solidarity") that was needed, as well as what "the people" desired. Hussein, in another round, took issue with Abdel Nasser's concept of "imperialism": instead, it was Communist imperialism that really threatened the Arabs, and Jordan would never relax its struggle against it. Abdel Nasser, after a long pause (he explained that he had thought Hussein did not expect a reply), concluded the exchange with accommodating generalities. The style of the four letters is courteous, sprinkled throughout with "brotherly" asides.

Hussein's reasons for initiating the exchange are not known. The original stimulus was an Arab League conference of foreign ministers at Baghdad from 30 January to 4 February 1961, at which a confrontation between the UAR concept of "unity" versus the "solidarity" of virtually all the other Arab states had put Abdel Nasser in a position of diplomatic weakness unprecedented in the Arab camp since 1955. It was thus tempting, and not particularly risky, to improve on the occasion. Hussein's rage over Majali's murder had evaporated long since, and he did not really believe that Abdel Nasser was personally a party to it. It also appealed to Hussein's vanity to appear before Arab opinion as a head of state conversing with the giant of the Arab world on equal terms. It would look good in Jordan, and, in particular, it would please the Palestinians. It would certainly please the new administration in Washington and raise Hussein's reputation there as a responsible statesman. Not the least consideration may have been that a civilized relationship with Abdel Nasser would smooth the difficulties likely to rise once Hussein's plan of a second marriage became public. Hussein was moderately successful. The basic realities did not change; Hussein cannot have expected anything else. Another truce between the media of the two countries commenced. UAR reactions to the affair ranged from shrugging to commendation.

But Hussein did miscalculate the effect of the correspondence on the Palestinians, in its intensity and possible dangers to himself. When Hussein's first letter to Abdel Nasser was made known, there were outbursts of jubilation "resembling those at the time of the dismissal of General Glubb in 1956."[15] Placards bearing the picture of Abdel Nasser appeared from nowhere and were carried through the streets of Amman and the West Bank towns, together, to be sure, with those of the king. Hussein read the signs; within a day, he had thanked the crowds for their loyalty and had the demonstrations dispersed.

The jolt that Hussein received from his success in establishing contact with Abdel Nasser was compounded at that time from the opposite end of the domestic spectrum. The beduin's loyalty to the state had been a constant for a generation, and throughout his trials Hussein relied on it implicitly. The beduin were the backbone of the army; they had saved him in crises, and more crises were probably prevented by the fame of their prowess and the fear of their wrath. However, Hussein knew that the generic term *beduin* covered a multitude of identities and self-identifications, of rivalries and ambitions going back into pre-Islamic times and extending in the present from the communal to the individual in a variety of nuances. There was never a certainty that the beduin might not one day fly at one another's throat and tear apart the army in the process. It was no small part of Hussein's kingcraft to watch for danger signs among the tribes, to mediate and to soothe, to promise and to threaten, and above all, to balance. Hussein was skillful and enjoyed respect, and he was usually successful in preventing outbreaks. However, one incident at this time did become public, rating a mention and brief analysis in foreign media.[16]

On 27 March 1961, 'Akif al-Fa'iz, the minister of defense, resigned. It was reported that the king had in fact dismissed him because of an intrigue aimed at replacing the commander in chief of the army, Lieutenant General Habis al-Majali, then on an official visit to the United States, together with Major General 'Akkash al-Zabin, commander of the armored corps and a Banu Sakhr kinsman of Fa'iz. The background of the incident was personal dislike and tribal jealousy. Only gradually was it revealed how near the "intrigue" had come to a conflagration: a conspiracy among northern beduin commanders to force the king's hand; the involvement of the Circassian chief of the general staff and assistant commander in chief, Major General 'Izzat Hasan; and the threat of Majali's half brother 'Atif to intervene at the head of his brigade. It took Hussein a confrontation with the unruly officers in their own camp to quell the uproar, and then it still required the dismissal of ranking Banu Sakhr officers from the army, together with the chief of the general staff. That the affair looks in retrospect like a tempest in a teapot is the measure of Hussein's success in dealing with it. His authority, his decisiveness in a real crisis, and his sheer pluck stand out again. The Banu Sakhr bore no lasting grudge; within two to three years, they were back in office and command and with the standing of the Majalis unimpaired.

The final event of that spring that seemed to threaten political upheaval was Hussein's second marriage. On 1 May 1961, the royal court announced that the king was engaged to marry Antoinette Avril Gardiner, the only daughter of Colonel Walker P. Gardiner of the British army's Royal Engineers, on loan to the Jordanian army as an adviser. "Toni" had become a Muslim, having received instruction from the venerable Shaykh Muhammad al-Shanqiti, minister of education and a friend of King Abdallah. She had also taken the name of Muna al-Husayn—"Hussein's Delight." Toni Gardiner evidently was the archetypal "girl next door," easier to sense than to describe. When Hussein, addressing his people that same night, spoke of the peace and happiness that he craved and that he was sure Muna would give him, his sincerity was evident.

The prophets of doom—especially at the Foreign Office and the State Department—who saw Hussein's marriage to an Englishwoman as political suicide, were confounded. There were grumbles and jeers in the media at Cairo and Damascus, but they were less poisonous than they could have been and were still to be. In fact, the marriage strengthened rather than weakened Hussein's position in the long run, if only because it once more vindicated his own instincts against those of his would-be guardians. Muna shunned a political role, no doubt by choice, and she never became queen. After the birth on 30 January 1962 of her first son, 'Abdallah, who was recognized for three years as the crown prince, Muna was styled the Hashemite equivalent of Royal Highness.

Early in 1961, a trend took shape that may have been triggered by Hussein's intended marriage and his perceived need to improve his image in the Jordanian public. The politicians and army officers who had come before the public as plotters and traitors and had been imprisoned or run away started to receive royal pardons. The prisoners were set free first, and the absconders permitted to return later; by 1967, there was hardly a malcontent who had made a name for himself as an enemy of the Hashemite Entity and who had not returned to the king's peace and been given, as often as not, a lucrative position. (The last of the lot was Rimawi, in 1971.) Again, Hussein's political instinct proved to be correct; he never had reason to regret his clemency. But this was a political rather than a humanitarian instinct, for common folk among the politically obnoxious were as liable as ever to be arrested and maltreated and to disappear without trial in the desert detention camps—sometimes for years, although not, it seems, "forever." (Imprisoned Communists—regarded by the king with a malice that he evidently did not feel toward his other enemies—were released on the condition that they foreswear their faith. No more than about half eventually did so, which was another indication of the steadfastness of the Communist cadre in Jordan as elsewhere in the Arab East.)

The summer that followed the Hussein–Abdel Nasser exchange was a period of uneasy truce, as the tenor of the exchange indeed presaged. Diplomatic representation remained at the chargé d'affaires level. The common Arab League enterprise in the late summer of 1961 in support of Kuwait against the pretensions of Qasim's Iraq did little to draw Jordan and the UAR together. Hussein was willing enough to show his accommodation to an Arab League resolution once he could do so without detriment to himself, but he also wanted to build up his new relationship with Iraq in case his relations with Abdel Nasser deteriorated once more. That eventuality materialized sooner than Hussein could have foreseen.

10

The Breakup of the UAR and After

The Syrian army çoup of 28 September 1961 and the breakup of the union between Egypt and Syria in its wake took Hussein as unawares as it took anybody outside the circle of conspirators immediately involved. Hussein's fear of this spectacular enhancement of Abdel Nasser's power had been known from the first. Hussein had never bothered to disguise it, and whenever his relations with Abdel Nasser reached yet another low, he and the Jordanian official media called on the Syrian people to rise up against its alien oppressors.[1] Subversion and sabotage activities emanating from Amman, feeble as they were, had not distinguished between the Jordanian defectors living in Damascus and Syrian objectives proper so long as those could be associated in any way with UAR activism. It is likely that a few individuals who later took a sizable, or even a prominent, part in the coup had received at some time money payments from Hussein.[2] But Hussein did not engineer the Syrian army coup—he had no means to do so.

When news of the coup reached Amman, Hussein became frantic. He immediately put the army on alert, but because the events in Damascus posed no conceivable military threat to Jordan, either this was a reflex reaction or Hussein seriously considered intervention, should Abdel Nasser try to restore the union by force. Western evidence supports the latter presumption, and again Hussein had to be restrained by the British and American ambassadors.[3] As on earlier occasions, we have no way of knowing whether Hussein had expected to be restrained.

Of greater significance were the political responses.[4] From the first, in the morning hours of 28 September, Radio Amman repeated, and thereby publicized, the communiqués given out by the insurgents in Damascus (except for the ninth communiqué, which for a few hours in the afternoon envisaged a settlement and the saving of the union). The following day, 29 September, Jordan formally recognized the seceded Syrian government of Ma'mun al-Kuzbari, within minutes of the announcement of its formation. The recognition was immediately followed by declarations of "joy" and "pride" made by Prime Minister Talhuni on behalf of the king, and soon by the king in person.

The UAR[5] broke off diplomatic relations with both Jordan and Turkey, the two countries that had recognized independent Syria before Abdel Nasser himself despaired of saving the union late on 29 September. Turkey's recognition could be rationalized, and was so rationalized, from the Cairo point of view as that of a powerful NATO country that had always cast covetous eyes on northern Syria and therefore aided any movement that would leave Syria weak and defenseless. Hussein's overt delight, however, was a bitter humiliation for Abdel Nasser. He chose what was probably the most dignified way out by admitting to the nation on 2 October 1961 that Hussein in his letters earlier that year had succeeded in deceiving him. Years later, Hussein was to concede for general consumption that his public joy had been ill considered.[6]

In the short-term view, the end of the union between Egypt and Syria under the aegis of Abdel Nasser undoubtedly meant monumental relief for Jordan, as it did for Israel, and Hussein's exultation is understandable. But it is more difficult to evaluate the breakup of the union in a wider historical perspective. A case can easily be made that the UAR of Egypt and Syria had been something of a paper dragon. Abdel Nasser was bound to find Syria more than he could digest. However, a Syria held and controlled—on the international scene at least—by Abdel Nasser meant the elimination of the regional upheaval that independent Syria had represented since the end of World War II. It does not need much imagination to argue that with the UAR intact, there would not have been either the Six-Day War or the Palestine Liberation Organization (PLO) as it evolved after the Six-Day War. And of course, the breakup of the UAR was not entirely accidental: Abdel Nasser in January 1958 had indeed taken on more than he could handle.

The fifth Chamber of Deputies, elected in October 1956 with a majority fundamentally disloyal to the Entity and changed beyond recognition in the wake of the royal coup six months later, reached the end of its term in October 1960. However, Hussein and Rifa'i were not prepared to expose the precarious calm gained by 1959 to yet another electoral convulsion, and a constitutional amendment easily passed by the National Assembly in January 1960 gave the king the right to extend the life of parliament "for a period of no less than one year and not more than two years."[7] Hussein issued the requisite decree.

A new elections law of 11 June 1960[8] increased the number of deputies to sixty, thirty from each bank, with the minorities still overrepresented. (The number of deputies had been increased from forty to fifty in the autumn of 1958, after the breakup of the federation with Iraq, to accommodate at least some of the Jordanian members of the federal parliament.) The elections for the sixth Chamber took place on 19 October 1961. The apprehensions of the king and Rifa'i, now president of the Senate, proved groundless, or rather, they were neutralized. The new Chamber was as uncontroversial in its composition as it had ever been in the halcyon days of Abdallah and Abu'l Huda, although the technique for achieving this desired result had become more sophisticated. Intimidation at the election booths and falsification of ballots seem to have been abandoned. Instead, the local authorities—district and subdistrict governors, police commanders, and security officers—working in unison, persuaded undesirable candidates to abstain from coming forward or to withdraw their candidacies, or at worst, they withheld the prospective candidates' necessary certificates of a noncriminal past.[9]

The result was that forty-seven of the sixty seats were determined by *tazkiyya,* or consensus, there being only one candidate, and of the rest most contests took place in constituencies that were conservative by tradition, such as Bethlehem, Hebron, and Tafila. It is a telling example of how the style of the king's governance had changed, even though its substance remained intact. The public accepted this wholesale falsification—no less false for being more subtle—with apathy. The authorities were ready, and were seen to be ready, to deal with troublemakers. Moreover, the appearance of only traditionalist candidates kept away the natural leaders of mass protest. And lastly, good luck also helped Hussein: the end of the union between Egypt and Syria less than four weeks before the elections, coupled with Abdel Nasser's loss of face, was bound to dampen the opposition, popular and intellectual alike.

The new Chamber—safe, docile, and loyal—had been sitting for three months when Talhuni resigned on 27 January 1962 to make way for Wasfi al-Tall, formerly the ambassador at Baghdad who had returned to Amman as a victim of Qasim's own Hallstein Doctrine.[10]

The first cabinet of Wasfi al-Tall, formed on 28 January 1962, is another milestone in the history of modern Jordan; indeed, in some respects it was the birth of modern Jordan. However, in one vital matter there would be no change, and here the new prime minister was to "out-Hussein" the king himself until his murder ten years later: Jordan remained authoritarian in the sense that no regard for parliamentarism, public opinion, or the broadening of the government base was ever permitted for long even to appear as challenging the fundamentals of the Entity, and as long as Tall prevailed, no such challenge was ever permitted for a moment.[11] This reservation in favor of conservatism must be kept in mind whenever Tall's work for Jordan, before 1967 or after, is considered.

Tall's appointment was not a complete surprise. He was well educated—a graduate of the American University of Beirut—outspoken, fiercely efficient, incorruptible, and of proven physical courage. His close relations with the king were well known. His past as a senior administrator and diplomat was impressive. His social standing as member of a leading Irbid family was an advantage. And the Palestinians were likely to respect him for his record as a fighting officer in the war of 1948.

It is less clear what made Hussein turn to Tall at just that time. Talhuni was doing well enough, and he certainly posed no challenge to either Hussein's power or his ego. But it was part of Hussein's statecraft to have available at all times a choice of prime minister candidates, and by 1961 this choice had been depleted: Rifaʿi was aging, and Abuʾl Huda, Hashim, and Hazzaʿ al-Majali were dead. Among the possibilities of the coming generation, Tall easily outshone his competitors. Added to this was the confusion created by the disruption of the UAR, which made it desirable, from Hussein's point of view, to have an activist and a foe of "Nasserite" nationalism as his chief policy adviser. As such, Tall had only recently proved himself by channeling, from Baghdad, Jordanian aid to the equally anti-Nasserite Nationalist Social party in Lebanon (originally the Parti Populaire Syrien), which had just attempted, unsuccessfully, to seize power in Beirut. (It is unlikely that Hussein, or Tall for that matter, was privy to the attempt, but their previous encouragement is on record. There are indications that Tall had contacts beyond the king's wishes and instructions.) And of course, with his dismissal from Baghdad, Tall was available, and although the choice of Tall may have been the king's there is no doubt that he was enthusiastically encouraged by the American ambassador, William B. Macomber, who knew Tall well.[12]

Hussein's letter of appointment and Tall's of acceptance were unsensational but, as it turned out, not meaningless, with their stress on administrative reform.[13] Moreover, the composition of the new cabinet was unprecedented: it contained no former ministers, and only one former member of parliament, and it was heavy with men of known administrative and professional experience.

The first six months of Tall's first cabinet were occupied by administrative rehabilitation that genuinely tried to get at the core, unlike past "purges" and "efficiency campaigns." From the beginning, Tall—we may suppose it was his initiative, although with the goodwill of the king—had an amendment to the civil service law passed by parliament that enabled him to deal with central and local authorities generally as he wished in accordance with the needs of the state. Clearly, Tall, although anything but a democrat, did not want to have to resort to extralegal measures. The continued release or recall of political offenders fitted well into the picture, although here Tall received credit for a process that the king had set in motion before his appointment. (The birth of Crown Prince 'Abdallah, Muna's firstborn, was the occasion for a general amnesty law.) Tall, however, failed in his effort—as valiant as it was hopeless from the outset—to establish a measure of civilian supervision over the army.[14] That he encountered the furious opposition of the commander in chief, Habis al-Majali, was probably less important than that Tall struck at a basic rule of the king, of keeping the army under his direct control.

It was in accord with the image of the new government and, in all fairness, its own character that economic development received prime attention. Here, too, Tall followed up a process that had started before his incumbency, but by concentrating official action on existing trends, he strengthened them and increased public belief in their viability.[15]

But administrative reform, economic awareness, and a judicious line of "let bygones be bygones" were not synonymous with pluralistic liberalism, as was demonstrated by the "Palestinian attitudes" of the king and his prime minister during this period. Here the core of the Entity as reconstructed in 1949 was at risk. The Hashemite kingdom spoke for the whole of its people on either bank, and a rival "entity" within its boundaries was out of the question. If exigencies took their toll, if lip service had to be paid on occasion to the concept of Palestinian rights, so be it. Nobody was really permitted to doubt that these were exigencies and lip service. No change was wrought in this respect during the first Tall ministry.

What did occur was a change in tactics: Tall took it upon himself to tackle the wolf, as it were, in his own lair. He may have been encouraged by Abdel Nasser's preoccupation with his domestic affairs during most of 1962, but more likely Tall acted in keeping with his innate impetuosity. However that may be, and the two explanations are not mutually exclusive, shortly after his accession to office and for many months, Tall pursued an active "Palestinian" line, with statements of policy and a series of discussion with Palestinian personalities like Ahmad Shuqayri who were uncommitted to the Jordanian Entity. These activities were meant to prove that it was Jordan that was the true repository of Palestinian aims and hopes. It was a mistake. The incompatibility between the sides was manifest and insoluble. Hopes were raised that had to be disappointed. Palestinian politicians who had for long prominently served the Hashemite Entity in sensitive posts were caught between conflicting demands and had to be disciplined or even discarded, with bad feelings on either side. The demotion in January 1963 of the Palestinian former minister Anwar Nusayba as governor of Jerusalem—Tall's own appointee—is a poignant example. The result was the first consolidation of Tall's image as a hater of Palestinians and, on a different level, the unnecessary disturbance of a domestic peace in which the regime more than anybody had an interest.

Hussein's euphoria during the year following the end of the union between Egypt and Syria reached its domestic climax in the elections for the seventh Chamber, which took place on 25 November 1962. Tall had evidently convinced Hussein that the tainted elections to the sixth Chamber were a blot on the record of the new era and were, moreover, unnecessary. Accordingly, official and semiofficial announcements that preceded the voting day stressed the virtues of untampered elections, including unimpeded candidacies, and their concomitant, a true though patriotic opposition. The number of candidates who contested the 60 seats was the largest ever by far, 166, with only 3 seats (apart from the 3 reserved for the East Bank beduin) going by *tazkiyya*. Participation, too, was the highest ever, a country average of about 70 percent, which posed a decent mean between the embarrassing indifference common to Jordanian elections in the past and the 99 percent already typical of "progressive" regimes throughout the Third World.[16] Government supervision had indeed been largely passive—observant but not oppressive—with less coercion than for any other elections in the history of Jordan except those for the "Nabulsi" chamber of 1956 (of which Nablusi himself had not been a member). Political parties indeed remained forbidden; this lesson was never unlearned.

The results were what the king and Tall should have expected but evidently did not; the number of first-time members was exceptionally high, twenty-one, and so was their formal education: both warning signals regarding the political order of things in Jordan. On the motion of confidence taken on 5 January 1963, with little as yet to excite the public except the remote Yemen civil war, eighteen members voted against the government, twelve of whom represented West Bank constituencies. For Tall, it was a shock that prepared for his resignation two months later, in an Arab situation that had dramatically worsened from the Jordanian viewpoint. In equal measure, his usefulness to Hussein decreased for the time being. Hussein on his part relearned the lesson that the West Bank was inherently unreliable and that "free" elections were a luxury he could not afford.

If Hussein's euphoria after the breakup of the UAR and, through his, Tall's, expressed itself on the domestic front in a mood of reform, on the Arab front it was characterized by a brashness that was Hussein's own brand of aggression.

Denigrations of the Egyptian leadership (Hussein rarely mentioned Abdel Nasser by name but frequently pinpointed him by description) were, of course, nothing new. What gave a twist to the attacks at that time was Hussein's tendency to pounce on Abdel Nasser while Abdel Nasser was preoccupied with setting his own house in order. Those were the days when Abdel Nasser geared his world, ideological and political, to "Arab socialism" rather than "nationalism," with a consequent shift of attention to domestic affairs. Those were the days of the "Arab Socialist Union"— vastly more important to Abdel Nasser than its predecessors, the "Liberation Rally" and the "Arab Union"—and of the National Action Charter.[17] It does not seem that Hussein tried to analyze what was going on in Cairo, but he rarely missed an opportunity to remind Abdel Nasser of his Syrian discomfiture. He made it clear that he regarded Abdel Nasser as unregenerate, and the political company that he kept as disreputable. Even the common venture in Kuwait was explained by Talhuni as the need to forestall an attempt by Egyptian troops to take over that country. It is true that Talhuni gave this insulting explanation to an Iraqi newspaper editor in what appears as a rather naive attempt to propitiate Qasim. But the interview naturally became common knowledge.[18]

At the same time, Hussein took pains to strengthen his ties with Saudi Arabia. It may have occurred to him that King Saud was nearing the end of the road, ill and discredited as he was, and that under these circumstances a "semiunion" between the two kingdoms was not likely to provide Jordan with additional resources. But Hussein's wish to insult Abdel Nasser seems to have been compulsive. A three-day meeting between the two kings at Taif, on 27 to 29 August 1962, culminated in a communiqué declaring immediate "complete military union" and "the establishment of a joint military command." Because there was no meaningful follow-up, the assertion, in the same communiqué, of "co-ordination. . . . in foreign and inter-Arab policies" was of greater significance, as it registered a genuine development in Middle Eastern alignments.[19] At about the same time, but not mentioned in the communiqué, negotiations started for redrawing the frontiers between the two countries, which would extend the Jordanian shore of the Red Sea to the south. However, the entente achieved an unforeseen reality when the civil war in Yemen broke out in the last week of September 1962.

When Imam Ahmad of Yemen died on 19 September 1962, Hussein ordered his court into mourning for fourteen days, out of a sense of monarchic solidarity and in recognition of the hatred for Abdel Nasser that the imam evinced after the incongruous "Union of Arab States" of 1958 between Yemen and the UAR had evaporated. A week later, a military coup at Sanaa proclaimed the birth of the Arab Republic of Yemen. Ahmad's heir, the new Imam Muhammad al-Badr, escaped from his capital and organized his forces among the Zaydi tribes in the north and east of the country. A civil war was afoot.

In important respects, the Yemeni coup repeated those takeovers elsewhere in the Arab world over the previous five years, whether completed or merely attempted. The mutineers considered themselves revolutionary Arab nationalists whose hero was Abdel Nasser. But Abdel Nasser had not organized the coup, nor is it probable that he had advance knowledge of its execution. All the same, like other such attempts, the coup vindicated what Abdel Nasser stood for in the eyes of his admirers and his own. His honor was involved in its success, and so its failure, without his doing his utmost in helping it, would utterly shame him. All this was in addition to the plain strategic advantage of having a friendly, perhaps even a docile, regime entrenched in the backyard of Saudi Arabia and on the doorstep of British Aden. Thus within two days, Cairo turned from being a powerful transmitter of the calls from Sanaa into an enthusiastic supporter of the revolutionaries' claims, and on 29 September the UAR became the first state to recognize the young republic. On 4 October, Abdel Nasser publicly pledged to Lieutenant Colonel 'Abdallah al-Sallal, the Yemeni revolutionary leader, the assistance of the UAR against attack or interference. By then, troops had already set out from Suez to give substance to the pledge. Five years of UAR military involvement in Yemen had begun.

From the first, Hussein turned Jordan into a center of support for royalist resistance. The Yemeni legation at Amman served as an early nucleus for a diplomatic rally. The king and the prime minister were lavish in their expressions of support for the new imam, who "expressed the desire of the Yemeni people [for reform]" and of condemnation for the UAR. The justification given for supporting al-Badr is rather curious, and it certainly bears Tall's stamp.[20]

Above all, from the start Hussein brought pressure to bear on a hesitant

King Saud "to intervene in force in Yemen before it was too late."[21] This particular problem was solved when Saud once more abdicated his operative responsibilities—this time definitely, as it turned out—to Amir Faysal, who again became the Saudi prime minister on 17 October 1962. Faysal energetically took up the royalist cause in Yemen, and the fronts were established. It was in keeping with the geographical facts that the Saudi Arabian presence in the civil war, in contrast with that of the UAR, came to lie less in massive ground support and more in logistics, rear bases, and the provision of strategic depth. Thus Hussein was not really put into the position of deciding whether or not to dispatch army units to Yemen, a decision that he might have found hard to make, despite all his passionate commitment. However, during the first weeks when the fate of Yemen was uncertain, he made ready to engage his tiny air force, the apple of his eye. Thereupon, its commander and two combat pilots, on 12 and 13 November 1962, defected to Cairo. It must have been one of the deepest humiliations in Hussein's career.

Of greater practical consequence to Hussein was the position taken by the Kennedy administration. It seems that from the first day, when it was clear that the coup of Sanaa had succeeded (and the early news exaggerated the scope of its success), both the White House and the State Department were in favor of speedy recognition.[22] Beyond the customary postulates—effective rule by a constituted government over most of the territory—considerations came into play that were not entirely rational. The imam's defunct regime had been widely characterized as "medieval," and the Kennedy administration was nothing if not forward looking. The desire to improve or at least to consolidate relations with Abdel Nasser, despite the Syrian secession, which was still monopolizing the Arab question, was rational as such. But improving relations with Abdel Nasser meant destabilizing the position of three solid allies of the United States— if not in reality, as the administration claimed, then certainly in their own estimate: Saudi Arabia, Jordan, and Britain, then engaged in evolving a policy in Aden leading up to the South Arabian Federation, anathema to Abdel Nasser. Washington's argument was that a speedy end to the civil war in Yemen through the consolidation of the republic meant eliminating centers of unrest dangerous to Saudi Arabia and Aden; it carried no conviction. After much diplomatic trafficking among Washington, Cairo, Riyadh, London, and even Amman, the administration obtained an "assurance" from Abdel Nasser that the UAR would withdraw its troops from Yemen, "as other external forces engaged in support of the Yemeni royalists are removed from the frontier and external support for the royalists is stopped."[23] On the strength of this assurance, the United States recognized the Yemeni republic on 19 December 1962. President Kennedy, in person and through his aides, endeavored to reassure his allies but was unsuccessful. The British government refused to recognize the new regime until Sallal solved the problem for it by closing the British legation in Taizz (the seat of foreign representations).[24]

In Jordan, Tall first and Hussein later expressed their disappointment in the United States in courteous but explicit terms,[25] the likes of which had not been uttered in public in respect to the United States since the special relationship was forged in 1957. In the end, Kennedy suffered over this affair the common fate of the appeaser. The war did not end; neither Abdel Nasser nor Sallal was won over; the Egyptian military presence in Yemen increased by leaps and bounds instead of phasing out; and the respect of all sides for the wisdom and forcefulness of American policy was put into question. American dithering over Yemen was at least in part responsible for the establishment of diplomatic relations between Jordan and the Soviet Union in August 1963. It seems from the developments, of both Soviet global politics and the dynamics in Jordan, that the step was inevitable. But it is also clear that it would have been delayed if Hussein had not felt that a snub to the United States was in order.

Hussein's involvement in Yemen was voluntary; whatever the inducements, they cannot be compared with the reasons that propelled the UAR and Saudi Arabia into action. But the same does not hold for the problem that gripped Hussein in the spring of 1963.

Qasim was toppled on 8 February 1963, and a regime dominated by chiefly civilian Ba'this took over in Iraq. Qasim, through his vagaries, had been friendless for years, and Jordan, like the world at large, hastened to recognize the successors. It was only to be expected that among Abdel Nasser's admirers in Cairo and elsewhere, high hopes would be expressed for Iraq's speedy return into the circle of Arab unity and even for a merger with the UAR. The Cairo press did not fail to predict Hussein's downfall as a logical sequence of Qasim's fall. However, with Syria ruled by "secessionists" like President Nazim al-Qudsi and Prime Minister Khalid al-'Azm, there was no need for immediate concern, and both Hussein and Tall preserved their equanimity, at least in public.

But the situation changed dramatically with the coup in Damascus on 8 March 1963. As in Iraq one month earlier, the army took care of the physical takeover, whereas Ba'th civilians provided the bulk of the new government, with Salah al-Din al-Bitar as prime minister. Now the cry for unity went up in earnest. After a preliminary visit to Damascus by 'Ali Salah al-Sa'di, the Iraqi deputy prime minister and secretary general of the Ba'th regional command at Baghdad, tripartite talks were held in

Cairo at the highest level from 14 to 16 March, with follow-ups between
the Egyptian and Syrian leaders until 21 March. The published results
were enthusiastic, the unofficial even more than the official. The rebirth
of an enlarged union composed of Egypt, Syria, and Iraq, embodying the
strength and eschewing the weaknesses of its forerunner, was expected.
And these expectations appeared justified when after final rounds of talks
in Cairo, the document proclaiming the new United Arab Republic was
signed by the three heads of government on 17 April 1963.

We now know that from the start the union rested on feet of clay. The
Cairo talks had not been a symposium of brotherly love,[26] and within two
months of its signature, the union agreement was consigned to the scrap
heap for all the world to see. The heritage of the first UAR—the resentment, suspicion, and, above all, the insight acquired by the partners
into their respective personalities—had created a chasm between Abdel
Nasser on the one side and the Ba'this on the other that could not be
closed.

Hussein was shaken by what he saw as the ring again closing around
Jordan. His abrupt descent from cockiness to evident alarm is another of
those phenomena that make his political nature so hard to define. It certainly was not his finest hour. Apparently, both Hussein and Tall rated
the coup in Damascus, coming as it did four weeks after that in Baghdad,
as nothing less than a disaster. Salvation seemed to lie in an instant and
unreserved attempt to curry favor (although not, be it stated at once, in
abandoning any of the principles of the Hashemite Entity). The new regime at Damascus was recognized within the day. Radio attacks on the
Cairo regime and its works ceased at once. "Egypt" became again "the
United Arab Republic," and Tall, in a hastily summoned press conference
on 9 March, found kind words for his "Ba'thi friends."[27]

On 16 March, Hussein addressed the central issue at an international
press conference.[28] The gist of the message was that "the latest events
have shown that our former critics are now copying our policy and attitude" and that "we want to cooperate with them and are willing to help
them with all our resources." He forestalled doubts about Jordan's being
a suitable partner for the union, with his proffered opinion that Jordan
was "more liberated than any Arab state." He played down his relations
with Saudi Arabia and with the royalists in Yemen, although he admitted
his sympathy for both. And because the recent coups had, after all, been
carried out by the military, he found it right to indicate the limit of his
complaisance: "We do not tolerate partisanship to infiltrate into our armed
forces. . . . We have always been against the indulgence of soldiers in
politics." That the king was in earnest in this matter, at any rate, was

shown by a well-publicized letter to Commander in Chief Majali regarding "certain measures against a number of officers involved in aspersions and allegations . . . "—clearly precautionary steps, as nothing is known of an actual army plot at that time.[29]

One thing was clear to Hussein at an early date: Tall had to go. It was difficult enough for Hussein to purchase an indulgence on his own behalf. But Tall as an additional handicap was too much. And so on 27 March 1963, Tall tendered the resignation of his government. In his letter to the king, he described the cause with a clarity that was rare in the political tradition of Jordan, even if it was ceremoniously circumscribed:

> I have had the honour of talking to Your Majesty during the past two weeks on new developments. These require a reassessment of the general situation and the creation of a new government to undertake the responsibility for such a study with the object of achieving Your Majesty's lofty aims of building the country [*balad*] and serving the nation [*umma*].[30]

It was a disappointing end to a high-spirited program.

On that same day, the king turned to Samir al-Rifaʿi, who now formed his sixth government and, as it turned out, his last. It is not necessary to look far for the reasons for Hussein's choice: an old hand with no-non-sense notions, incomparable experience, and an unassailable loyalty to the Hashemite monarchy. Unless the king wished to appease his foes by appointing one of Abdel Nasser's sympathizers—and Nabulsi had been a lesson that the king never forgot—Rifaʿi had no peer. His health and presumably his stamina had been on the decline for some time, but a young man of twenty-seven must be excused if he has no intuition in this sphere. Rifaʿi's cabinet was in keeping with his political persona. There was no experimenting now; Hussein and Rifaʿi played it safe. Saʿid al-Mufti was back as vice premier; Talhuni was reinstated as chief of the royal cabinet; a Majali was at the Interior Ministry; and ʿAkif al-Faʾiz of the Banu Sakhr returned to the government from which he had been absent since the fracas with the Majali: the tribal confederations must have understood that this was no time for internecine feuds. It is of interest that the only newcomer to the cabinet was Hasan al-Kayid of Irbid, who much later was to become prominent—and hated—as an enemy of the Palestinian organizations.[31]

After the announcement of the tripartite agreement on 17 April 1963, mass rallies formed in the main towns of the West Bank, in Irbid, and in Amman. Ostensibly expressions of support for unity, they soon turned into demonstrations against the regime. By 20 April, Jerusalem and Nablus were out of control, and the army went in to clear the streets.[32] The

king was in earnest. The units employed were handpicked for their loyalty; prominent among them the beduin Desert Patrol, successors to the
original "Glubb's Girls," in robes and ringlets.[33] A strict curfew—not
applied to tourists—did the rest, and order was generally restored. A total
of six people had been killed in the clashes, according to official figures.[34]
Among the public figures taken into preventive custody was Sulayman
al-Nabulsi.

Success in the battle of the streets—undoubtedly Hussein's first concern during this crisis—went with failure where he may not have expected it. On 13 April 1963, Rifaʿi addressed the Chamber before a vote
of confidence that he demanded. The thesis of his statement was his professed belief in "the inevitability of unity." However, the nature of this
belief was indicated by Rifaʿi's emphasis on "the peculiar contribution
which the Jordanian community" could make.[35] The debate and the voting
were deferred to 20 April. When the time arrived, the riots were at their
peak. Again the kingdom's survival seemed to hang in the balance. It
was not for nothing that Tall had prided himself on the freedom with
which the seventh Chamber of Deputies had been elected. Member after
member rose to attack the prime minister on his record—with what mixture of sincerity and opportunism it is impossible to determine, although
the lead of a few West Bank deputies stands out.

After thirty-one deputies, an absolute majority of the Chamber, had
voiced their distrust, the prime minister announced his resignation. It is
the only time so far that a government has resigned in Jordan for losing
the confidence of parliament. There was no actual vote of confidence;
Rifaʿi resigned before that. This point is important. Political tradition in
Jordan being what it was, the prime minister might have asked the speaker
to end the debate. The prime minister could then have used the customary
measures to persuade members to change their minds, or the king might
have dissolved parliament. It stands to reason that Rifaʿi in his prime
would have done so. But Rifaʿi was no longer in his prime, and with his
resignation, he vanished from the political scene.[36] One need not sym-
pathize with Rifaʿi's aims and means throughout his public career to feel
a tinge of regret that the old war-horse should have disappeared so meekly.

Hussein, however, had no time to waste on Rifaʿi. He asked his great-
uncle Sharif Husayn bin Nasir (Ibrahim Hashim no longer being available) to form a caretaker government before holding new elections, the
behavior of the "late" Chamber having resulted from "personal rivalries
and an attempt to seek selfish benefits. . . . "[37] Hussein's optimism,
combined with his measures, paid off. By 29 April 1963, the atmosphere
of the towns everywhere could be described as normal, and daytime re-

strictions were removed. But Jordanian citizens leaving the country had
to obtain a permit from military area commanders, apparently as the result
of assaults—ostensibly by Jordanian students—on Jordanian embassies
in several Middle Eastern capitals. Already on 28 April, Hussein had
summed up the recent events by attributing them in public to "a group
of people who do not believe in this country and this nation [*umma*].
Whenever we have difficulties, that group used to abandon us. . . . I
assure you that I shall not tolerate, and shall not allow the toleration of,
any prejudice to our aims. . . . "[38]

The elections for the eighth Chamber of Deputies were duly held on 6
July 1963. They were as tightly managed as those for the sixth Chamber
had been in October 1961, and the results were as satisfactory from the
king's viewpoint.

Although Hussein weathered this storm, as he had that of July 1958
(which was also triggered by a stunning success for Abdel Nasser on the
Arab front), this time he never lost faith in his survival, as he apparently
had for a while on the former occasion. But it seems that the same cannot
be said for his great ally in the West.

At first glance, the official American reaction to the unity agreements
of 17 April 1963 and their repercussions in Jordan was satisfactory from
the Jordanian view. At a foreign policy briefing for newspaper editors on
22 April, Phillips Talbot, the assistant secretary of state for Near Eastern
and South Asian affairs, said that the United States believed that Jordan
would "continue to be a separate state" because of its importance to the
stability of the Middle East and because of its close ties with countries
outside the region, "including the USA." Also, the projected new United
Arab Republic still had to prove that it was workable.[39]

It takes some reading between the lines and perhaps an inside knowledge of State Department cogitations concerning Jordan since 1956 to
realize that "a separate state" of Jordan is not synonymous with "the
Hashemite kingdom" and that Hussein, the linchpin of that kingdom and
a known ally of the United States, went unmentioned. The formulation
of Talbot's announcement was undoubtedly carefully considered, in particular as to what it left unsaid.

Already on 19 April 1963, as rioting in Jordan was approaching its
height, the prominent Tel Aviv daily *Haaretz* reported that President Kennedy had told Israeli Deputy Defense Minister Shimon Peres earlier that
month that the United States would continue to give full backing to the
Arab unification trend, without prejudice to the security needs of Israel.
At the same time, *Haaretz,* quoting "an [American] diplomat," stated that
U.S. policy might persuade Hussein "without difficulty" to leave Jordan,

as the United States was "now" convinced that the days of the monarchy were numbered in Jordan (and Saudi Arabia).[40] The report was promptly denied by the State Department, which asserted that "any suggestions that the United States is working for the abdication of King Hussein of Jordan and the inclusion of Jordan in the UAR are totally false and without any foundation whatsoever." But this denial denied what had not really been claimed. Peres dismissed the report as "sheer speculation" and "a figment of the imagination."[41]

It is perhaps in this context that an otherwise enigmatic statement by Salah al-Bitar, the Ba'thi prime minister of Syria, should be read: he stated to the U.S. and British ambassadors in Damascus, and distributed the statement to the press on 16 May 1963, that Syria rejected "all forms of trusteeship in Jordan and the Arab states . . . whatever happens in any Arab state is a purely domestic affair."[42] By then, at the latest, Bitar had become skeptical of the new Arab union. Any American backing of "Arab unification," resting as it did on the premise of Abdel Nasser's power and attraction, would rouse Bitar's resentment and perhaps his contempt of American obtuseness. President Kennedy and his aides may not have seen through Bitar's motivation; if they did, they may have rejected it as counter to historical trends in the Arab Middle East. What matters is that in a crisis, the State Department, despite this particular administration's ideological proclivities, still maintained that the separate existence of Jordan was useful to the United States, even though the Hashemites there might be a hindrance rather than an advantage.

A position paper written when the crisis was well past summarized the return to a more conservative attitude in the upper reaches of the U.S. administration regarding Jordan:

> Our support for Jordan is based on the conviction that collapse of the government or chaos there could set up severe tensions leading even to renewal of Arab–Israel hostilities . . . we would not be opposed to some political realignment in the Near East which would link Jordan more closely with its Arab neighbors leading hopefully to a reduction in the burdens we now carry to preserve Jordan's independence. Under these circumstances King Hussein and his regime appear to represent the best hope for stability in Jordan.[43]

In fact, Hussein survived by means of his own actions, and the United States was not prepared to undermine his position.

When the crisis was still in recent memory, Hussein denied in public that he would ask for military help from Great Britain, as he had done in 1958.[44] Early in June, the U.S. government ordered units of the Sixth

Fleet to proceed toward the eastern shore of the Mediterranean in a show of support for King Hussein. The rationale for the maneuver and its timing is not quite clear. The ambassador at Amman, not previously informed, complained to the president at a later meeting at the White House that "we should not throw it [i.e., demonstrative solidarity with Hussein] around when he does not need it [any more]."[45]

The crisis of April 1963 started another ball rolling. The Israelis, especially Prime Minister Ben-Gurion, viewed the disturbances with apprehension. The Hashemite kingdom might break up at any moment, and the chances that it would do so were rated high. An Israeli intervention would then be necessary, considering the concomitant of an Egyptian-Syrian-Iraqi federation or union under Abdel Nasser's aegis.[46] And so the Israeli general staff devised Plan Granite for the occupation of the West Bank. A military commander there received his contingency appointment as military governor—Major General Chaim Herzog, a former director of military intelligence and future president of Israel—and rudiments of an administration began to be thought out.[47] The American government, cognizant of what was going on, tried to calm Israeli fears and, more especially, to dissuade Israel from taking "sudden action" if Hussein should disappear.[48] The crisis soon ended in Jordan. But the measures that Israel took or considered left their mark when the storm did break four years later.

A new departure in Israeli–Jordanian relations—under American prodding—developed later in 1963: the renewal, after a break of twelve years, of purposeful contacts, in regard to which the Six-Day War was a mere hiatus.[49] The basic attitudes were not new. On the Israeli side, the view prevailed that Hashemite Jordan was better than any conceivable alternative and that it might even be made to serve Israeli's interests. Hussein, on his part, had inherited his grandfather's lack of anti-Zionist zeal. Beset with existential dangers as he was, he responded to a favorable atmosphere that did not, after all, demand overt action and that might, moreover, afford him additional protection. And naturally the desire to please an activist American administration was woven into these considerations.

The breakthrough—if this is not too strong a word—came in the summer of 1963, after Ben-Gurion's final retirement as prime minister and minister of defense, and his replacement in both capacities by Levi Eshkol. Eshkol, at one with Ben-Gurion in politics and ideology, differed from him in temperament. He believed in the innate virtue of opponents talking, as, up to a point, did Hussein. And so in September, a meeting took place in London between the king and Ya'acov Herzog, then deputy director for Middle Eastern affairs in the prime minister's office. Others followed, such as a meeting, in Paris, between the king and Foreign Minister Golda Meir, in the autumn of 1965. These meetings had their agendas and did make some progress. There were renewed understandings regarding the division of the Jordan and Yarmuk rivers. There was a written agreement by Jordan in 1965 that American Patton tanks delivered to the Jordanian army should not enter the interior of the West Bank which had been a condition for Israeli acquiescence to the sale in the first place. Indeed, the very limitation of problems under discussion made limited successes possible.

In the main, however, these talks merely served as "atmosphere," an attitude that was as characteristic of Eshkol as it was of Hussein.[50] There was no talk of formal peace or nonbelligerency (apart from pious phrases): even if Jordan had been interested which it was not, its position in the Arab world would have made such a proposition unthinkable. The "Palestine question" or "territorial compromises" of the kind that strained contacts after 1967 naturally were not on the agenda. In May 1964, the U.S. embassy in Tel Aviv assessed the Israeli position: " . . . re Jordan, Israel plays protective role eagerly, and can be expected [to] react sharply to almost any change in status quo there."[51] It is a fair summation, and Hussein drew similar conclusions, at least until the Samuʿ raid in November 1966. To him, it was entirely a matter of intelligent opportunism, until the last week of May 1967 when all former assessments became irrelevant.

After the April riots had petered out and during the remainder of 1963, Jordan was in the position of being a country that made no headlines. Significantly, Sharif Husayn bin Nasir stayed in office after the July 1963 elections, constitutionally no longer as prime minister of a caretaker government. He would not have survived if the king had feared a renewal of difficulties. The appointment of Saʿid al-Mufti as deputy prime minister and Samir al-Rifaʿi's (final) translation to the senate underscore this reading.

The drawing together of the Baʿthi regimes in Syria and Iraq during 1963 did not trouble Hussein or, conversely, excite the latent opposition in Jordan; it was too obviously a further demotion of Abdel Nasser's standing on the Arab scene. In consequence, it was good policy to defuse what remained of the tensions of March and April with as little ado as possible. At home, all recent detainees were released by early autumn. Student demonstrators who appeared before the State Security Court received light sentences: weeks and months of imprisonment, usually rescinded at once. (The wedding of Amir Muhammad and the birth of Hussein's second son, Prince Faysal, during this period were appropriately

Hashemite occasions for the exercise of clemency.) Nabulsi, released from his renewed detention, found himself elevated—perhaps deflated—to the Senate, together with other National Socialist ex-ministers of his cabinet. In the Arab world, Jordan's relationship with Saudi Arabia steadily improved. Crown Prince (also Prime Minister) Faysal had stood by Hussein's side during the spring troubles, a significant departure from his position in the summer of 1958. Jordan and Saudi Arabia now exchanged ambassadors for the first time. The Jordanian ambassador at Riyadh was Shaykh Muhammad al-Shanqiti, and evidently he was welcome at the Wahhabi court. Relations with Ba'thi Syria and Iraq were in a state that passed for normalcy with these regimes; both Damascus and Baghdad were quietly eager to strengthen their ties with a country that might be expected to side with them in their new quarrel with Abdel Nasser.

Jordan's relations with the UAR during that half-year were unpleasant, but well below the danger level reached in earlier times. For once, Hussein was interested in a détente. In a lengthy meeting with the editor of Egypt's *al-Ahram,* Muhammad Hasanayn Haykal, in Paris, it was Hussein who was anxious to appear accommodating, without giving away the essentials of his position, and it was Haykal who, according to his report in *al-Ahram,* was caustic and ill humoured.[52] It is possible to see here the respective stances of the tactically stronger versus the weaker side. Hussein had some reason to feel confident, whereas Abdel Nasser, with Haykal, was also the loser on the secondary Jordanian front, at a time when his energies were taken up by a variety of difficulties: the stillborn tripartite union with Syrian and Iraq, the war in Yemen, the transition to "Arab socialism" at home, and a cooling in his relations with the United States without precedent since Kennedy's accession.[53] Above all, there was the dilemma of dealing with Israel's diversion of water from the Jordan—played up as the major threat to Arabdom for generations to come—without seeming to be soft on Israel, on the one hand, and without slithering into an untimely war in the wake of Ba'thi aggressiveness, on the other hand.

The answer that Abdel Nasser found to these challenges was to propose, on 23 December 1963, a meeting at Cairo of all Arab rulers. The problem posed by President Kennedy's newfound aversion to Abdel Nasser had been solved in Dallas thirty-one days before.

11

Summitry

On 23 December 1963, Abdel Nasser, addressing a mass rally at Port Said commemorating the seventh anniversary of the city's evacuation by its British and French invaders, called for a meeting of all Arab heads of state to consider the impending diversion by Israel of water from the Jordan River. A meeting of the chiefs of staff or of the Arab Defense Council, he said, would not suffice, because the question was political in essence rather than military.[1] It was an ingenious response to a serious challenge. Syria had recently come under the direction of a group of Ba'thi army officers headed by Major General Amin al-Hafiz, who had replaced the veteran party leaders around Bitar. Ever since the aborted Nasserite coup of July 1963, Damascus had been taunting Abdel Nasser for dragging his feet over a properly aggressive reply to the Israeli project.

Now Abdel Nasser put himself—his leadership and his prestige—at the spearhead of a coordinated effort against Israel that camouflaged his main objective of preventing matters from sliding into war at an inopportune time. But there were complementary reasons for the new departure. The recent ouster of the Ba'th in Iraq and its replacement by a regime effectively headed by 'Abd al-Salam 'Arif, a genuine admirer of Abdel Nasser, had for the first time created conditions for cooperation between Egypt and Iraq based on mutual trust, without the threat of imminent domination by the one side and servility on the other. On the debit side, the pan-Arab aspects of revolution, as proclaimed by Abdel Nasser after the breakup of Syria in September 1961 and especially in the "Charter for National Action" of May 1962,[2] had clearly proved counterproductive. The Yemeni morass was one spectacular proof, and on a different level, the worsened relations with the United States was another. To use his still unrivaled prestige in the Arab world to put up an all-embracing "unity of ranks," with himself at its head, instead of the discredited "unity of aims," was therefore a promising idea, constructive as much as tactically clever.[3]

A universal acceptance could be foreseen; in the prevailing circumstances no Arab government could have taken upon itself the onus of remaining aloof. It is worth noting that Hussein was the first, and Faysal the last, ruler to accept, although they were by then close partners in their Arab and international alignments. Faysal had the Yemeni royalists to consider, whereas Hussein would always welcome the chance to gain legitimacy by visibly figuring in the Arab camp. But Faysal's gravity and Hussein's ebullience probably played a part, too, in determining their respective responses.

The first summit took place at Cairo from 13 to 17 January 1964. It proved a significant event in the contemporary history of the region. It created "summitry," a concept that still exists. It helped diminish the constant abuse back and forth, an accomplishment that distinguishes the present generation on the Arab scene from that of the late 1950s and early 1960s.

The first summit also produced a unanimous decision—despite complaints by General Amin al-Hafiz, now president of the Syrian Revolutionary Council—to ignore all differences in the face of the Israeli danger. The summit set up the Unified Arab Command under a UAR general, ʿAli ʿAli ʿAmir, but without a specific commitment to action, in itself as good a solution to Abdel Nasser's immediate predicament as he could have wished. The summit also established the Arab Jordan Diversion Authority and began the institution of the Palestine Liberation Organization (PLO) through an announcement by ʿAbd al-Khaliq Hasuna, the Arab League secretary general, that the conference had decided on "organizing the Palestinian Arab people to enable it to play its role in liberating its country and determining its future."[4] It seems that Hussein and Faysal had been successful in excluding this announcement from the final communiqué, but they had failed to exclude Ahmad al-Shuqayri from discussions among the national leaders. In general, Abdel Nasser's personal and political ascendancy was unimpaired throughout the summit.

During the following year, the Jordanian Entity appeared integrated in the Arab political family, if we see that family through the eyes of Abdel Nasser with himself at its head. The first concomitant was the reestablishment of diplomatic relations between the UAR and Jordan on 15 January 1964, while the summit was still in session. The advantage to Hussein was obvious. There was a price to pay, in installments, and he paid it, painful though some of the installments were. More Baʿthi and nationalist detainees were released from Jafr camp, possibly the last still kept after previous amnesties over the past two years. The most prominent among the Ba'this was Dr. Munif al-Razzaz, soon to be chosen secretary general of the Ba'th National Command in Damascus. The arch-traitor, 'Abdallah al-Tall, was permitted to return from his Egyptian exile,[5] as were 'Ali Abu Nuwar and 'Ali al-Hiyyari. An even older opponent of the Entity, if less a conspirator, Dr. Subhi Abu Ghanima, was appointed in a symbolic gesture as the Jordanian ambassador to Syria, to which he had retired in Abdallah's days. Salah Shara' was also pardoned.

Jordan's diplomatic relations with the Soviet Union were activated after the formal announcement of their establishment in August 1963, and the exchange of ambassadors with other Communist countries in Europe, but not with China, soon followed. (Hussein ignored the pressure from Cairo to try to negotiate a major Soviet arms deal—MIG-21s were mentioned—financed through the United Arab Command; rather, he used that pressure to obtain F-104 fighter-bombers from the United States, together with other military hardware. It was a good example of Hussein's adroitness in getting the best of two worlds.[6] At the same time, Hussein agreed to the visit in Moscow by a mixed group of Jordanian radicals; with the situation at home well in hand there was no particular risk involved.) Finally, Hussein, by a royal decree on 22 July 1964, transferred Jordan's recognition from the royalist to the republican side in the Yemeni struggle, leaving Saudi Arabia as the only Arab government recognizing the royalists. Prime Minister Talhuni explained that the decision proved that the king was "placing all of [Jordan's] resources to make inter-Arab relations as friendly as they should be, . . . above all other considerations,"[7] a fairly straightforward comment on what must have been a distasteful step. The king himself seems to have kept silent.

A result of Jordan's accommodation to UAR policies was a show of personal cooperation between Hussein and Abdel Nasser. This was highly desirable to Hussein; indeed, it was the main benefit that came to him from the summit. It was no benefit to Abdel Nasser, but it was a price he had to pay for his initiation of the summit, and he paid it with as much grace as he could muster. Thus Hussein made two visits to Cairo, between the first and the second summit, both taken up with meetings between the two heads of state, private conferences, and nothing in particular decided. (A visit by Abdel Nasser in Amman was rumored briefly after the Cairo summit and probably promoted by Hussein. But the rumor came to nothing; not surprisingly, Abdel Nasser would not stoop that low.)[8]

Hussein used every opportunity to cast himself as a mediator among

Arab governments or as a spokesman for the Arab states: it was, and remained, a favorite stance of his, but in 1964 it had a better chance of being accepted at face value than it did earlier or later. There certainly was no dearth of opportunities for mediation: between Egypt and Saudi Arabia over Yemen; and Egypt, Syria, and Iraq over the unity agreements of 1963. Hussein's posturings came to nothing, but his public at home may have been impressed.

Of greater interest are Hussein's meetings with President Lyndon B. Johnson in Washington in April 1964 and with President Charles de Gaulle in Paris in November after the second summit. Both times, Hussein carried with him the "message" of the Arab governments, and his authorization to do so was valid on the whole. The Paris visit especially was a highly formalized affair. The king met his host twice in private. The official speeches and the final communiqué are steeped in satisfaction at the significance of the visit, not merely to the two countries, but also to world peace. This was one of the first occasions when de Gaulle registered in public his determination to clear a new path for France in the Middle East by creating a special relationship with the Arab states, inevitably with no great regard for Israel.

In the light of the controversies soon to crop up, it is of interest to note that during the second summit, Hussein, when asked whether he would agree to have Arab troops on Jordanian territory if the Unified Arab Command advised this, answered, "Certainly."[9] Hussein's confidence in thus assenting to a hypothetical step that he knew perfectly well he would tolerate only under extreme duress can be explained in the genesis of Arab summitry: "summitry" had been created to obviate just such an emergency that would make necessary the stationing of Arab troops in Jordan, and so far the strategy had worked.

But the real test of the summit's achievement lay for Hussein in his ability to deal with the nascent Palestine Liberation Organization, in a way that would basically satisfy both Abdel Nasser and the believers in a Palestine entity but not endanger the Hashemite state—with Hussein as the judge.

From the outset, the task looked like squaring the circle. The Hashemite Kingdom of Jordan was a sovereign state of the twentieth century, intent on preserving its attributes, and with two-thirds of its citizens putative "Palestinians," Arabic-speaking natives of the defunct mandated territory west of the Jordan River, or their descendants. (There were always some Palestinians who claimed that Transjordanians too were Palestinians, according to the criteria of geography, history, and "destiny.") And this did not take into account the pecularities of the Jordanian Entity, for decades a fact of political life and accustomed to harrowing tests of survival. The Palestinian entity, though, made no sense unless it promised the politically motivated public of Palestinians the means of determining their own fate as Palestinians, while the core homeland was now part of the Hashemite kingdom. Finally, this did not take into account the abrasive personality of Ahmad al-Shuqayri, the leader of the PLO, who through the vagaries of circumstances had stepped into this position as a matter of course.

However, a brave attempt was made on both sides to achieve coexistence or even a show of blood alliance, and for a matter of months the attempt succeeded beyond what might have been expected.[10] Fundamentally this was so because the sides restricted their acknowledgment of each other to semantics and declarations. When their success demanded an advance into action, this mutual toleration broke down.

Ahmad al-Shuqayri had attended the Cairo summit *ex officio* as the Palestinian representative on the Arab League Council, successor since September 1963 to the recently deceased Ahmad Hilmi. Shuqayri's credentials were by then well established, at least since his terms as the U.N. representative of first Syria and then Saudi Arabia. His Saudi Arabian employment had come to a precipitate end in August 1963 when Shuqayri refused to criticize Abdel Nasser in defiance of orders from Riyadh.[11] This fact, with its implications for Abdel Nasser and Faysal, should be remembered when considering the PLO under Shuqayri.

Shuqayri regarded Hasuna's announcement at the summit, in regard to the PLO, as giving him a free hand to proceed. From then until the second summit at Alexandria in September 1964, he embarked on a bout of creative organizing that should claim the respect of the historian. Shuqayri's optimism proved justified. The second summit ratified his conduct retroactively—including the founding of the PLO itself—over the reservations of Syria and Saudi Arabia; in the end, Shuqayri received unanimous support. (In between the summits, Saudi Arabia had constantly complained that Shuqayri was exceeding the authority vested in him by the first summit. Although literally true, in practice this was mere grousing. Shuqayri's later difficulties were due to other causes.)

Within the eight months, the Palestine Liberation Organization was constituted as it still exists in the main, with its principal institutions; the first version of the Palestinian Covenant signed; and the constituent assembly held in Jerusalem,[12] welcomed by Hussein in person, with worldwide attention, and inspired by a general feeling that a turning point of Palestinian history had been reached. It was Shuqayri's success, even though the foundation laid in the early 1960s must not be ignored. The members of the leading bodies as well as the commander of the Palestine Liberation Army (as yet to be raised) were selected by him rather than elected by any constituency.

The one real hurdle that counted at this stage was Hussein's attitude, and here Shuqayri showed considerable ingenuity. He realized that even though their aims were fundamentally irreconcilable, for the time being Hussein could be conciliated at not too high a price, which was explicitly recognizing Jordanian sovereignty on both sides of the Jordan River, and Shuqayri kept paying that price with a flourish: "The emanation of the Palestinian entity in Jerusalem does not aim at carving the West Bank from the Hashemite Kingdom of Jordan. . . . We are in no way touching on the Jordan entity. For the sake of unity any political, military or economic aid to Jordan is aid to recover Palestine."[13] This quotation from Shuqayri at the opening of the founding congress of the PLO on 28 May 1964 shows him going as far in reconciling Hussein as he would ever go; one might say as far as he could go without incurring liabilities irredeemably damaging his credibility as the Palestinian leader. The explicit abnegation of a territorial status at the expense of Jordan is repeated in a separate paragraph (number 24) of the National Covenant as adopted by the congress.[14] (It was dropped in the 1968 version.)

Hussein, on his part, showed sophistication in extracting his own safeguards. Indeed, the ubiquity of his security agents at the congress was for all to see.[15] And instead of the 150 handpicked "Palestinians" (by Shuqayri's definition), the congress was attended by 388 delegates, of whom 242 were living in Jordan and whom the king expected to prove "prudent and moderate," thus ensuring to him a reasonable guarantee that the proceedings would not get out of hand.[16] Moreover, Shuqayri's conciliatory efforts angered Palestinian groups for whose adherence he was anxious.

In the end, the Qawmiyeen (Arab Nationalist Movement, later to give birth to George Habash's Popular Liberation Front) joined the congress as a body, motivated less by faith in Shuqayri's leadership than by loyalty to Abdel Nasser. Even so, the Qawmiyeen's attitude toward the emerging PLO always remained ambivalent. Members of Yasir Arafat's al-Fatah attended the congress as individuals only. Also, the preponderance of delegates presumably under the thumb of Hussein did Shuqayri no good—if for different reasons—at Damascus and Riyadh. Needless to point out, Shuqayri's difficulties were advantages to Hussein and facilitated his concession to permit the congress at all.

Hussein's opening address to the congress was florid and noncommital. He dubbed the occasion "a new stage of planned effort."[17] But he also referred to the congress as an extension of the recent summit, a reminder to Shuqayri and his followers that they would do well not to get carried away.

Trouble in the relationship first came to public notice when Shuqayri had to turn to functional tasks. But even before such moves came out into the open, the Jordanian authorities worked hard to keep the PLO and its sympathizers under surveillance.[18] The substitution in July 1964 of the elderly Sharif Muhammad Hashim as director of security by the Circassian Brigadier Hikmat Mihyar, formerly commander of the metropolitan police, served to ensure that the game would be played by the proper rules. The same motive may be ascribed to the exchange that Hussein made that same month between Prime Minister Sharif Husayn bin Nasir and the chief of the royal cabinet, Bahjat al-Talhuni, a man much younger, in better health, and with a more active personality. The exchange, in turn, confirmed the appointment of the Transjordanian Salah Abu Zayd as the information—that is, propaganda—minister, a position that was established only five months before and that Abu Zayd was to hold, on and off, for six years. Since the 1950s, Abu Zayd had worked for Radio Amman, where he had orchestrated the anti-Cairo propaganda. His promotion now might indicate to Hussein watchers that the king was having second thoughts about summitry. A possible pointer in the same direction was Talhuni's own replacement by Wasfi al-Tall on 13 February 1965: Hussein's commission mentions the right of each Arab state to manage its domestic affairs as it saw fit,[19] and Tall's reckless identification with Hussein's anti-Nasser bout at the time of his former term as prime minister surely was remembered in Cairo. But Tall fell in with the mood that still prevailed on the surface, even to the point of being presented by the king to Abdel Nasser within a week of his reappointment, and his meeting Shuqayri at Amman another week later, a meeting reported as all brotherliness.

The PLO became officially operational on 4 October 1964 when its executive, chaired by Shuqayri, assumed its responsibilities. A new factor entered the scene three months later when Palestinian militants independent of the PLO—Fatah or Fatah directed—staged a raid into Israel across the Jordanian lines, although evidently based in and supported by Syria. The raid itself was insignificant. What made it significant was both the claim that, at last, the Palestinians were taking the liberation of their homeland into their own hands, by violent action, and the responses to this claim by Jordan, the PLO, and Israel, each of which felt threatened. But these responses took months to develop, by which time the Cairo atmosphere of January 1964 had evaporated.

The signs—again, in retrospective reading—that the era of goodwill was ending came with two events that were peripheral to what concerned Hussein most but that to him added to the overall strains under which the "unity of ranks" first showed cracks. These events were Tunisia's President Habib Bourguiba's visit to the Mashreq, the Arab East, in February 1965, and the establishment of diplomatic relations between Israel and the Federal Republic of Germany discussed at the same time.

Bourguiba had long outlived his image as a freedom fighter against French colonialism. Although so far a generally conforming member of the Arab League, his Western acculturation and that of the Tunisian ruling class, together with the conviction of what served his country best, had stamped him as the most accommodating among the "liberated" leaders in the Arab world. The result of Bourguiba's visit was his public proposal, made in Tunis on 21 April 1965, that the Arabs recognize Israel within the boundaries of the United Nations' partition resolution of 29 November 1947, together with the repatriation of refugees.[20] It was a sensational statement for an Arab head of state to make at that time. The proposal roused a torrent of rage and led to the ostracism of Tunisia throughout the Arab world as far as Abdel Nasser's influence carried. Bourguiba's "stab in the back"[21] was not as unexpected as it might seem. His statements during his journey and shortly after his homecoming, advising "the Arabs of the East" to give priority to rationality over sentiment and cautioning them not to provoke West Germany needlessly over Israel,[22] should have been indications.

When the storm broke, Hussein refrained from identifying with Bourguiba. But he did not condemn him either, and the cordiality of Bourguiba's reception at Amman, with its unmistakable undertones of true fellowship, still lingered in the air. Haykal, editor of Egypt's *al-Ahram*, who had the task of spelling out the unpleasantries that Abdel Nasser found it impolitic to utter in person, stated that "Bourguism solutions" appeared only after Bourguiba had visited Riyadh.[23] The insinuation was directed at an opponent of Abdel Nasser, King Faysal[24] of Saudi Arabia, but Faysal was not likely to have encouraged Bourguiba to propose an Arab recognition of Israel even on stringent terms. Nonetheless, the political road from Riyadh to Amman was short, and Bourguiba had gone to Amman straight from there. The inference regarding Hussein was clear.

The second event, pertaining to West Germany, bears a similarity. At the beginning of March 1965, it became known that West Germany was about to recognize Israel officially. In May, the two countries announced their decision to establish full diplomatic relations, and in August 1965 the ambassadors took up their posts. The Arab states (with the exception of Libya, Morocco, and Tunisia) followed the UAR's lead in first withdrawing their ambassadors from Bonn and soon after breaking off diplomatic relations. Again Hussein went along, but his unhappiness over the enforced break with a country that he admired and respected was manifest, and he did not, like Abdel Nasser, ostentatiously flirt with recognizing East Germany.

It was at this time that Haykal pontificated in *al-Ahram* that Jordan did not after all have "in the long run" the essentials of a "natural and independent" entity,[25] which, after eighteen months of acceptance, was a portent of things to come. Haykal may have acted on his own. But it is more likely that he acted on orders from Abdel Nasser, who wanted to give Hussein a warning. This seems to have been Hussein's view, for his response was similarly conveyed through a somewhat contemptuous rebuttal by Prime Minister al-Tall, who took care to state at the same time that he understood Haykal to have merely given his personal view as a journalist.[26]

But the peace, or its pretense, lasted through 1965. As before, the price to Hussein must have been unpleasant, such as a measure of cooperation with Abdel Nasser during the latter's renewed campaign against the Muslim Brothers in the autumn of 1965. However, one important, and ostensibly constructive, event during the second half of 1965—the Jedda Agreement of 24 August 1965 between the UAR and Saudi Arabia, which aimed at restoring peace in Yemen—may have posed in Hussein's eyes as a political threat. Eventually, the agreement was not carried out, but at the time the prospective release of around 60,000 Egyptian troops for assignments nearer home was no comfort to Hussein.

With the shadows lengthening over the summit, Hussein took measures in two directions, one external and the other domestic. Saudi Arabia was still the foremost barrier between the Hashemite Entity and another *qawmi* onslaught. Hussein therefore set out to reactivate his entente with King Faysal. If he could do so by innocuous means, all the better, but if he had to risk incurring Abdel Nasser's displeasure, so be it. Faysal was agreeable. From his point of view, Abdel Nasser's reformation was a chimera, as was the self-abnegation over Yemen recently negotiated.

The first tangible result of the new impetus were the signature on 9 August 1965 and the subsequent ratification of a Jordanian–Saudi frontier delimitation treaty.[27] The treaty involved exchanges of territory by which each country gained: the Jordanian shoreline on the Red Sea was extended from six to twenty-five kilometers,[28] and Saudi Arabia received a piece of desert that smoothed out most of the Jordanian bulge that had jutted into Saudi Arabian territory between Mudawwara and Wadi Sirhan. But the treaty's significance went beyond the worth of the territorial exchanges to either signatory, considerable as that was: it was the first time that the Saudi state had formally acknowledged the right of the Hashemite state to a presence on the Red Sea shore. Abdel Nasser might have been worried or annoyed, but he could not openly take umbrage on ideological grounds.

It was different when Hussein joined Faysal in cooperating with the Johnson administration and its allies in the region.[29] Faysal's visit to the shah of Iran in December 1965 came soon to be understood, correctly, as a step by which Faysal sought to put himself at the head of an "Islamic" alternative to Arab nationalism. Hussein had as early as June 1965 called for a congress of Islamic heads of state in Mecca.[30] He may not have acted on a hint from Faysal, but it is beyond doubt that he was currying favor from him. The very concept of a such a congress, a rival summit, was a challenge to Abdel Nasser, and although Abdel Nasser showed restraint for the time being, the era of goodwill was clearly drawing to an end.

Hussein's measures of entrenchment at this time were rounded off on 1 April 1965 by the appointment as crown prince of his youngest brother, Amir Hasan, just turned eighteen, together with the necessary amendment of the constitution.[31] It was then conjectured that Hussein considered a half-British crown prince an unacceptable political liability or that he and his wife wished to protect the young Abdallah from the dangers inherent in being crown prince. However, it seems that Hussein's own explanation, that he had made the change in order "to choose the most suitable for the task, and to prepare the one who can continue carrying the responsibility,"[32] is the truth. Prince Abdallah was only three years old, and Amir Muhammad, Hasan's elder brother, was unsuitable.

Hasan's installation as crown prince was celebrated by the publicized burning of twenty thousand personal files kept at the Directorate of Public Security. But that awe-inspiring figure instead draws attention to the ubiquity of the department, and some of the names mentioned—Bahjat al-Talhuni, Sharif Husayn bin Nasir—suggest that the step was less than revolutionary in character.[33]

12

In the Sign of the PLO

The day came when Shuqayri answered Hussein's customary assertion, "Jordan is Palestine, Palestine is Jordan," with the counterclaim that the annexation of the West Bank after 1948 had in fact annexed the East Bank to Palestine.[1] It was malicious repartee, but it also made it clear how well the contestants understood what separated them. At that time, Shuqayri complained in an interview to a Lebanese paper that "certain Arab states" had as yet done nothing for the PLO; the context pinpointed Jordan.[2] This combination of resentment with an unwillingness to advertise the break was a significant stage on the road downhill. The ambiguity was not based on courtesy on either side. The summit atmosphere to which both Hussein and Shuqayri owed much had not yet vanished beyond restoration. More important, Abdel Nasser still showed restraint in his dealings with Hussein, and Shuqayri had to act accordingly. Also, Shuqayri still hoped that Hussein's unwillingness to grant the PLO more latitude in its actions was temporary. But here he underrated Hussein's intelligence in assessing the stakes at any given moment, and he overestimated Abdel Nasser's readiness to strain his own relations with Hussein for Shuqayri's sake. Both miscalculations were characteristic of Shuqayri.

By then, the king and Wasfi Tall had taken preventive measures. At the beginning of March 1965, the National Guard (al-haras al-watani)—a militia of about 40,000 men based chiefly in frontier-line villages in both banks, first established under the aegis of Glubb in 1951—was disbanded. Its members, as far as feasible, were transferred to the regular army in which they were put into newly raised infantry brigades.[3] By June 1967, there were five of these, as against four infantry and two armored brigades in the old army.[4] The government clearly feared that the National Guard would be the nucleus of whatever forces Shuqayri might succeed in raising.[5] This apprehension was rational at the time.

An additional, though related, reason for the dispersion of the National Guard probably was the start of the Fatah raids against Israel or, rather, Israel's expected reaction: border villagers with military training were more easily controlled inside the regular army. (The reasoning did not hold. The Fatah raids continued, and on 27 May 1965 Israel retaliated with its first major action for some years against Jordanian targets. There is, of course, no way of knowing whether the situation would not have been worse with small National Guard detachments in position along the border.) In Israeli military circles, there was some worry whether the new formations might not be more highly motivated in the defense of the West Bank than the "old," largely East Bank army would have been—and this apart from the sharp increase in the order of battle as such. However, it seems that the reorganization made no appreciable difference in the fighting in June 1967, let alone its outcome.[6]

The incompatibility between the PLO and Jordan came into the open after the third summit conference at Casablanca from 13 to 17 September 1965. Shuqayri presented the conference with a report stressing the progress made in training units of the Palestine Liberation Army in "Gaza, the UAR, Iraq and Syria"; the omission of Jordan stands out. Shuqayri also demanded, as a matter of right, that recruitment for the Palestine Liberation Army among Palestinian refugees should be compulsory, in addition to freedom of movement and maneuver for the units thus raised. It was a demand that no sovereign state could be reasonably expected to accept, but Shuqayri had not attained prominence by being reasonable. The test case was obviously the events in Jordan, and in a statement on 30 September 1965, Shuqayri singled out Jordan for criticism.[7] His tone was moderate by his standards, but the issues involved ensured that public criticism meant total criticism, and the facade of collaboration was shattered.

The Jordanian government and press replied with a concerted counterattack, not particularly well reasoned and therefore all the more convincing in its hostility. On 4 October 1965, Hussein himself entered the fray when he spoke to members of the National Assembly, ostensibly on the summit, by now weeks past, but really to defend and define his position vis-à-vis the PLO.[8] His argument went to the heart of the confrontation: "East Jordan" and "West Jordan" were one and would not be divided; PLO members were welcome in top military and civilian positions, but within the structure of the Hashemite state. As for any role to be played by the PLO as such, "no organization should act outside the framework of the Unified Arab Command," possibly a dangerous commitment for the future, but at present a good refutation of PLO pretensions.

From then on, the mood continued to deteriorate on both sides, although care was taken for some time to refrain from abuse or charges of treachery. At a press conference on 10 October, Tall characteristically dwelt on the duplication of effort that the PLO demands entailed. Also characteristically, he leveled personal criticism at Shuqayri, which the king had so far abstained from doing.[9] By now, the main charges and their refutation were clear. The PLO demanded permission to recruit freely for its liberation army, a levy of 6 percent on the salaries of "Palestinian" officials to be deducted at the source, and "popular action" to be organized.[10] Hussein saw these demands as virtual treason, as they "split the country and divided the army."[11] (One wonders how the identity of "Palestinians" would have been settled if the demand for separate taxation had been accorded. The official PLO definition of "Palestinian Arabs born in mandatory Palestine before 1948 and their descendants" was ideologically satisfactory, but it would have led to untold complexities in real life: the problem of intermarriages; Transjordanians in the West Bank; and, most important of all, "Palestinians" who did not identify as such in the public eye, among them "official" Transjordanian families like the Rifaʿi and the Touqan.)

However, the two sides were not ready for a complete break, or rather, the political disadvantages of such a break were still deemed greater than its advantages. Also, there still was a residue of the summit atmosphere that both sides hesitated to wipe away. And so, with the blessing of Abdel Nasser and under the prodding of the Arab League, an agreement was signed at Cairo on 1 March 1966 after a week of high-level talks, the first of many to come.[12] The agreement purported to settle equitably the two main quarrels, and on the face of it, the agreement was sensible. "Summer camps for military training and moral guidance" were to be set up under instructors provided by the army and confirmed by the PLO. A tax for the benefit of the PLO of from 0.5 percent to 2 percent would be levied on the income of all individuals and companies in Jordan, through the agency of the state. One hour per day would be allocated to the PLO on Radio Amman, supervised by the Ministry of Information. Discussions for the implication of these and other points were to follow. The agreement was signed by Shuqayri for the PLO and by ʿAbd al-Wahhab al-Majali, minister of the interior, for Jordan.

The deterioration of the accord followed in step with a deterioration on the general Arab scene. In Damascus, a rival branch of the military

Ba'th had taken over from Amin al-Hafiz on 23 February 1966. It made clear that it would outdo its predecessor in "central democracy and collective leadership," that is, in doctrinaire leftism. It also taught a lesson to those who thought that in aggressiveness and irresponsibility—defining these terms as Abdel Nasser himself evidently understood them at the time—any change from Amin al-Hafiz could only be an improvement. Although the change was in degree and not in kind, it was significant. For the historically most relevant case, that of Israel, it turned out that the difference between Hafiz and Salah al-Jdid, who replaced him, meant the displacement at Damascus of a practice that was just tolerable to Israel by one that was not. This lay in the future, but the heightened tension, including that between Damascus and Amman, was felt at once.

At the same time, the Jedda agreement crumbled between Egypt and Saudi Arabia concerning Yemen. Clearly, it had not been a constructive compromise; its crux, the departure from Yemen of all foreign troops, was understood by both sides to spell the ascendancy of its own Yemeni allies. When that assumption threatened to be untenable, the agreement plainly became a snare. Abdel Nasser, who through the withdrawal of his own troops across the sea was expected to make a more striking show of good faith, was the first to say so in public.[13]

But the first disruptive development was King Faysal's alleged determination to establish an Islamic alliance. It is difficult not to believe that Abdel Nasser's reaction was not entirely rational and that in his display of hostility he relived the days when his fight against the Baghdad Pact had lifted him to eminence and power in the Arab world.[14] Faysal always denied that he intended to set up a front against Arab nationalism. It did not matter. If the acknowledged leader of Arab nationalism chose to see Faysal in the role, then that image would become political reality.

The facts are that Faysal had called for an "Islamic summit" during a state visit to Tehran in December 1965, which was, after all, more significant than Hussein's doing more or less the same in Amman at a gathering of 'Ulama'. While Faysal was visiting Amman at the end of January 1966, Hussein took care to stress the "spiritual" ties between the Islamic states, which it behooved him and his guest to strengthen by the side of "our Arab nationalism" (*qawmiyya*). But Hussein's underlining the need to wean that same Arab nationalism away from the dangers of polytheism (*shirk*) and apostasy (*ilhad*) was bound to arouse Abdel Nasser's resentment and perhaps his contempt for Hussein's clumsy phrasing: *shirk* and *ilhad* were deadly sins, and it was surely proper to denounce them at a meeting of Muslim heads of state who took pride in their impeccable orthodoxy. But Hussein's credentials for impeccable orthodoxy were none too strong, and Faysal, who was above reproach, kept away from such verbal extravaganzas. Also, Hussein's description of Jordan and Saudi Arabia as "twins" left no doubt about where Jordan's position was in the rift that was widening again between the radical and conservative regimes in the Arab world.[15]

Commentators from the periphery, however motivated, justified Abdel Nasser's growing conviction that a new conspiracy was afoot.[16] But as far as Jordan was concerned, both Abdel Nasser and Shuqayri—the latter possibly restrained by the former—still hesitated to burn their bridges. Abdel Nasser chose this juncture to reopen the UAR consulate in Jerusalem on 21 March 1966, shut since the convulsions of 1958. Shuqayri went out of his way to thank Hussein for implementing the March agreement. Hussein, however, clearly did not wish to be singled out from Faysal for preferential treatment, which in any case was bound to be temporary, and so he acted accordingly.

On 13 April 1966, the minister of the interior, Majali, who had so recently set his name to the settling of difficulties with the PLO, announced the arrest of a large number, which he gave as "about one hundred," of "party-men" (*hizbiyyun*) whom he identified as Communists, Ba'this, and Arab Nationalists. He denied that the PLO was involved.[17] In fact, Jordanian security documents make it clear that the detainees were indeed largely members of the named illegal parties, but especially those who were using the PLO as a front. It looked like a last-minute attempt to separate chaff from wheat within the PLO. Some of those detained were released within days; others were referred to the state security court and then quietly set free; and still others remained in prison until the Six-Day War. The operation was the particular responsibility of Major General Muhammad Rasul al-Kaylani, recently appointed director of military intelligence after a rapid rise since he had first proved his worth to the Entity during the trial of General Shara'.[18]

After another month of uneasy tension during which Shuqayri declared, significantly at Damascus, against the "Islamic pact" (which did not exist) and in favor of the "progressive forces,"[19] Hussein on 14 June 1966 crossed the Rubicon. The occasion was trivial, unless we assume that Hussein particularly wanted to frighten a sector that was proverbially unsafe from his viewpoint: a teacher's graduation ceremony at Ajlun, in the heart of Transjordan. The key sentence of his long speech[20] was that "all hopes have vanished for the possibility of cooperation with this organization [i.e., the PLO] in its recent form." The vehemence—expressions like "be the hand cut off that menaces the integrity of Jordan" and "be the eye gouged"—is uncharacteristic of Hussein and suggests Tall's authorship. But that did not matter once Hussein had made it his own.

The impossibility of cooperation between Jordan and the PLO soon materialized. The parliament at Amman joined the king in condemning the PLO.[21] Tall forbade the holding of elections for the PLO National Council, to which Shuqayri had agreed after much agonizing, and dispersed the election committees.[22] Shuqayri on his part denied ex cathedra that Jordan had a right to exist.[23] The Voice of Palestine stopped transmitting from Amman, apparently on Shuqayri's orders.[24] But the PLO's headquarters in Jerusalem remained open for the time being, closely watched.

The near elimination of the PLO from public life caused in Jordan little reaction. Clearly, Shuqayri's appeal was immeasurably inferior to both Abdel Nasser's before the 1967 war and that of the transformed PLO afterward. Shuqayri's call to the Palestinian members of the Jordanian cabinet to quit[25] was ignored (compare this with the attitudes of Palestinian ministers during the Baghdad Pact crisis). Soon afterward, Shuqayri declared the PLO to be "a revolutionary organization."[26] To him, this was chiefly another obeisance toward Abdel Nasser, who was then cementing his fateful alliance with the new, radical Damascus regime. On his Jordanian constituents, Shuqayri's pronouncement had little effect. Occasional reports of that time of campaigns in support of the PLO at Nablus and elsewhere in the West Bank are unimpressive. Significantly, none refers to places south of Jerusalem. When the regime did get into trouble in November 1966, the causes were not connected with what the PLO either did or suffered, and neither was the atmosphere of mounting tension that marked the six months that followed.

Shuqayri, although a talented political tactician, organizer, and orator, was not a leader. His position vis-à-vis the heads of Arab states, ostensibly as their equal, gave the impression of posturing that derived its significance from an agreed-upon pretense. In regard to the Palestinians, Shuqayri appealed first and last to would-be politicians, would-be organizers, and would-be orators—his peers. His elevation at the first summit and his brief ascendancy until the third were basically a result of circumstances. His subsequent decline meant that Hussein had called his bluff. And his return to the headlines on the eve of the Six-Day War was an irrelevance. It was not thus that his successor Yasir 'Arafat (formally his successor by one remove) came to play his role.

At the time of the PLO's virtual elimination from Jordan, Abdel Nasser announced his disenchantment with summitry. He had been cheated by the reactionaries, he declared, who had used him to insinuate themselves back into the Arab family, under false pretenses. (Abdel Nasser had certainly been cheated in his expectations, and it is a measure of his declining influence that he bemoaned his misfortune in public.) The demise of this first age of summitry was made official when the acting secretary general of the Arab League announced on 22 July 1966 the indefinite postponement of the fourth summit, due to convene at Algiers on 5 September. It was a concomitant of Abdel Nasser's disappointment with summitry that the two member states that strenuously opposed the decision were Saudi Arabia and Jordan.

The newly found zeal of Saudi Arabia and Jordan for institutionalized Arab cooperation outside the Arab League had a more practical aspect than public protest. If the summits were sabotaged, then there was no sense in wasting money on their official offspring. And so Saudi Arabia, already a chief financier of common Arab undertakings, stopped its allocations to the PLO and the Unified Arab Command, generally seen as products of Abdel Nasser's policy.

Hussein then further poisoned the political atmosphere by permitting, perhaps instigating, mass manifestations of grief when three leaders of the Muslim Brothers were hanged in Cairo in September 1966, among them Sayyid Qutb, possibly the greatest intellectual ever to arise in their midst.[27] Only a year earlier, Hussein had given diplomatic support to Abdel Nasser against the Brothers; his change now was a return to an old functional alliance. The same pattern—showing up the recent two years of goodwill as a mere abberration—recurred when Hussein's government withdrew its recognition of the Yemeni Republic on account of its "inhuman persecution of the Yemeni people."[28] Because this inhumanity had as its most conspicuous feature Egyptian poison-gas attacks, this was a spectacular blow at Abdel Nasser. A rerecognition of the Yemeni imam had, though, become anachronistic, and Jordan remained unrepresented on either side until the resolution of the civil war in 1969. Jordan's restoration of diplomatic relations with West Germany on 4 March 1967 in defiance of the Arab League ban, although part of the same pattern, was less of a challenge. Hussein was merely jumping the gun in anticipation of a general Arab decision.

Hostile relations between Hussein and Abdel Nasser during this period present nothing new as such. There was the requisite vituperation, with Abdel Nasser harking back to Abdallah's fate. There was a temporary recall of ambassadors, but no break in relations. The diminution of relations was less in ill will as in their vigor and viciousness, when compared with earlier downturns in the relationship.

It was the Syrian complex that presaged the cataclysm to come, and Hussein was partly responsible. The summer of 1966 had been relatively quiet. Possibly Syria's Zu'ayyin-Jdid-Atasi regime still had to find its feet. Be that as it may, Hussein provoked the dangers inherent in the ultraradical government at Damascus by involving himself in an attempt at its ouster. It is not certain, although it is likely, that he helped a group of officers, stationed conveniently near the Jordanian frontier, turn against their new chiefs. However, when the coup failed, Hussein granted both asylum and access to the media to the coup leader, the Druze Major Salim Hatum, after he crossed into Jordan on 9 September 1966 with a number of accomplices.[29] (Hussein later enabled Hatum to prepare for a second attempt, which Hatum carried out with catastropic results to himself and his comrades on the eve of the Six-Day War.)

At about the time of Hatum's coup, Syria returned to its traditional role of spoiler. A Syrian rapprochement with Abdel Nasser entailed another pact of mutual defense, signed on 4 November 1966, which allowed the Syrians a kind of insurance against the possible consequences of their own recklessness.[30] The superficially cordial relations that Abdel Nasser had with the "extremists" at Damascus put him, paradoxically, at greater risk than had the tension that had generally prevailed since the summer of 1963 between him and their "bourgeois" predecessors: he could no longer ignore the cries for action from Damascus, just when those cries came to signify a situation that was in reality more dangerous.

The core of that reality was Israel. The new rulers at Damascus were temperamentally incapable of preventing the armistice lines from exploding. Their backers at Moscow egged them on, for reasons not known even today—possibly no more than ignorant opportunism. The Israeli leadership worried about domestic morale and tended to be jittery. And Fatah, after an interval of relative inactivity, returned to its chosen battlefield. It had the blessing of the Syrian authorities, who hoped both to destabilize Israel and to involve it with Hussein by sending in guerrillas across the Jordanian border.

13

The Descent into War

In the morning hours of 13 November 1966, a composite Israeli force of brigade strength with air support attacked the West Bank village of Samuʿ south of Hebron, in retaliation for the death of three Israeli soldiers who had been killed two nights before when their vehicle ran on a mine in that sector in Israeli territory. Samuʿ was devastated, and twenty-one Jordanians, most of them soldiers, were killed.[1] It was not disputed that the mine had been laid by Fatah members—their culminating success in months of mounting activity on the Israeli side of the armistice lines. The Israeli government felt compelled to hit back. A strike against Syria, the known rear base of Fatah, was believed to put relations with the Soviet Union under an untenable strain, in view of the latter's special link with the new regime at Damascus. But it had always been an Israeli argument that a distaste for involvement in fighting should not give a neighboring state immunity against its failure to police its own ground. Intelligence that Samuʿ had for some time served Fatah as an advance post provided the rationale for the choice of target.

The significance of the Samuʿ raid cannot be brought under one heading. It relieved for the moment domestic pressure on the Israeli government and satisfied the feeling—always latent in Israel—that "Jewish blood is not free to shed." It brought on Israel the reproaches of its traditional friends for having brutally overreacted—condemnations that aroused anger in Israel as yet another example of the double standard that the democracies were wont to apply to the Palestine conflict.[2] (In any case, these condemnations had no fundamental effect and were reversed by the events that preceded the 1967 war.) It did not change the Soviet Union's aversion to Israel, by now well known. And it did not alleviate Hussein's position vis-à-vis the Arab radicals, whether they saw him as a culpably weak victim or as a traitor scheming to leave his country defenseless.[3] It once more shattered the semblance of the West Bank's integration into the Jordan Entity, which had been noted ever since the unity riots of April 1963.

For weeks, the towns of the West Bank and the refugee camps seethed with hatred for the regime that seemed to abandon its Palestinian stepchildren to slaughter and dishonor, and they cheered the Palestinian republic and the PLO. (The distinction of Fatah from the PLO, its leader, and his ways were not then generally understood.) Damascus and Cairo—the former predictably more so than the latter—with Shuqayri to the fore, fanned the unrest to the best of their ability. However, the administration and the army reexerted their control in the traditional way, and by the beginning of the new year, quiet was restored. The East Bank had remained virtually unaffected, except in that a distaste for the West Bank caused insults and some violence to Palestinian residents of Amman and other urban centers. After Samuʿ, the Israeli–Jordanian armistice lines quieted down. Tightened Israeli security and mounting tension along the Syrian lines played their part, together with an increased vigilance by the Jordanian authorities.

The greatest effect of the raid was its impact on Hussein. He could not understand the Israeli action except as proof of an Israeli desire to bring down the Hashemite Entity or, at least, to conquer the West Bank. President Johnson tried to reassure him in a secret personal message that combined strong disapproval of the Israeli action with advice for restraint and a circumscribed American guarantee against Israeli territorial aggression.[4] Hussein was not impressed. Empathy was never his strength. He could not see how Israel, instead of punishing Syria, the most committed of its enemies and on all accounts responsible for its present troubles, should lash out at himself, unless Israel's leadership wished for his destruction. This suspicion never entirely left him.

After the Samuʿ action, Israel is said to have transmitted a message to Hussein through American channels: no malice intended, but the action was necessary, as he, Hussein, had lost his grip on the situation.[5] Hussein remained unappeased.

On the broader Arab scene, Jordan maintained its position as a supporter of the conservative camp until the fourth week in May 1967, well beyond the onset of the crisis that descended into war. Clearly, Hussein had no premonition that his vaunted solidarity with the Arab cause would soon be called to the supreme test, and this at the behest of his enemies in the Arab camp. As often before, although the situation was fundamentally not of his making, Hussein's tactics were aggressive rather than responsive.

Hussein's line was that the all-Arab summits should be reconvened instantly and that no half-measures were of use. Because summitry had been Abdel Nasser's invention, just as it was Abdel Nasser who had first abandoned it, this was a clever ploy to beat Abdel Nasser at his own game. This earned some diplomatic dividends in that it provided the conservative camp with a plausible rallying point: less provocative than the Islamic "pact," demonstrated friendship for the West, or issues concerning "progress," whether economic or social. Saudi Arabia, Sudan, Lebanon, Morroco, and Kuwait signified their approval.

At the same time, Jordan refused to attend sessions of Arab League bodies or institutions devised by the earlier summits. Hussein asserted that with the breakdown of summitry, Arab League institutions had been emptied of content and merely served to legitimize the illegitimizable—the selfish ambition of a "certain Arab power." The Egyptian–Syrian defense agreement of November 1966 in particular served Hussein as an example for the malfunction of the Unified Arab Command (although it is historically more correct to say that the agreement became necessary, from the viewpoint of Cairo and Damascus, when the UAC had proved to be unworkable because of Jordanian and Saudi Arabian suspicions). Hussein's insistence on a return to summitry was perceived even then as an ideological misappropriation. But Hussein clung to it with zeal, and Wasfi al-Tall supported him to the hilt.

Hussein resurrected his old claim that Arab radicalism and the politicians, organizations, and regimes that embodied it were a cloak for Marxism and thus inimical to all that true Arabism stood for. Here Hussein undoubtedly spoke with sincerity, although he skirted the issue of his country's developing relations—on the official level, at any rate—with the Soviet Union. In 1957 the two issues, softness on Marxism and the Soviet Union, had served Hussein in one and the same cause. But as in 1957, the anti-Communist battle cry merely convinced those who were Hussein's allies in any case.

Concerning the fight against Israel, Hussein's position was difficult, as it had always been when his relations with the radical camp were critical. His interest in keeping quiet his border with Israel was entirely rational and of course well known. But whenever the regional situation deteriorated, and with it the public's capacity to view the present exigencies with circumspection, this need did not easily lend itself to mass-media parlance. Hussein did his best. As usual, his best was aggressive. although defensive arguments, like the need for patience and the discouragement of uncoordinated sabotage, were not absent. Yet the emphasis was on the service his opponents at Cario and Damascus, and of course the PLO leadership, did to Israel and its patrons. Except for one line of argument, Hussein's reasoning seems unconvincing, but he probably believed in the force of reiteration. The exception was his repeated taunt that it was Abdel Nasser who had been actively contributing to the security and development of Israel since the Suez war, when he handed over the supervision of the Sinai frontier and the Tiran Straits to a United Nations force and thereby wittingly deprived Egypt of the capacity to threaten Israel along its chief front.[6] This accusation hit home. It probably helped Abdel Nasser decide in May to demand the instant recall of the United Nations Emergency Force, with immediate political results that Hussein should have foreseen and had every reason to dread. It is another case—the most striking of all—of Hussein's propensity to ignore the future implications of his own tactics when a short-term gain, however limited, beckoned, or perhaps of his deficiency in imagination.

One episode appears at that time as a ghostly codicil to Hussein's policy of undermining his enemies' position. On 1 March 1967, Hajj Amin al-Husayni, president of the practically defunct Supreme Arab Committee, former mufti of Jerusalem, and King Abdallah's deadly enemy, turned up in Jerusalem by Hussein's invitation, after thirty years of exile (except for fleeting stays in Gaza). The king showed him all honor. He facilitated his meeting with notables, religious as well as secular, and he put his own residence at Beit Hanina, north of Jerusalem, at Hajj Amin's disposal. After a sentimental stopover in Jerusalem, Hajj Amin proceeded to Amman, where Hussein received him for a talk. Afterward, Hajj Amin told reporters that he supported the king's Palestinian policy and that they had discussed an alternative to the PLO. After a further fortnight's stay in Jerusalem, Hajj Amin departed for Saudi Arabia, where he was welcomed as an enemy of Abdel Nasser with impeccable Islamic and Arab nationalist credentials. The interest of Hussein and Hajj Amin in this interlude—so incongruous at first sight—is obvious. Hussein wanted a stick to beat Shuqayri and, if not to beat, then at least to bait or perhaps to frighten. He also needed any residual credit that Hajj Amin might have with the Palestinians to strengthen his own standing in the West Bank, in the aftermath of Samuʿ. Hajj Amin, on his part, never ceased to scheme for a comeback.[7] Nothing tangible emerged from the event.

The outcry after Samuʿ induced Hussein to introduce compulsory national service, by a law of 23 November 1966.[8] The law provided for ninety days of military service a year for all Jordanians between eighteen and forty years of age, with rather liberal exceptions and the possibility of *badl,* an exemption payment of one hundred dinars (£ 100) to be expended "on front line fortification." By the time war broke out in June, a few recruitments had completed their three months of training. The idea itself was uncongenial to the Entity, with its reliance on a professional army whose fighting cadres were preferably Transjordanian if not beduin. But Hussein believed that the measure suited the public mood. More congenial to the tradition of the Entity was a retroactive rise in pay for the noncommissioned army ranks,[9] not for the first time in a period of political tension.

Another fresh start in that period that can be related to the tense atmosphere was the Press Law of 1 February 1967, which came into effect on 21 March.[10] The law, to "provide new guarantees for the freedom of the Jordanian press . . . and enable it to guide the regime,"[11] ordered the closing of all existing newspapers and periodicals and provided for the conditions under which their successors might come into existence. Eventually, two new Arabic dailies appeared, *ad-Dustur* at Amman and *al-Quds* at Jerusalem. The government was to hold 25 percent of the shares. Among the victims of the law was the venerable *Falastin,* which hailed back to Ottoman times. The editors of the affected papers protested, although somewhat lamely, and complied. They did not contest the law's constitutionality, as distinct from its crudity and unfairness.

It is not quite clear what made Hussein take a step that was bound to show him up as a petty tyrant, that made light of his claim to have the confidence of the educated public, and that did not even promise to suppress printed disaffection. The nonparty press had never given him—or his grandfather before him—any particular trouble, although without a doubt it was lukewarm in pursuing his feuds with Abdel Nasser or Shuqayri, especially the former. Wasfi al-Tall may have had a part in the decision, with his penchant for ordered efficiency and his suspicion of uprooted intellectuals. Basically Hussein disliked the press,[12] for all his affectation of liberalism and, on a different plane, his unaffected pleasure in seeing himself a center of media attention. Lately, dissatisfaction with the authorities' ability to protect border villages in the West Bank from Israeli aggression had been noticeable in the press. This was a sensitive point, and it may have triggered the law.[13]

The last event on the domestic scene during those troubled months was the resignation of Tall as prime minister in conjunction with elections for a new Chamber. The eighth Chamber of Deputies was dissolved by royal decree on 22 December 1966, about half a year before its constitutional expiration. Elections were set for 15 April 1967. Six weeks before, on

4 March, Tall handed in his resignation, which the king accepted. Tall's published motive was a constitutional regulation concerning the wish of certain ministers to run as candidates. The real reason seems to have been Hussein's feeling that after more than three months of "strong" government—strong even by Jordanian standards—the time had come for a prime minister whose image was more accommodating. Tall himself seems to have cooperated willingly, and in any case his subsequent appointment as chief of the royal court gave him direct and official access to the king.

The acting prime minister, charged with overseeing the general elections was again the king's great-uncle, Sharif Husayn bin Nasir, who was succeeded on 23 April, with the elections safely past, by Saʿd Jumʿa, of a noted Tafila family. It was Jumʿa's first premiership, although he had had much experience in the upper ranks of diplomacy and administration, and his record for conformity was impeccable. In fact, critics of the Hashemite monarchy branded him as an "American agent" when he assumed office, presumably because he and his brother Midhat had spent time in Washington. Jumʿa's chief virtue lay in his inoffensiveness, coming as he did after a prime minister with a particularly sharp personality. Jumʿa's cabinet presented no new departures; only Radi ʿAbdallah's appointment to the crucial Ministry of the Interior deserves comment as further proof of his rehabilitation.

The elections were uneventful, being strictly supervised by the authorities. Clearly, the times were not fit for a display of liberalism. The results produced a Chamber that would not be expected to give trouble. Four newly elected members did have a genuinely political stamp: two Muslim Brothers sitting for East Bank constituencies and two known associates of Hajj Amin al-Husayni's Arab Higher Committee, both representing Jerusalem.[14] With the renewal of political warfare against Abdel Nasser, the Muslim Brothers were back in the regime's good graces: Emile Ghoury and Muhi al-Din al-Husayni owed their elevation to the uncompromising hostility that the Arab Higher Committee had shown to Abdel Nasser since 1959 and Shuqayri's PLO from the start, and to Hussein's wish to extend courtesy to the ex-mufti after his recent visit.

One note from the sidelines of the elections is appropriate. During the preliminary stage, Prime Minister Tall remarked at a press conference that women could not vote, although they had the legal right to do so, as their participation would "necessitate a national census and the issue of identity cards."[15] It is as revealing a light on the sociopolitical ambiguities of the Entity as can be found.

The events that led to the involvement of Jordan in the Six-Day War have often been analyzed, although Jordan usually takes its place on the sidelines.[16] In contrast with the picture that Hussein himself drew later, his conversion to the united front consolidating against Israel, with its call of "now or never," came long after the onset of the crisis.[17]

The attitude of Jordan to the Egyptian and Syrian regimes did not change as it had hardened over the preceding eighteen months, until almost the brink of war. This is not surprising. With Damascus speaking in terms of a "popular liberation war," which explicitly included Hussein among the enemies,[18] and Abdel Nasser pointedly refraining from naming Jordan among the long list of Arab states rising to the historic occasion,[19] a professed change of heart at Amman would have lacked credibility. Indeed, when the king sent his chief of the general staff, Lieutenant General ʿAmir Khammash, to Cairo on 21 May, this was the reception that Khammash met.[20] It is more surprising—and an indication of the emotional storm that was sweeping the Arab world—that Hussein was accepted into the Arab front when he himself turned up in Cairo on 30 May.

On 28 May, Hussein inquired, through the Egyptian embassy in Amman, whether his visit in Cairo would be acceptable in order "to coordinate our defence measures in view of the Israeli menace."[21] Abdel Nasser's assent arrived the following day, and on the morning of 30 May the king, accompanied by Prime Minister Jumʿa and General Khammash, flew to Cairo. It seems that Hussein and Abdel Nasser did not easily overcome the awkwardness of their relationship: the abuse of the recent months—not to go back further—signified more than just an expediency to be wiped out by other expediencies in a changed constellation. But this did not affect the business of the day.

"Coordination" was settled by Hussein's and Jumʿa's putting their names to a bilateral defense pact with Egypt along the lines of the Syrian—Egyptian Defense Pact. This in itself was hardly more than symbolic ritual—significant through its timing, to be sure—as the general Arab defense agreement signed in the wake of the first summit had never been abrogated, and the Arab League Collective Security Pact (which Jordan had joined belatedly in 1952) also held good. But the operational importance of the understanding lay in Abdel Nasser's appointing an Egyptian as "commander of the Arab forces on the Jordanian front," Lieutenant General ʿAbd al-Munʿim Riyad, a former assistant commander of the Unified Arab Command. Relations between Jordan and the UAC had been strained for the past eighteen months, and the references of Hussein and Tall to its achievements had been uncomplimentary. This meant that in the future, decisions affecting the defense, indeed the existence, of the Entity would be made either by an Egyptian whose loyalty did not lie with Jordan or by divided counsel, which might prevent decisions from being made at all.

There can be no doubt that this provision, quite possibly suggested by Hussein, was the prize that made Abdel Nasser agree to readmit Hussein onto the team. After this concession, the appearance of Shuqayri, summoned hastily from Gaza, whom Abdel Nasser pressed on Hussein as a travel companion back to Amman, was hardly more than an additional annoyance, showy but for the moment unsubstantial. Hussein felt constrained to order the release of PLO (and Fatah) detainees and to permit the reopening of the PLO office in Jerusalem. Sharif Nasir bin Jamil, by now deputy commander in chief, took Shuqayri on a tour along the lines, to impress his guest with the competence of the Jordanian army guarding the country's frontiers—without help from the Palestine Liberation Army (PLA), as Shuqayri thought, probably correctly.

In the same spirit, Hussein refused a request from Shuqayri to permit the entry into Jordan of PLO units stationed at Deraa, in Syria just across the frontier. Hussein explained to Shuqayri that doing so would arouse "certain feelings" in the army.[22] However, Hussein assented to the reestablishment of full diplomatic relations with Syria. In part, this was a concomitant of the reconciliation with the PLO, and it also fitted in with the euphoria of those days.

On Monday, 5 June 1967, Hussein ignored Prime Minister Eshkol's request that Jordan stay out of the war that had that morning broken out between Israel and the UAR.[23] Two days later, he accepted the ceasefire call issued by the United Nations. By then, the West Bank was lost and his field army shattered.

What were King Hussein's considerations when he took Jordan into the war on the side of Abdel Nasser? As often with such questions, pivotal yet abstract, the answer leaves much to an outsider's preferences. Moreover, it stands to reason that Hussein, never introspective, would not himself be able to give a satisfactory account.

To start, Hussein had not one but two moments to exercise his "free will" (the limitations duly understood): first when he flew to Cairo and then when he rejected Eshkol's appeal. It needs little analysis to realize that the second decision flowed largely from the former, but still Hussein conceivably had the opportunity to reverse a trend or at least delay for a while, had he so wished. The raging war fever clearly must be taken into account, just as it must be considered when accounting for Abdel Nasser's actions. The difference between the two was that there was an interplay between Abdel Nasser and the Arab public in this respect, whereas there was none, or as good as none, regarding Hussein.

Did Hussein come to believe at any stage during the crucial month before the war that victory over Israel was likely? Again, there is no clear-cut answer. His public pronouncements once the war seemed all but certain exuded confidence, indeed triumphant joy. But not too much should be made of that, although anybody—particularly someone as mercurial as Hussein—in a comparable situation might become convinced by self-persuasion. In striking power, including that of the air force, the UAR alone was certainly much superior to Israel, an important consideration.[24] It is known that Hussein was impressed—just as uncounted Israelis were shocked—by the bathos of Prime Minister Eshkol's address to the Israeli public on 28 May,[25] but it is not known whether his approach to Abdel Nasser on the following day owes its timing to this impression and, in its wake, to a lessened respect for Israeli prowess. Also, Hussein was aware of the enormous boost that victory over Israel would give to Abdel Nasser in the Arab world, and hence of the danger it represented for the Hashemite Entity. Even with Jordanian participation, a victory would owe much, in propaganda at least, to Arab contingents on Jordanian soil. UAR commandos—well advertised—had arrived in Amman; an Iraqi brigade had crossed the eastern frontier; Saudi Arabian forces were approaching; and even from Syria "brotherly help" could be expected. (During the fighting in the West Bank, a Syrian brigade did cross into Jordan, to be precipitately recalled when Israel attacked on the Golan Heights.)

In regard to the risk of defeat, Hussein has never ceased to assert since the war that he was always pessimistic, that he had expected defeat all along, although indeed he "had never imagined that Israel could win that easily."[26] There is independent evidence that this indeed was his prevailing mood right up to the outbreak of fighting. He had a low opinion of Arab armies in general, on grounds that were in part irrational—an inheritance of King Abdallah's Hashemite superciliousness. Besides, whatever the Arabs' intrinsic fighting capacity, Hussein did not believe that the allied Arab formations would be in battle position in time and, if they were in time, in sufficient strength. Moreover, there was indeed a defense plan prepared in cooperation with the Unified Arab Command in 1965, but it was rudimentary, and no staff cadres existed. Hussein did have a high opinion of his own army, its beduin units at any rate, but its infrastructure was clearly unsuited to a major war; its armored force was weak; its air force was weaker; and its air defense was almost nonexistent. Just as important, Hussein had a well-grounded horror of what the casualty rate, certain to be high, would mean for the morale of his supporters and the stability of the Entity, even if military defeat were averted.

He had much respect for the Israeli army, although he may not have properly understood the sources of its strength and inspiration. He just as firmly believed the Johnson administration to be committed to Israel— if not to an outright Israeli victory, at least to preventing an Israeli defeat.[27] It was a belief that Hussein shared with other Arab governments, but placed as he was, his position was particularly frustrating.

Then why, on balance, did he go to war? First, at the operational level, Hussein had no real alternative. When the war began, Riyad was installed at general headquarters in Amman as commander of the Jordanian front, with his personal staff, his communications with Cairo, and the towering prestige of Abdel Nasser to support him. His authority might have been superseded. But with the unassailable legality of Riyad's position, this would have amounted to a coup. In the prevailing atmosphere—public excitement mounting by the hour, the army's martial ardor at a peak, and Hussein himself in all probability affected even against his better judgment—such a coup would have demanded superhuman single-mindedness, and even then it might well have collapsed, together with the Entity. Hussein did not have that single-mindedness. During the morning of 5 June, when Hussein arguably still had some freedom of choice, he was fed disinformation from Cairo regarding Egyptian successes. Later Hussein asserted that the disinformation was at least in part responsible for faulty dispositions at Amman.[28] He did not suggest that it played a part in Jordan's decision to go to war, and it is unlikely that it did, at that late hour.

Beyond the question of operational calculations, Hussein may have felt that if he went to war and, as he later said he foresaw, lost, he would still save the core of his kingdom; an Israeli invasion of the East Bank was improbable; and none of his Arab allies was likely, in the event of common defeat, to be a serious risk to him.[29] (The PLO, so soon to become a mortal danger to his survival, was of no account in this respect under Shuqayri's control.) If, however, Hussein refrained from going to war, he might well expect an uproar that would sweep him away, whether Israel was victorious or defeated. An imponderable was at stake, and Hussein may be credited with enough intuition to realize how this imponderable would affect his survival. It was the shame attached to the shirker. When the U.S. secretary of state, Dean Rusk, urged Hussein on 5 June not to open another front, with unpredictable consequences, Hussein replied that he was sorry but his honor left him no choice. Dean Rusk, no romantic, felt that although this may not have been the whole truth, it was that part of the truth that mattered.[30]

The thesis of this book is the danger to the Hashemite Entity from Arab secular radicalism, chiefly as Arab nationalism under the aegis of Gamal Abdel Nasser. After the Six-Day War, that danger receded dramatically—in part because of the price that Hussein had been willing to pay for his demonstration of solidarity. A long chapter in the history of Jordan had been closed.

Conclusion

So far it has been explained how Hussein and the Hashemite Entity survived those years of peril, against heavy odds and the expectation of practically every observer. It remains to discover why. In the following, the components of that answer will be marshaled, and a synthesis will be presented, in the knowledge that even if the components are reasonably uncontested, the synthesis will be wide open to debate.

The first component is the personality of King Hussein, as the Hashemite ruler of the Entity. Since early 1957, he had been referred to as "the brave little king," ad nauseam, in those media that were not fundamentally hostile. Like many such clichés, this one contains some truth; and to some extent it has proved self-fulfilling. Hussein *is* brave, and being an extrovert much concerned with his public image, he undoubtedly took care to live up to the praise. A complement of his "courage" is his faith in the role that devolved on him as the standard-bearer of the Hashemite house and his resulting determination never to give up.[1]

Obviously, Hussein has other qualities that have helped him survive, some temperamental, others intellectual, some inherited, others acquired. He can dissimulate, and he can be hard of hearing when he chooses.[2] He knows how to bide his time, and he knows when to hit hard. Also, although Hussein is not soft, he is not a hater, and above all, he is not paranoid. He is apt to mete out punishment that is less than would have fitted the crime. When he forgives, he forgives completely, although he rarely restores a forgiven enemy to a position in which he can do political damage. (An interesting exception is Sharif ʿAbd al-Hamid Sharaf, Hussein's distant relation, who after an active membership in the Qawmiyeen returned to the fold in 1961 and died as prime minister in 1980.) By now it is possible to judge that Hussein's customary and temperamental clemency was wise, as it did not refuel hatreds that later tended, if not to die down, then at least to burn low.

Lastly, Hussein has an instinct for making decisions and accepting responsibility. This must have been inherited from many generations, with perhaps an element of his own. It was not acquired through experience, as his personality in this respect appears to have been fully formed from that day in May 1953 when he began his constitutional duties. He can be influenced and he has made mistakes, but he has felt and acted the ruler from the first.

The resources of the state are at Hussein's disposal according to the ground rules of the Entity. Moreover, those supporters of the state that possess the legal authority and the means of maintaining the Hashemite monarchy are also those that support it not merely because of their corporate and individual interests but also because of traditions and convictions openly held: the elite units of the army, the security services, the senior civil servants, and the religious establishments, both Muslim and Christian. (The Jordanian free officers of 1953 to 1958 were *hadari* and, as such, atypical. Thus however dangerous they may have been, they were never "the army.")

Jordan's sociopolitical character has helped in Hussein's survival. Hussein did not then lead a nation conscious of its identity, which put in him its trust once he had established his legitimacy in the public mind and his high qualities as a leader. But throughout the settled population of Jordan, in both banks, there is a tradition of passive obedience.[3] The government—meaning the king—is expected to govern, and if the government meets certain expectations, if it is Muslim, if it shows reasonable respect for the subjects' privacy, if it is not unbearably rapacious, and above all if it is self-reliant, then the people will not be a congenial breeding ground for radicalism and subversion. When Hussein denounced *fitna,* he showed his sound insight. The refugees and the beduin must indeed be excluded from this presumption of quietism, for differing reasons. But it was not the least part of Hussein's statecraft during those years that he knew how to deal effectively with both.

From 1955 to 1967, Hussein and the Entity had their supporters abroad whose material aid or political attitude was vital to their survival. But they were supporters rather than friends. Few cared for the survival of the Hashemite monarchy because of a sense of moral obligation or traditional ties. They all had their well-considered reasons of state, whose point of departure was the appraisal that Hussein was worth the investment, however risky the investment might have looked. The United States, Britain, and Saudi Arabia, and Israel up to a point, are examples. Again, it was Hussein's statecraft that kept those supporters as partners whose advantage tallied with his own, rather than patrons on whose bounty he depended. This brings us to those who could have brought down Hussein and the Entity with him. Why were they, all told, ineffective?[4]

On the home front, first mention must go to the excellence of the Hashemite security services. Generally, they were highly professional, loyal, and well paid. Their suppression of the opposition to the regime was not particularly harsh by some standards of the times. Their instructions as well as their practice varied according to the situation and also according to varying moods that were not always connected with the domestic situation. However, their vigilance was unceasing, their proficiency in penetrating circles of doubtful loyalty inspires awe; and they could certainly act swiftly and decisively.

The strength of the security services was balanced by some peculiar weaknesses of their targets or, better, their victims. Jordan—both banks—had no tradition of "party" consciousness and all that goes with it, in the modernist sense that had become relevant by the period under review here. In mandate times the "parties" had centered on the leading families (the Communists and the Muslim Brothers were marginal exceptions), but by the 1950s, these families were rapidly losing their power and attraction. Moreover, even as far as these assets remained, they were by no means in the forefront of opposition to the Entity. Party consciousness and activities also tended to concentrate in the West Bank, far off the center of the state. The leaders of the opposition, whether or not they belonged to the traditional elite, did not relish the idea of martyrdom, even if it did not entail the ultimate sacrifice, again with the exception of the Communists and Islamic fundamentalists.

The high tide of pan-Arab nationalism was connected to the acceptance of Abdel Nasser as its symbol and its captain. The two organizations in Jordan at the time that counted in this context were the Ba'th party and the Arab Nationalist Movement, or the Qawmiyeen, the former being more closely identified with the impersonal aspects of pan-Arabism and the latter with Abdel Nasser. Both exemplify the general weaknesses of the opposition. But their presence remained; their presumed influence on students and the population of the refugee camps remained; and the authorities could never cease to regard them as a potential threat to the existence of the Entity. The two groups' ally of convenience, the National Socialist party, might—and did in 1956 and 1957—provide a valuable strengthening. But on its own, it was no danger to the Hashemite monarchy, as it was led by notables with a stake in the existing order.

The Communists and the Islamic fundamentalists were a different mat-

ter. Their ideologies, although admittedly it is difficult to put Islam and
Marxism-Leninism under the same conceptual roof, were far better defined than was pan-Arabism. Also, their proponents, both leaders and
followers, were ready to uphold their faith, whatever the cost to themselves. But they too suffered from a dearth of activists, their number
being far below what experience has shown might constitute a critical
mass. The Communists also were stigmatized by their confessed atheism
and their readiness to concede to Israel the right to exist, even though
they came to de-emphasize both points as time went on. An additional
handicap in Jordan was Hussein's deep dislike of them. The Islamic fundamentalists were divided. And the Muslim Brothers were too preoccupied with their quarrel with Abdel Nasser to turn their attention to the
Hashemite regime, a situation that the regime knew well how to use. The
Tahrir party seems to have had the most constancy among the recognized
opposition groups, but it was one of the smallest. In assessing the combined influence of the Islamic fundamentalists, it must also be remembered that their time had not yet come and that they professed a dedication
to nonviolence that may have cost them the support of forces that rushed
to join their successors in the late 1970s.

It was Abdel Nasser who gave his name to an epoch in Arab history,
the period under review here. It was he whom Hussein came to regard
as the incarnation of the forces embattled against himself. It was he who
was universally regarded at that time as Hussein's implacable enemy,
almost certainly his nemesis. There could be no doubt about his immea-
surable superiority over Hussein in material and spiritual resources. And
yet it was Hussein who survived. Where did Abdel Nasser fall short?

In retrospect—things looked different at the time—an important factor
is that Abdel Nasser did not return Hussein's fear and hate with equal
measure. Of course, he disliked Hussein. He saw him as an impedi-
ment—one of several—to the achievement of his goals. He reacted angrily to Hussein's charges and, worse, his jeers. He expressed a contempt
that was probably genuine. There can be no doubt that had Hussein fallen,
Abdel Nasser would have exulted—and expected to gather the full fruits
of his fall. The critical point, however, is that Hussein was never remotely as important to Abdel Nasser as Abdel Nasser was to Hussein.[5]
This was understandable: Egypt, or the UAR, under Abdel Nasser was
of vital consequence to Hussein, but Jordan under Hussein was to Abdel
Nasser only an irritant and a reproach.

But the matter goes deeper, to the roots of Abdel Nasser's qualities as
a statesman and his record as a politician. There is a discrepancy between
Abdel Nasser's persona as a man of action, and historic reality. Through-

out his years as ruler of Egypt, Abdel Nasser was reluctant to embark on risky departures, but he was apt to be persuaded, to join, or to follow up when he came to believe that in a given situation he had to act according to his image. This mattered less after the Six-Day War when such situations were fewer and less dramatic. But it was crucial during the twelve years after 1955, when Bandung and the Czech arms deal catapulted him into the role of the avenger.

Time and again, a purposeful lead by Abdel Nasser might have made the difference between Hussein's overthrow and a mere coup attempt, or a "coup situation" that was not utilized. It is as good as certain that Abdel Nasser never gave the lead, as distinct from, at most, his presumed blessing or his generalized knowledge of plots in the offing. His underlings went much further, but nothing could replace his own active involvement.

The last point is the hazards of accident. Disregarding the medical aspect—Hussein was never as robust as he looked and acted—he was for years a target of assassination attempts. It was more than just taking vengeance on a "traitor" and removing an enemy: it stands to reason that right up to 1967—in fact, until it seemed that a capable successor to Hussein had grown in the person of Amir Hasan—Hussein's disappearance would have meant the disappearance of the Hashemite monarchy, with what to follow none can tell. The prize would have been enormous. Although Hussein's security service was good, he was not invariably careful; this was his nature as well as the image of himself that he wished to impart. We know of attempts on his life that almost succeeded, and there certainly were others that went unpublished or even undiscovered. Only chance allowed Hussein to escape unhurt.

Hussein thus survived because of his singleness of purpose in wanting to survive and because he knew how to marshal his resources for this purpose: the resources of the traditional society that was his home ground and the resources of his personality. Hussein survived because his most dangerous adversary, Gamal Abdel Nasser, lacked the singleness of purpose in wishing his destruction and because other enemies who may have had that singleness of purpose lacked the resources. He survived by good luck. The three did not depend on one another, and each was indispensable.

Epilogue

How does the present pertain to this study? And what are the lessons, if any?

Some elements of the Jordanian existence up to 1967 have disappeared or changed beyond recognition. Abdel Nasser is dead and has no heir. The West Bank has been lost to the Hashemite kingdom; many would say forever. The Palestine problem and the Palestine Liberation Organization as "sole legitimate representative of the Palestinian people" have changed so much as to constitute a virtually new factor. Economically, Jordan is substantially better off, when compared with both the 1950s and the 1960s and other poor countries in the Middle East today.

But in the ever-changing Middle East, what remains valid is even more striking as far as Jordan is concerned: the Entity is still there. Nationalist and Muslim-fundamentalist radicalism are still the two prongs of the ideological onslaught on the Entity, and it is unsafe to debate their force, whether relative to the Entity or to each other. (In 1979, Muslim fundamentalism seemed to be the wave of the future; in 1983, it looked as if the wave had passed its crest; today Muslim fundamentalism looks strong again.) The United States is still Jordan's mighty friend, and still not by treaty. Israel's attitude toward Jordan is ambivalent, as it was before 1967: officially, and supported by public opinion in general, not actively hostile but with a strong undercurrent of existential rejection. Saudi Arabia is an ally, for the old reasons. Syria is hostile most of the time and always suspect. The dynasty seems as secure as ever since Transjordan gained its freedom from the mandate in 1946. Al-Husayn bin Talal reigns and rules.

All the same, this continuity does not render much help in understanding the present and in dealing with it. History does not repeat itself, and too much has changed even within the continuity. The Entity has indeed survived, but a transformation has taken place. The sense of Jordanian statehood has developed by the side of, and perhaps overlaying, the sense of loyalty to the Hashemite ruler and the sense of belonging to an ageless, traditional society, the first being active by nature, the last two rather passive. This sense of statehood was not unknown in 1967, and its beginning goes further back. But its growth since 1967 appears to have effected a qualitative change whose significance for the future I cannot gauge.

The United States also has changed since 1967: its self-image, its domestic centers of power and influence, and its place in world affairs, including the Middle East—all preclude analogies with a past twenty to thirty years ago. The Israel ruling the West Bank is not the Israel confined to the Green Line in 1949, with all that this means for Jordan. Saudi Arabia and Syria have existential problems today that differ from those then and that may affect their relationship with Jordan in a crisis. And above all, Hussein in his fifties is not Hussein in his twenties and early thirties. The point is obvious, but it is not trite. Apart from accumulated experience and changing appreciations, growing older must have wrought changes of personality as well as of health, and these will affect attitudes, initiatives (or their absence), and responses—we cannot know for sure.

If asked wherein lies the justification for this work, all I can say is that it behooves us to study the past for its own sake. If my subject has peculiar elements of proximity and of associations with our present condition, so much the better. And if I am asked whether there really are, after all, no lessons to be learned, I will say that this book shows once more that in history the individual plays a role, that the battle is not always to the strong, and that luck comes in, too.

Notes

Introduction

1. This paragraph is based on U. Dann, "'The Jordanian Entity' in Changing Circumstances, 1967–1973," in I. Rabinovich and H. Shaked, eds., *From June to October: The Middle East Between 1967 and 1973* (New Brunswick, N.J.: Transaction Books, 1978), pp. 231–44.

2. Abdallah's aspirations regarding Syria, Iraq, and Palestine are common knowledge. His close companion and adviser Alec S. Kirkbride—from 1939 and until Abdallah's death in 1951 British resident and later minister at Amman—believed that Abdallah always hoped that he would regain the Hijaz.

3. For Abdallah's *Weltanschauung*, see Israel Gershoni, "The Arab Nation, the Hashemite Dynasty and Greater Syria in the Writings of 'Abdullah" (in Hebrew, with an English abstract), *Hamizrah Hehadash* 25 (1975).

4. A good introduction to this theme is Howard C. Reese et al., *Area Handbook for the Hashemite Kingdom of Jordan* (Washington, D.C.: American University, 1969).

5. The constitution was originally promulgated in *Jarida Rasmiyya (Official Gazette)* (Amman), no. 1093, 8 January 1952. I have also used the English translation in Muhammad Khalil, ed., *The Arab States and the Arab League* (Beirut: Khayats, 1962), vol. 1, pp. 55–75. Although the constitution is still in force, the observations in the text do not in all cases fit the practice as it has evolved *since* 1967; for example, the Chamber is now hardly ever convened.

6. *Jarida Rasmiyya*, no. 646, 2 September 1939.

7. *qa'id a'la*, not "commander in chief" (*qa'id 'amm*), as in Khalil, *The Arab States*, vol. 1, p. 60.

8. Properly "National Assembly" (*majlis al-umma*), "Assembly of Notables," (*majlis al-a'yan*), and "Assembly of Representatives" (*majlis al-nuwwab*), respectively. I shall use the shorter forms.

9. For the role of parliament in Jordan, see Kamel S. Abu Jaber, "The Jor-

danian Parliament," in Jacob M. Landau, ed., *Man, State and Society in the Contemporary Middle East* (New York: Praeger, 1972), pp. 91–121.

10. The Municipal Elections Law, by contrast, stipulated a minimum tax qualification, thus giving an advantage to conservative elements and disfranchising many of the refugees. Women were given the franchise in 1973. See also Chapter 13, note 15.

11. For these amendments to the constitution, see *Jarida Rasmiyya*, no. 1179, 17 April 1954, and no. 1243, 16 August 1955.

12. There are many competent studies of Jordanian society. For the years 1955–1967, I have found the following comprehensive surveys particularly useful: A. Konikoff, *Transjordan: An Economic Survey* (Jerusalem: Economic Research Institute of the Jewish Agency for Palestine, 1946), and Raphael Patai, *The Kingdom of Jordan* (Princeton, N.J.: Princeton University Press, 1958). The Transjordanians (including the beduin) are discussed in Kamel S. Abu Jaber et al., *Bedouins of Jordan: A People in Transition* (Amman: Royal Scientific Society, 1978); Gabriel Baer, "Land Tenure in the Hashemite Kingdom of Jordan," *Land Economics* 33, no. 3 (August 1957): 187–97; Peter Gubser, *Politics and Change in Al-Karak, Jordan* (London: Oxford University Press, 1973); Jane M. Hacker, *Modern 'Amman* (Durham, Eng.: University of Durham, 1960); Paul A. Jureidini and R. D. McLaurin, *The Impact of Social Change on the Role of the Tribes* (Washington, D.C.: Praeger, 1984); Daniel Lerner, *The Passing of Traditional Society: Modernizing the Middle East* (London: Free Press, 1958); Frederick G. Peake, *History and Tribes of Jordan* (Coral Gables, Fla.: University of Miami Press, 1958); Seteney Khaled Shami, "Ethnicity and Leadership: The Circassians in Jordan" (Ph.D. diss., University of California, Berkeley, 1982); and Ahmad Yousef al-Tall, *Education in Jordan* (Islamabad: National Book Foundation, 1979). For the Palestinians (including the refugees); see Clinton Bailey, "The Participation of the Palestinians in the Politics of Jordan" (Ph.D. diss., Columbia University, 1966); Zeev Bar-Lavie, *The Hashemite Regime 1949–1967 and Its Status in the West Bank* (in Hebrew) (Tel Aviv: Shiloah Center for Middle Eastern and African Studies, 1981); Eliezer Be'eri, *The Palestinians Under Jordanian Rule* (in Hebrew) (Jerusalem: Magnes Press, 1977); Yoram Ben-Porath, Imanuel Marx, and Shimon Shamir, *A Refugee Camp in the Mountains* (in Hebrew) (Tel Aviv: Shiloah Center for Middle Eastern and African Studies, 1974); Amnon Cohen, *Political Parties in the West Bank Under the Hashemite Regime (1948–1967)* (in Hebrew) (Jerusalem: Magnes Press, 1980); Abdulla M. Lutfiyya, *Baytin: A Jordanian Village* (The Hague: Mouton, 1966); Moshe Ma'oz, *Palestinian Leadership on the West Bank: The Changing Role of the Arab Mayors Under Jordan and Israel* (London: Cass, 1984); Shaul Mishal, *West Bank/East Bank: The Palestinians in Jordan, 1949–1967* (New Haven, Conn: (Yale University Press, 1978); Avi Plaskov, *The Palestinian Refugees in Jordan, 1948–1957* (London: Cass, 1981); Avraham Sela, *The Palestinian Ba'ath* (in Hebrew) (Jerusalem: Magnes Press, 1984); and Shimon Shamir et al., *The Professional Elite in Samaria* (in Hebrew) (Tel Aviv: Shiloah Center for Middle Eastern and African Studies, 1975). For a representative statement of the Palestinian case against the Hashemite En-

tity, see 'Isam Ahmad al-Fayiz, *Al-nizam al-hashimi wa 'l huquq al-wataniyya lil-sha b al-filastini* (The Hashemite system and the national rights of the Palestinian people) (Beirut: Dar Ibn Khaldun, 1974).

13. There has been no Jewish settlement in Transjordan since later Roman times, although some Jews worked in Abdallah's amirate or served there with the Transjordan Frontier Force. But by 1948, none remained.

14. The studies by Israeli authors mentioned in note 12 are based in part on Jordanian security files captured in 1967. They afford a fascinating insight into the aims and methods of the Hashemite security services.

15. One major exception were the Baghdad Pact riots of December 1955 and January 1956.

16. Plascov, *The Palestinian Refugees,* pp. 20–22.

17. In 1961, UNRWA recognized in Jordan 635,000 ration cards. It was generally realized, even by the UNRWA officials, that this number considerably exceeded the number of "needy refugees," principally because the cards of deceased holders were rarely returned.

18. For the agreement that Jordan and UNRWA signed on 14 March 1951, see Plaskov, *The Palestinian Refugees,* pp. 214–18. Plaskov also reproduces a document that throws light on the peculiar relationship between the two sides and the problems that it might raise (pp. 224–25).

19. This had not always been the case. Older servants of the Entity would remember Abdallah's early days in Transjordan when Kerak had been a trouble spot.

20. The establishment of the Palestine Liberation Organization in 1964, with the conditional blessing of the Jordanian state, complicated the situation, but the king never wavered from the principle.

21. The Education and Instruction and the University of Jordan (i.e., of Amman) laws (*Jarida Rasmiyya,* nos. 1763 and 1764, 26 May and 1 June 1964) are examples of the authorities' gingerly approach. "Political activity" was permitted to teachers and students; or it was prohibited; or it was permitted with safeguards—even though political parties were strictly illegal.

22. See Naim Sofer, "The Political Status of Jerusalem in the Hashemite Kingdom of Jordan, 1948–1967," *Middle Eastern Studies* 12 (January 1976): 73–94.

23. *Jarida Rasmiyya,* no. 1166, 17 January 1954, and no. 1223, 3 April 1955. For the then valid anti-Communist law (*qanun muqawamat al-shuyu'iyya*), see *Jarida Rasmiyya,* no. 1164, 16 December 1953. For an English translation, see Aqil Hyder Hasan Abidi, *Jordan: A Political Study, 1948–1957* (London: Asia Publishing House, 1965), pp. 223–30.

24. For the "Political Tenets" of the Tahrir party, see in Landau, ed., *Man, State and Society in the Contemporary Middle East,* pp. 183–88. The party was never licensed, but until 1957 it seems to have met with little interference.

25. Pieter Lieftinck et al., *The Economic Development of Jordan* (Baltimore: Johns Hopkins University Press, 1957), and Eliyahu Kanovsky, *Economic Development of Jordan* (Tel Aviv: Tel Aviv University, 1976) are indispensible when studied in conjunction, although both seem to understress the sheer poverty

of the country. See also Kamel S. Abu Jaber and Manabu Shimizu, *Economic Potentialities of Jordan* (Tokyo: Institute of Developing Economies, 1984).

Chapter 1

1. The annual report for 1954 dispatched by the British embassy at Amman to the Foreign Office on 5 January 1955 attributes the dismissal of the "liberal" prime minister Fawzi al-Mulqi to Hussein's alarm at Fawzi's failure to oppose in the Chamber of Deputies a motion of thanks to Soviet foreign minister Andrei Vishinsky (Public Record Office, London, Foreign Office [FO] 371/115635).

2. Abdel Nasser, strongman of Egypt since the 1952 coup, was prime minister from April 1954 to June 1956, when he became president. (He also was acting president after Neguib's deposition in November 1954). His domination of Egypt was unchallenged except by the Communists and the Muslim Brothers. See especially Panayiotis J. Vatikiotis, *Nasser and His Generation* (London: Croom Helm, 1978), and Raymond W. Baker, *Egypt's Uncertain Revolution Under Nasser and Sadat* (Cambridge, Mass.: Harvard University Press, 1978).

3. Keith Wheelock, *Nasser's New Egypt* (London: Atlantic Books, 1960), pp. 218–19. For the roots of pan-Arabism in Egypt, which antedate the free officers' revolution, see Israel Gershoni, *The Emergence of Pan-Arabism in Egypt* (Tel Aviv: Shiloah Center for Middle Eastern and African Studies, 1981).

4. Under the monarchy, the Order of the Nile had been third in precedence. But the prime minister of the young republic would no longer award the Order of Mohammad Ali or the Order of Ismail.

5. It seems that the Queen Mother had considerable influence on Hussein's personal affairs until the late 1950s.

6. Fedayeen activities up to February 1955 were undoubtedly sponsored by local Egyptian command posts in the Gaza Strip, in conjunction with the ex-mufti of Jerusalem, Hajj Amin al-Husayni, then living in Cairo. It is not clear to what extent the central Egyptian authorities were involved, but apparently it was less than the Israeli government claimed at the time.

7. *Ahram* (Cairo), 28 April 1955.

8. Actually Syria made its own "Czech" (literally so) arms deal about a year before Egypt did. But Atasi's Syria was not the same as Abdel Nasser's Egypt, and Syria at the time preferred discretion.

9. On 4 October 1955. For the text of the resolution, see Naseer Hasan Aruri, "Jordan: A Study in Political Development, 1921–1965" (Ph.D. diss., University of Massachusetts, 1967), p. 279. The only dissenter on that occasion was Shaykh Ahmad al-Da'ur of the Tahrir party, who regarded as evil any political trafficking with infidels.

10. For unofficial translations of the pacts, see *Middle East Journal* 10 (Winter 1956): 77–79.

11. Royal Institute of International Affairs, *Survey of International Affairs, 1955–1956* (London: Oxford University Press, 1960), pp. 282–83; Hazza' al-Majali, *Mudhakkirati* (Jerusalem, 1960), pp. 152–53. The memoirs of the two

chief British protagonists, Eden and Macmillan, are silent on this; Eden, in particular, is positively misleading. (*Full Circle* [Boston: Houghton Mifflin, 1960]) For the story of the British official attitude toward Jordan's accession, see Uriel Dann, "The Foreign Office, the Baghdad Pact and Jordan", *Asian and African Studies* 21 (November 1987): 247–61.

12. As early as 14 April 1954, when the first of the Northern Tier treaties (between Turkey and Pakistan) was signed, a senior British Foreign Office official wrote in a secret minute, ". . . the Arab Legion would be used on our side in the event of a Russian attack on the Middle East . . ." (FO 371/11094).

13. Abu'l Huda died in July 1956.

14. The onslaught is well described in Macmillan's autobiography, *Tides of Fortune, 1945–1955* (London: Macmillan, 1969), pp. 653–55. Macmillan characterizes King Faysal II and Crown Abdul Ilah as "loyal."

15. Robert R. James, *Anthony Eden* (London: Weidenfeld & Nicolson, 1986), p. 429. The official documents convey an impression—difficult to substantiate—that it was Macmillan who egged on Eden throughout the crucial weeks of November and December 1955.

16. This expression appears repeatedly in the British departmental correspondence of those days.

17. This derisive phrase is found throughout the Foreign Office minutes of that time.

18. Templer's secret *Report* to the foreign secretary after his return to Britain requires close study, and not just for its subject matter (FO 371/115658). But Templer was "progressive" by his own lights. On a previous occasion, he had grown honestly indignant at what he felt was the insufficient respect shown by the British soldiers stationed in Jordan and Libya to the national armies, and he was ahead of Glubb in regard to the "Arabization" of the Arab Legion officer corps (June 1955, FO 371/115681).

19. "Templer flies to see for himself again"; "With typical Templer dash . . ." (*Daily Mail* [London], 7 December 1955) are good examples of the semipopular British press of those days.

20. The Islamic Conference was established by Egypt in August 1954, in cooperation with Saudi Arabia and Pakistan as impeccably anti-Communist counterweights to oppose imperialist aspirations of continued dominance. At the same time, it helped Abdel Nasser refute the propaganda of the Muslim Brothers, who were rapidly becoming his deadly enemies. On this, as on Sadat's visit, see Martin Kramer, "Sadat's Visit to Jerusalem, 1955" (Lecture in Hebrew given at a symposium, "Jerusalem's Place in Islam," Jerusalem, 15 April 1986). For a glimpse of ʿAmir in Jordan, see P. J. Vatikiotis, *Politics and the Military in Jordan* (London: Cass, 1967), p. 122. Also see M. I. Faddah, *The Middle East in Transition* (London: Asia Publishing House, 1974), p. 247.

21. ʿAmir naturally sought the company of Jordanian officers in the Arab Legion. Sadat, a strict Muslim, concentrated on religious matters (and on an Islamic conference under Egypt's aegis), although not exclusively so.

22. And longer, perhaps. At their meeting at Amman, Sadat and Hussein took

a dislike to each other, which may have had a bearing on events as late as the Camp David period.

23. For the British draft agreement and the Jordanian counterproposals, see Templer's *Report*, and Hazzaᶜ al-Majali, *Qissat muhadathat Templer* (Story of the Templer talks), (Amman, 1956), pp. 7–10. The two versions are close, although not identical. For an English translation of Majali's work, see FO 371/121492.

24. The British embassy in Amman believed that the Palestinian ministers had been persuaded to resign—even bribed with £9,000—during a meeting with Sadat (FO 371/121476). The "persuasion" is probably true, but it must be remembered that these ministers were in a state of mind in which persuasion was easy. A monetary bribe seems out of context, although a "contribution" is possible. Sulayman Musa's biographical studies of Hazzaᶜ al-Majali, Sulayman al-Nabulsi, and Wasfi al-Tall, *Aᶜlam min al-Urdunn* (Amman: Ihsan Kamil Swis, 1986), reached me too late for my manuscript.

25. For the sack of Musa al-ᶜAlami's model farm near Jericho, see Geoffrey Furlonge, *Palestine Is My Country* (London: Murray, 1968), pp. 188–91.

26. FO 371/115640. For the government's indecision at this stage, see Glubb in *Daily Mail*, 16 March 1956, after his dismissal. Majali gives his side of the story in *Mudhakkirati*, pp. 165–74. For Duke's and Wikeley's views of the Arab Legion's conduct, see their reports to the Foreign Office of 19 December 1955 (FO 371/115657, 115524).

27. "This dance it will not further go." Hussein assuredly did *not* use these words when he spoke to the ambassador. But a student of history interested in both twentieth-century Jordan and eighteenth-century England—there may be such—will find strange similarities between the Baghdad Pact and the Excise Scheme crises, and their aftermaths. For Duke's interview with the king on the night of 19 December 1955, see Duke to Foreign Office (FO 371/115657).

28. The protest against the dissolution was signed by a group of deputies. Even if they were not manipulated by the authorities, their action was interpreted otherwise, and reasonably so.

29. "The king's blood was up!" commented Ambassador Duke in his report. He was instructed by return to compliment Hussein in the name of the British government (FO 371/121464).

30. *The Times* (London), 11 and 12 January 1956. Under Glubb (and under the terms of the Anglo-Jordanian Treaty of 1948), the dispatch of British troops to Jordan in an emergency was far less sensational than it would be later, in the summer of 1958.

31. An amusing example is an epigram coined by the Turkish foreign minister, who told Macmillan that King Saud had recently distributed in Jordan £750,000 "to the poor. It was not known how much the Saudi Arabians had given to the rich" (FO 371/115654).

32. FO 371/121563, 2 February 1956. See also *Asian and African Studies* 21 (July 1987): 213–20, with my annotation.

Chapter 2

1. Not "commander in chief," as Hussein in a curious error styles Glubb in his autobiography, although Glubb had been "Officer Commanding, Arab Legion," under the Mandate, like F. G. Peake before him. Hussein, as the sovereign, was the supreme commander.

2. See James Lunt, *Glubb Pasha: A Biography* (London: Harvill Press, 1984), p. 217.

3. And for Colonel Patrick Coghill. See P. Coghill, "Before I Forget," Mimeograph (Copy in the Private Papers Collection, Middle East Centre, St. Antony's College, Oxford, 1960), pp. 125–8. Coghill knew no Arabic, and when he accepted the job in 1951, he made it clear that he "did not intend at [his] age to learn it" (p. 100).

4. See also John B. Glubb, *A Soldier with the Arabs* (London: Hodder & Stoughton, 1957), p. 383. The embassy's "Annual Review for 1954" already gloomily observes that "the close and confidential relationship inherited from Mandatory times is being gradually eroded."

5. Anthony Nutting, *No End of a Lesson* (London: Constables, 1967), p. 29. Nutting was at the time minister of state at the Foreign Office. He resigned over the Suez Canal crisis in November 1956.

6. I agree with Peter Snow that Major 'Ali Abu Nuwar, Hussein's friend and senior aide-de-camp, may have informed Abdel Nasser a few hours in advance (*Hussein* [London: Barrie & Jenkins, 1972]; p. 88). As Glubb himself knew, there was even then no dearth of channels of instant communication with Cairo for officers who were so inclined.

7. Minute by C. A. Thompson, 14 April 1954 (FO 371/110924).

8. Snow, *Hussein*, p. 83.

9. It stands to reason that the enthusiasm was not shared by all. But there were no demonstrations of support for Glubb. Before his departure, Glubb, and his British subordinates, ordered the strict maintenance of discipline. Glubb's successor as CGS, the elderly police colonel Radi 'Innab, is on record as having then and there expressed his own gratitude for Glubb's work. After his dismissal from the cabinet in May 1956, Rifa'i said in an interview that Glubb need not have been sent away with so much "yelling" (*dajja*). Moreover, the absence of precautionary measures had exposed Jordan to an unwarranted risk from possible Israeli aggression (*Jarida* [Beirut], 27 May 1956). I am obliged to Ms. Ayala Munk for drawing my attention to this information.

10. Glubb counseled restraint as soon as he arrived in Cyprus from Amman in the morning of 2 March (FO 371/121540).

11. British cabinet file (CAB) 128/50, pt. 1: cabinet meeting of 9 March 1956. See also Kirkbride's thoughtful elaboration in his "Note . . . on Visit to Jordan," 4 April 1956 (FO 371/121466).

12. See a somewhat personal but still authoritative memo from Lieutenant Colonel C. E. Phipps, Current Intelligence Unit, Joint Chiefs of Staff, to Rear Admiral E. T. Layton, Deputy Director of Intelligence, 27 April 1956, distrib-

uted to the Joint Chiefs of Staff without rousing much interest, as far as is known (*Declassified Documents Quarterly Catalog [DDQC]*, 1980, p. 268C).

13. Ambassador Duke in a "secret" appraisal, 5 March 1956 (FO 371/121154).

14. There was a spate of brawls and cases of insubordination in the summer of 1956, but they did not constitute a "movement."

15. *Al-Husayn bin Talal* (Amman, 1957?), quoted in M. I. Faddah, *The Middle East in Transition* (London: Asia Publishing House, 1974), p. 205.

16. According to *Majlis al-umma al-urdunni fi khamsin 'am 1921–1971* (The Jordanian parliament in fifty years) (Amman: Wizarat al-thaqafa wa'l a'lam, 1976), p. 23.

17. The enthusiasm was joyously described in the Jordanian press.

18. In his autobiography Hussein does not mention the nationalization. Prime Minister Ibrahim Hashim told Duke that the official expressions of gratification were mere lip service, made necessary by the general atmosphere of enthusiasm (FO 371/121497).

19. The Suez war that followed has attenuated the memory of the tension, not to say the panic, that the situation on the Israeli–Jordanian armistice line had caused during the preceding weeks. Secretary of State John Foster Dulles and FBI Director J. Edgar Hoover easily convinced President Dwight D. Eisenhower that "it seems to be taken internationally as a foregone conclusion that Jordan is breaking up," chiefly because of "the recent savage blows of the Israel border armies." Israel must be strongly admonished to desist, but "at the same time I [Eisenhower] have Foster's promise to have ready a policy or plan that would guide our action in the event that the dissolution of Jordan would actually take place and thus create a new situation in the world." ("Memorandum for the Record," 15 October 1956, initialed D. D. E., Eisenhower Library, Ann Whitman File, Diary Series, Box 18, *DDQC*, 1981, p. 625A.)

20. Sir Michael Wright, British ambassador at Baghdad, to Prime Minister Nuri al-Sa'id, 3 October 1956; Foreign Office to Ambassador Duke, 17 October 1956, (FO 371/121499).

21. Knowledgeable observers would add "with the elections to the seventh chamber in November 1962 as a reasonable contender for second place."

22. In a conversation with Ambassador Duke (3 July 1956, FO 371/121468); *Jarida Rasmiyya*, no. 1287, 30 July 1956.

23. *Gumhuriyya* (Cairo), 23 October 1956.

24. Hussein, *Uneasy Lies the Head* (London Heinemann, 1962), p. 127.

Chapter 3

1. For the exchange of letters, see *Jarida Rasmiyya*, no. 1302, 30 October 1956.

2. Nabulsi affirmed this to Peter Snow (*Hussein* [London: Barrie & Jenkins, 1972], p. 100).

3. Ibid., pp. 100–101.

4. *Difa'* (Jerusalem), 3 November 1956. Duke, dumbfounded by the evolving British part in the drama, arranged with the Italian embassy to take care of British

interests should Jordan break off relations and consulted Abu Nuwar regarding the concentration, protection, and evacuation of the British community under the auspices of the Jordanian army (1 November 56, FO 371/121599).

5. *Falastin* (Jerusalem), 28 November 1956.

6. Ambassador Johnston in his memoirs elaborates these points (Charles Johnston, *The Brink of Jordan* [London: Hamish Hamilton, 1972], pp. 33–36).

7. For the text, see *Ahram*, 20 January 1957, and *New York Times*, 21 January 1957.

8. *New York Times*, 21 January 1957; *Christian Science Monitor*, 22 January 1957.

9. Radio Amman, BBC (Summary of World Broadcasts) (SWB), pt. IV, 17–19 November 1956; *Mideast Mirror* (Beirut), 8 December 1956.

10. *New York Times*, 17 December 1956.

11. Ibid. Much later, in 1974, Nabulsi denied in an interview that when he was prime minister he believed in forming "blocs" with any Arab state, particularly Egypt, or that he had joined Egypt in ganging up against Iraq (Marius Haas, *Husseins Königreich* [Munich: tuduv, 1975], p. 625). This is not so.

12. Amnon Cohen quotes a directive issued by the Directorate of general security on 13 January 1957 to prepare lists of prominent members of all political parties (*Political Parties in the West Bank Under the Hashemite Regime (1948–1967)* [Jerusalem: Magnes Press, 1980], p. 1). I doubt Cohen's inference that we have here Hussein's decision to outlaw the political parties once he had given them additional rope to hang themselves. Of course, there is no sharp division between "contingent precautions" and radical policy decisions demanding undercover preparation months in advance.

13. For example, *New York Times*, 18 January 1957; *Mideast Mirror*, 20 January 1957.

14. Cablegram from Eisenhower to Dulles, 12 December 1956 (*DDQC*, 1984, p. 000385).

15. Ibid. Eisenhower went on to say that "one of the measures that we must take is to build up an Arab rival of Nasser, and the natural choice would seem to be the man you and I have often talked about." This man, according to former Assistant Secretary of State William M. Rountree, was Nuri al-Saʿid (letter to me, 25 July 1984). According to Steven L. Spiegel, *The Other Arab–Israeli Conflict* (Chicago: University of Chicago Press, 1984), p. 83, and to Stephen E. Ambrose, *Eisenhower: The President* (New York: Simon and Schuster, 1984), p. 317, it was King Saud.

16. For the seriousness with which this possibility was regarded, see a naval top secret "Memorandum for the Joint Chiefs of Staff," 13 November 1956, which envisaged the unilateral use of force by the United States to prevent the notional volunteers from disembarking (*DDQC*, 1978, p. 371B).

17. U.S. Department of State, *U.S. Policy in the Middle East, September 1956–1957* (Washington, D.C.: Government Printing Office, 1957), pp. 419–20.

18. These deliberations have since been declassified to a large extent. See *DDQC*, 1980, pp. 153A–153C, 155A.

19. Paul E. Zinner, ed., *Documents on American Foreign Relations 1957* (New York: Harper & Brothers, 1958), pp. 214–15. See also Spiegel, *The Other Arab–Israeli Conflict*, pp. 83–87.

20. An amusing example is that of Congressman Albert H. Bosch of New York, who referred in the House on 22 January 1957 to the Jordanian request for $30 million as "tops in gall"; Bosch more or less expected Hussein to spend the money on "the sport cars he fancies" (*Congressional Record*, app., vol. 103, p. A331).

21. The "National Covenant" of 22 April 1957 demanded Mallory's expulsion but not that of British Ambassador Johnston. It is a sign how the seat of power behind the throne had changed in the public imagination over the previous year.

22. Since the revelation (*Washington Post*, 18 February 1977) that Hussein had been secretly receiving millions of dollars each year since 1957 and Hussein's indirect admission of such payments (*Newsweek*, 7 March 1977), tables detailing official U.S. financial aid to Jordan are of no great significance to the political historian. For a detailed survey of 1955 to 1967, see Stephen S. Kaplan, "United States Aid and Regime Maintenance in Jordan, 1957–1973," *Public Policy* 23 (Spring 1975): 189–217.

As late as 31 January 1957, the Joint Committee on Programs for Military Assistance described the "present government" of Jordan as "very unstable" and hence probably not eligible for U.S. aid. The text makes it clear that the originators were not aware of the ongoing polarization, with Hussein as one focus of power and the Nabulsi cabinet as the other (*DDQC*, 1980, p. 153B).

According to Donald Neff, CIA payments to King Hussein started as early as October 1956, "[as] part of the plan to build up anti-Nasser states" (*Warriors at Suez* [New York: Simon and Schuster, 1981], p. 317). Although Hussein may have accepted the money, I do not believe that he would have wittingly agreed at that date to the purpose mentioned.

23. Sir Harold Caccia, the British ambassador in Washington, quoting Dulles in a report to the Foreign Office of 25 December 1956 (FO 371/121525).

24. Caccia's advice to the Foreign Office, 26 December 1956. On the margin the prime minister scribbled: "I agree. A.E. 28.12.56." Thirty-five years earlier, a British colonial secretary had settled the future of Anglo-Jordanian relations—and of the Hashemite Entity—by similarly putting his decision on the margin of a departmental memorandum: "Do we, or do we not, wish to see Abdallah settle himself firmly in the Transjordanian saddle?" In that case, the answer had been, "Yes. W.S.C." (CO [Colonial Office] 733/8, pp. 460–61, 2 February 1922). See also Uriel Dann, "T. E. Lawrence in Amman, 1921," in *Studies in the History of Transjordan, 1920–1949* (Boulder, Colo: Westview Press, 1984), p. 44. It is also a curious closing of a circle.

25. *Treaty Series no. 39 (1957)*, Cmnd. 186. Britain later largely waived the payments, when Nabulsi was a phenomenon of the past.

26. For the text of both cables, see Radio Ramallah, SWB, 10–12 January 1957.

27. For a good example of the approach, see Hussein's speech on his return from Cairo, 25 January 1957 (*Falastin,* 24 January 1957).

28. Radio Ramallah, SWB, 2–4 February 1957.

29. For example, Hussein in his interview with *L'Orient* (Beirut) quoted Radio Baghdad, SWB, 2–4 May 1957. As early as mid-March, Kennett Love identified the ring leaders among the "politicized" officers: Shahir Yusuf, Mahmud al-Mu'ayta, Turki al-Hindawi, Ahmad Za'rur, and Mazin al-'Ajluni (*New York Times,* 16 March 1957). All five got into trouble when the crisis broke a month later. None were in any way Communists.

30. *Mideast Mirror,* 31 March 1957.

31. *Mideast Mirror,* 3 and 10 February 1957.

32. "I never act; I only react" (Robert St. John, *The Boss* [New York: McGraw-Hill, 1960], p. 107). This confidence of Abdel Nasser is as close to the historical truth as such aphorisms can be.

33. Radio Amman, SWB, 26–28 February 1957.

34. According to the well-informed Arab New Agency of Beirut (*Mideast Mirror,* 7 April 1957).

35. *Mideast Mirror,* 5 January 1958. Here, too, Hussein's argument was that the Nabulsi government was about to hand over Jordan to Communism or the Soviet Union. The Syrian government replied that the enemy was Western imperialism, that the Soviet Union was friendly, and that Communism was a world-wide phenomenon and not peculiarly Arab. The Syrian note was restrained, although it held the suggestion that Hussein might let himself be exploited for antinationalist purposes. It was only when Syria published the note ten months later that it was cited as evidence for Hussein's return to the imperialist fold.

36. *Falastin,* 26 March and 4 April 1957.

37. *Falastin,* 26 March 1957, quotes extensively from three of Nabulsi's "momentous" speeches.

38. According to the U.S. assistant military attaché in Amman (DA Intelligence Report, no. R-230-57, ID no. 2047279, 16 April 1957, National Archives, Washington, D.C., Modern National Field Branch).

39. In the presence of Maurice Fischer of the Concilation Commission. See *Foreign Relations of the United States (FRUS), 1951,* pp. 735–37, and Dan Schueftan, *A Jordanian Option* (in Hebrew) (Yad Tabenkin: Hakibbutz Hameuhad, 1986), p. 224.

Chapter 4

1. Named after Hussein's and Dina's baby daughter. Queen 'Aliya was King Faysal II's mother and Abdul Ilah's sister, who had died in 1950. The Hashemites are closely knit even in their given names.

2. For a good concise account of the crisis of April 1957, see Richard H. Sanger, *Where the Jordan Flows* (Washington, D.C.: Middle East Institute, 1963) pp. 381–87. Sanger at the time was the American deputy chief of mission at Amman.

3. *Falastin,* 11 April 1957.

4. Not except, in my view, the Six-Day War and Black September 1970.

5. *Mideast Mirror,* 14 April 1957.

6. Two examples representing the opposing sides are "The people of Jordan will vindicate its rights against British aggression and imperialist intrigue!" (*Gumhuriyya,* 12 April 1957), and "Today . . . this artificial kingdom . . . is being slowly ground into oblivion" (*New York Times,* 14 April 1957).

7. Cited by Radio Damascus/Israeli monitored, 13–14 April 1957; the tenor of the source is that the king had accepted. For Mufti's putative cabinet, see *Difaʿ,* 15 April 1957; it is much more innocuous, from Hussein's viewpoint, than Nimr's.

8. For Razzaz, an intellectual, as opposed to the lightweight demagogue Rimawi, see I. Rabinovich, *Syria Under the Baʿth, 1963–1966* (Jerusalem: Israel Universities Press, 1972), and J. F. Devlin, *The Baʿth Party* (Stanford, Calif.: Stanford University Press, 1976).

9. Hashim, Rifaʿi, and Abuʾl Huda were Palestinians by birth who had become "Transjordanians" through the careers of a lifetime.

10. *Jarida Rasmiyya,* no. 1325, 15 April 1957.

11. Hussein, *Uneasy Lies the Head* (London: Heinemann, 1962), p. 127.

12. I should add that being Western myself, I believed for a long time in the "plot situation" rather than the "plot." Abu Nuwar, now a prominent businessman in Amman, has since denied on many occasions his intention to plot against the king.

13. It must have been part of Abu Nuwar's personality that he inspired confidence in newcomers not predisposed in his favor. Reports from Amman and Cyprus throughout 1956 record the pleasant surprise of senior British negotiators at finding him courteous, reasonable, and basically pro-Western. It is to the credit of the new British ambassador, Johnston, that within less than two weeks of his arrival, he wrote of Abu Nuwar: "Tricky customer . . . I would not trust him out of sight" (FO 371/121500, 25 November 1956).

14. The semibeduin Majali of Kerak were among Abdallah's earliest supporters in Transjordan. It may be true that Hussein even then saw the apolitical Hiyyari as a stopgap, with Habis as his slated supplanter (*New York Times,* 20 April 1957). Personally, I think this is overcontrived.

15. The names appear in Aqil Hyder Hasan Abidi, *Jordan: A Political Study 1948–1957* (London: Asia Publishing House, 1965), p. 161, with that of Hikmat al-Masri added, who does not figure in the copy in my own hands.

16. For Hussein's broadcast to his "dear people," which introduced the royal takeover, see *Difaʿ,* 26 April 1957; English text, BBC/SWB, 26 April 1957.

17. *New York Herald Tribune,* 25 April 1957.

18. *New York Times,* 30 April 1957.

19. *New York Herald Tribune,* 25 April 1957.

20. Ibid. Loyal as the beduin were, then and later it was always considered unsafe to delay their pay.

21. *New York Times,* 17 and 30 April 1957. The quotation is from 30 April.

22. "Egypt informed the Jordanian government on 21 April that her first half-yearly instalment . . . would soon be available as arrangements were made *to open credits for Jordan* [my emphasis] in European countries" (*Mideast Mirror*, 28 April 1957).

23. An annotated but incomplete summary of the measures appears in Abidi, *Jordan*, pp. 162–63.

24. *Difaʿ*, 28 April 1957; English text as monitored from Radio Ramallah, SWB, 29 April 1957.

25. DA Intelligence Report, no. R-261-57, ID no. 2047967, 28 April 1957. National Archives, Washington, D.C., Modern National Field Branch.

26. *New York Times*, 26 April 1957. The front page headline is even more explicit: "King Scores Cairo."

27. Ibid., p. 3.

28. Compare Richard P. Stebbins, *The United States in World Affairs 1957* (New York: Harper & Brothers, 1958) pp. 183–84.

29. According to the *New York Herald Tribune*, 29 April 1957.

30. "The Eisenhower Doctrine is an attitude [*sic*]. . . . We have great confidence in . . . King Hussein. . . ." Secretary Dulles at a press conference on 24 April 1957 (*Documents on American Foreign Relations, 1957*, p. 231).

31. Steven L. Spiegel, *The Other Arab–Israeli Conflict* (Chicago: University of Chicago Press, 1984), p. 86.

32. Nadav Safran, *From War to War* (New York: Pegasus, 1969), p. 71.

33. The sequence of releases from the State department during these days and afterward gives some clues to this.

Chapter 5

1. *Difaʿ*, 1 May 1957; *Mideast Mirror*, 5 May 1957.

2. As paraphrased in *Mideast Mirror*, 15 September 1957, with the full text in *Jihad* (Jerusalem), 12 September 1957.

3. *Mideast Mirror*, 4 August 1957.

4. *Jihad*, 26 September 1957. ʿAli Abu Nuwar and ʿAli al-Hiyyari were sentenced to fifteen years each, and Mahmud al-Musa and Mahmud Muʿayta to ten years—all in absentia. Muhammad Muʿayta and Maʿn Abu Nuwar were among those acquitted.

5. In the summer of 1958, with stabilization achieved, the police came back under the minister of the interior. Occasional bickering resulted, but nothing worse.

6. For detailed studies of this subject, see Avraham Sela, *The Palestinian Baʿath* (in Hebrew) (Jerusalem: Magnes Press, 1984), and Amnon Cohen, "Political Parties in the West Bank Under the Hashemite Regime," in Moshe Ma'oz, ed., *Palestinian Arab Politics* (Jerusalem: Jerusalem Academic Press, 1975).

7. The temporary shutdown of *al-Kifah al-Islami*, the organ of the Muslim Brothers, in October 1957, can be viewed as symptomatic of the political stabilization since April. During the crisis the Brothers, in Jordan as elsewhere possessed of greater independence of mind than the secular parties, had closely collaborated with Hussein, and so by autumn, they evidently felt they could again

lash out against the regime's Western proclivities in a style that was impermissible. Not many editors in Jordan dared to offend thus at the time.

8. *Jarida Rasmiyya,* no. 1333, 26 May 1957; see also Naseer Hasan Aruri, "Jordan: A Study in Political Development, 1921–1965," (Ph.D. diss., University of Massachusetts, 1967), pp. 176–77.

9. On Hussein in Egyptian caricature, see Moshe Gershovitz, "King Hussein in Egyptian Political Caricature, 1957–1967" (in Hebrew) (Seminar paper, Tel Aviv University, 1985). I am obliged to Mr. Gershovitz for permission to quote.

10. *Falastin,* 2 October 1957.

11. They were Fa'iq Warrad, Communist member for Ramallah, sentenced to fifteen years' imprisonment; Ya'qub Ziyadin, Communist member for Jerusalem, sentenced in absentia to nineteen years' imprisonment; Rimawi, sentenced in absentia to fifteen years' imprisonment—the only civilian to have come before the special military court; Sa'id al-'Azza, secretary of the National Socialist party and member for Hebron, sentenced in absentia to one year's imprisonment; 'Abd al-Khaliq Yaghmur, independent member for Hebron and under detention pending trial; Yusuf al-Bandak, independent member for Bethlehem; Shafiq Rashidat, National Socialist member for Irbid; and Kamal Nasir, Ba'th member for Ramallah (the last three apparently made good their escape). All were expelled from the Chamber.

12. Before the year was out, Hussein improved on his "best" by having five of the abstaining delegates removed, officially by resigning their seats. Shaykh Ahmad al-Da'ur of the Tahrir party stayed on for the time being, undaunted, and cast his vote against the government in a vote of confidence on 16 October, one of two delegates to do so.

13. *Mideast Mirror,* 28 July 1957.

14. 28 May 1957, Eisenhower Library, Ann Whitman File, Diary Series, Box 24; *DDQC,* 1983, p. 001393.

15. *Department of State Bulletin* 36, 10 June 57.

16. At his press conference of 2 July 57 (*Department of State Bulletin* 37, 22 July 57).

17. Charles Johnston, *The Brink of Jordan* (London: Hamish Hamilton, 1972), p. 79.

18. Ibid., pp. 70–71.

19. With respect to Egypt, this was entirely true; to Syria, less so.

20. My own interpretation is largely deductive. The scraps of direct evidence in my possession are contradictory. The British ambassador, Johnston, mentions Hilal's "terrorist activities" (see Charles Johnston, *The Brink of Jordan,* p. 81). But this needs elaboration to be convincing.

21. An excellent example is the statement put out by the government information office on 28 July 1957 attacking Abdel Nasser for his speech at Alexandria two days before, on the first anniversary of the Suez Canal nationalization (*Mideast Mirror,* 4 August 1957). The statement is attributed to "an important political source"; as the *Mideast Mirror* surmised, the source was Rifa'i. Abdel

Nasser had referred to Jordan only obliquely, and he had not mentioned Hussein.

22. Ibid.

Chapter 6

1. From the preamble of the union agreement, 1 February 1958, as translated in Muhammad Khalil, ed., *The Arab States and the Arab League* (Beirut: Khayats, 1962), vol. 1, p. 601.

2.¹ His situation was embarrassing. On 21 January 1958, the "opposition" deputy Fa'iq al-'Anabtawi complained in the Chamber that a radio commentator had attacked the proposed union between Egypt and Syria. Rifa'i expressed his disapproval but denied government responsibility, as the "commentaries represented the view of the commentators" (*Mideast Mirror*, 26 January 1958).

3. See *Bilad* (Jerusalem), 8 February 1958, for the rationale of a Jordanian-Iraqi-Saudi Arabian federation, obviously inspired from above.

4. *The Times*, 17 February 1958, quoting interlocking Cairo sources.

5. As translated in Khalil, ed., *The Arab States*, vol. 1, p. 79.

6. Ibid.

7. Ibid., pp. 80–90.

8. Royal Institute of International Affairs, *Documents on International Affairs, 1958* (London: Oxford University Press, 1962), p. 241. A prestigious Lebanese politician asserted that King Faysal cabled a reply—at the dictation of 'Abdul Ilah and over the protests of his foreign minister—that intimated that Abdel Nasser was not qualified to talk of Arab unity; only the Hashemites were. Bustani surmised that this insult was one reason for Abdel Nasser's change of attitude toward the federation. (Emile Bustani, *March Arabesque* [London: Robert Hale, 1961], pp. 113–14).

9. *The Times*, 17 February 1958, quoting *Al-Shaab* (Cairo).

10. *The Times*, 17 February 1958.

11. Public speech at Cairo, 20 March (*Mideast Mirror*, 23 March 1958).

12. *Ahram*, 14 February 1958.

13. *Hayat* (Beirut), 19 February 1958.

14. *Jihad*, 30 and 31 March 1958.

15. *Mideast Mirror*, 9 March 1958.

16. *Mideast Mirror*, 18 May 1958.

17. *Mideast Mirror*, 4 May 1958, quoting *Akhir Sa'a* (Cairo).

18. For example, *Falastin*, 26 February 1958.

19. *Jihad*, 21 May 1958.

20. *Urdunn* (Amman), 20 May 1958.

21. *Mideast Mirror*, 16 February 1958.

22. The following is chiefly collated from originally top secret and secret documents of the Joint Chiefs of Staff, recently declassified. For detailed source references, see the cumulative indexes in *DDQC*, 1979, 1980, "Middle East."

23. Thus the Jordanian army was held to be incapable of withstanding an Is-

raeli offensive on the West Bank for more than six days—not a bad prognostication in 1957.

24. According to Dulles at a cabinet meeting, 18 July 1958 (Eisenhower Library, Ann Whitman File, Cabinet Series, Box 11; *DDQC*, 1981, p. 628A). There is no reason to doubt the sincerity of Dulles's presentation, although its self-centered formulation is extraordinary. For example, the United States had for long "hoped" that Abdel Nasser would "adopt . . . the moral obligations of civilized nations."

25. According to William M. Rountree in a letter to me, dated 25 July 1984.

Chapter 7

1. Much of the affair is still in doubt. My own account is collated from a number of sources in a way that I believe gives the essentials. See especially Andrew Tully, *CIA: The Inside Story* (London: Barker, 1962), pp. 75–76, 82–83. Although this book is not totally trustworthy, its factual assertions are usually correct. Second, on the Baghdad coup, it agrees with the presidential briefings on 14 July 1958, recently declassified though heavily "sanitized"—that is, published with deletions.

2. Hussein, in his autobiography, makes much of the detailed information concerning the projected Iraqi coup, which he says he passed on to King Faysal and the Iraqi chief of general staff, Lieutenant General Rafiq 'Arif, which the Iraqis coolly disregarded (*Uneasy Lies the Head* [London: Heinemann 1962], pp. 160–61). This is largely an afterdramatization. The Jordanian plotters had no concrete knowledge of Qasim's plans, although like many others, they sensed the atmosphere inside the Iraqi officer corps. Under examination, they may have said more than they knew.

3. The UAR authorities had a score to settle with Radi 'Abdallah. He had been the Jordanian military attaché in Cairo in 1955 where he became known for his skeptical views regarding the revolutionary regime.

4. The juridical aftermath of the conspiracy may be related here: Rusan and fifteen accomplices were tried early in 1960, and those who had absconded, in absentia. The brothers Shara' were not among the sixteen. Their involvement was revealed in 1959, by which time Sadiq was the army chief of general staff and Salah brigade commander, soon to be transferred to Bonn as military attaché. They were convicted, it appears, on trumped-up charges of plotting said to have taken place a year after their real transgressions.

Radi 'Abdallah, after his rehabilitation, was appointed assistant director of security in 1962 and, shortly afterward, director of investigations. By then, he had certainly acquired inside knowledge. (He died when this chapter was being written, in the summer of 1986).

5. Majid Khadduri surmises that the brigade was "to reinforce the Jordan army against alleged threats to Jordan from Israel" (*Republican Iraq* [London: Oxford University Press, 1969], p. 38). But the relations between Israel and Jordan at that time, tense as usual but not particularly so, make this explanation doubtful.

6. Synopsis reported to the president, 19 July 1958 (Eisenhower Library,

Ann Whitman File; *DDQC,* 1984, p. 000638). The quotation refers to the United States, but it may be assumed that Hussein spoke to the British chargé d'affaires in similar terms.

7. "Cypress," as it appears in Eisenhower's personal diary of these days more than once. It may have been a typist's idiosyncrasy that passed undiscovered and provides a moment of light relief for the student of history.

8. Macmillan, in making the announcement in the House of Commons on 17 July, protested rather too much when he stressed that on the previous night he had got "the first news . . . that King Hussein and the Prime Minister of Jordan [Rifaʻi] had made a request for the immediate despatch of British forces to Jordan" (Royal Institute of International Affairs, *Documents on International Affairs, 1958* [London: Oxford University Press, 1962], p. 296). Literally, however, this was correct.

9. Secretary Dulles at a White House conference, 14 July 1958 (*DDQC,* 1984, no. 2, p. 1391).

10. *American Foreign Policy, Current Documents 1958* (Washington, D.C.: Government Printing Office, 1962), p. 981.

11. *New York Herald Tribune,* 20 July 1958.

12. An authoritative indicator is the "timetable of events . . . July 14–19" compiled for President Eisenhower, under 18 July 1958 (Eisenhower Library, Ann Whitman File, Box 10; *DDQC,* 1981, p. 629B).

13. At the time of the Iraqi revolution, President Nasser was visiting Yugoslavia. He decided to fly to Moscow when American marines landed in Lebanon; British paratroopers entered Jordan; and Turkish forces concentrated along the Syrian borders. First Secretary Nikita Khrushchev told him that "under the present circumstances anything was possible . . . and frankly the Soviet Union was not prepared to indulge in a clash with the West the consequences of which were unknown." (*Ahram,* 22 January 1965, quoted in *Mideast Mirror,* 23 January 1965).

14. Descriptions of the Amman scene during those days consistently convey this impression.

15. *Falastin,* 17 and 18 July 1958.

16. ". . . essentially a state of rebellion *against the divine law* [my emphasis] in which the weak always run the risk of being trapped . . . *ahl al-sunna wa'l jamaʻa* [i.e., Sunni Muslims] have the strict duty to obey the legitimate sovereign so long as his orders do not run counter to the Qurʾan, and to shun all *fitna*" (L. Gardet, *Encyclopedia of Islam, New Edition* [Leiden: Brill, 1965], vol. 2, pp. 930–31).

17. *Difaʻ,* 18 July 1958.

18. *Majzarat al-Rihab,* the slaughter at Rihab Palace to the west of Baghdad, became common coin.

19. The careful circumscriptions of Ambassador Johnston are especially convincing. See his *The Brink of Jordan* (London: Hamish Hamilton, 1972), pp. 105–6.

20. A memo to the White House from the Policy Planning Staff at the State

Department states as late as 9 August 1958 that "we ... believe ... that Hussein could be quickly persuaded to make a gesture of this sort" [i.e., "step aside for the benefit of the people"] (*Declassified Documents Retrospective Collection, 1976*, p. 683E). The tenor of the memo indicates that Hussein was half convinced.

21. For example, in Cairo, 22 July 1958. The headline in *Gumhuriyya*, 23 July 1958, screams, "Treason to perish!"

22. Allen Dulles, director of the CIA, to congressional representatives, 14 July 1958 (*DDQC*, 1979, p. 12D).

23. This defeatist appraisal appears at its most authoritative in the National Security Council's "U.S. policy toward the Near East" of 4 November 1958 (NSC 5820/1, *DDQC*, 1980, p. 386B), from which the quotations are taken. But the appraisal is in a line with ruminations since mid-July.

24. It was, of course, the British appraisal that turned out to be correct, and for once the humorous condescension of British Middle Eastern hands, when contemplating the lack of experience of their American colleagues, does not jar (e.g., Johnston, *The Brink of Jordan*, passim).

25. Culled from my talks with persons who had intimate information about the subject.

26. On Prince Muhammad's personality, see *Time*, 15 February 1960. The report is essentially true, despite the angry denial by Hussein, a loyal brother. Another denial signed by Wasfi al-Tall, then director of broadcasting and national guidance, was more objective and hence more effective; it may have helped win him the king's trust and esteem. See *Time*, 7 March 1960.

27. *New York Herald Tribune*, 27 July 1958.

28. Baha al-Din Touqan resigned in a huff at thus being displaced.

29. *Public Papers of the Presidents of the United States: Dwight D. Eisenhower, 1958* (Washington, D.C. Government Printing Office, n.d.), pp. 606–15.

30. Here, too, Eisenhower meant what he said. "Defense Comments" in the National Security Council appraisal of 4 November 1958 state that "no U.S. military aid is now programmed for Jordan for FY 1959 or beyond," although provisions for economic aid were generous (and escape clauses were included concerning military aid as well).

31. Royal Institute of International Affairs, *Documents on International Affairs, 1958*, pp. 327–29.

Chapter 8

1. A foreign diplomat who was close to Hussein at the time has described to me the "glassy look" in Hussein's eyes the moment the conversation turned to details of finance, however important.

2. Hans E. Tütsch, *Swiss Review of World Affairs*, February 1961, p. 6.

3. *Neue Zürcher Zeitung* (*NZZ*) (Zurich), 31 August 1958. Then and later,

the *NZZ* was particularly well represented in the Middle East by its reporters Hans E. Tütsch and Arnold Hottinger.

4. *United Nations Treaty Series* (Secretariat) 315, 1958, no. 4564, pp. 125–33, registered 18 November 1958.

5. *Mideast Mirror*, 24 August 1958.

6. On this, see Hava Lazarus-Yafeh, "An Inquiry into Arab Education," *Asian and African Studies* 8 (1972): 1–19. Lazarus-Yafeh proceeds with great caution and takes care to put the various data into their psychological and environmental context. But the fundamental message is clear, all the same.

7. Memorandum by Secretary of State John Foster Dulles, 26 September 1958 (John Foster Dulles, "Papers, 1952–1959," General Correspondence and Memoranda Series, *DDQC*, 1983, p. 001026).

8. The secretary of state's "Memorandum for the President," 15 January 1959 (Department of State memoranda, *DDQC*, 1981, p. 00343).

9. Department of State memoranda, *DDQC*, 1982, pp. 0–0299; "Memorandum of Conversation," 25 March 1959 (Eisenhower Library, Ann Whitman File; *DDQC*, 1979, p. 196A). Present with Eisenhower were the acting secretary of state, Christian A. Herter (Dulles was in the terminal stage of his illness), and the assistant secretary for Near Eastern affairs, William M. Rountree. Midhat Jum'a, who apparently kept silent during the meeting, is not to be confused with his more prominent brother, Sa'd Jum'a, later the prime minister at the time of the Six-Day War.

10. An American well acquainted with the Jordanian scene told me that Rifa'i was ready to come to terms with Israel, which might have been acceptable to both, but Hussein would not hear of it.

11. Hussein, *Uneasy Lies the Head* (London: Heinemann, 1962), pp. 196–97; Peter Snow, *Hussein* (London: Barrie & Jenkins, 1972), pp. 133–34

12. The Majali, with their power base in the city of Kerak, were not nomads, as the Banu Sakhr predominantly still were in Abdallah's days. Yet in sentiment and social organization, they were tribal.

Chapter 9

1. See also Majali's declaration at a special session of the Chamber of Deputies in Jerusalem on 19 January 1960 (*Falastin*, 20 January 1960).

2. Actually applying the resolution would have been awkward, as the Jordanian government soon realized. Within less than two weeks, it was officially explained that countries with established refugee agencies like UNRWA were excluded (i.e., the UAR and Lebanon, where the overwhelming majority of Palestinian refugees outside Jordan resided). Finally, the requisite amendment to the Jordan Nationality Law was never passed (*Falastin*, 5 February; *Hayat*, 13 February; and *Difa'*, 16 February 1960). However, a few Palestinian residents of the Persian Gulf area eventually acquired Jordanian citizenship, presumably on the strength of the February 1960 resolution.

3. Radio Amman, 16 March 1960, quoted in *Middle East Record [MER]*, *1960* (London: Weidenfeld & Nicolson, n.d.), p. 322.

4. Hussein, *Uneasy Lies the Head* (London: Heinemann, 1962), pp. 186 ff.

5. Hans E. Tütsch, *Swiss Review of World Affairs*, February 1961, p. 8.

6. The speech is rendered in full in Hussein, *Uneasy Lies the Head*, pp. 200–207.

7. Radio Cairo, 5 October 1960.

8. For the American "Memorandum of Conversation" between Abdel Nasser and the president on 26 September 1960, see *DDQC*, 1983, p. 001436. It is clear that Eisenhower was at pains to assuage Abdel Nasser's vanity, and Abdel Nasser, on his part, was all relaxation and common sense.

9. *Jihad*, 2 November 1960.

10. Iraqi News Agency, 15 October 1960, quoted in *MER, 1960*, p. 160.

11. As authoritative a study of Kennedy's foreign policy as that of Roger Hilsman (an insider), *To Move a Nation* (Garden City, N.Y.: Doubleday, 1967), does not mention the Middle East, any Middle Eastern country, or Abdel Nasser or any other Middle Eastern personality in its table of contents and index. Arthur M. Schlesinger, Jr., one of Kennedy's closest collaborators, devoted only two pages to Abdel Nasser in his thousand-page account—*A Thousand Days* (Cambridge, Mass.: Harvard University Press, 1965)—in a subchapter entitled "North Africa." (But Schlesinger explains that he himself "had little to do with the Middle East.") Another piece of evidence by default is the general absence of the Arab East and Israel from the agenda of National Security Council meetings during Kennedy's presidency, in contrast with Turkey, Iran, and Pakistan. In general (most of the actual proceedings are still classified), the tone seems to have been optimistic in regard to "Nasserism" (National Security Files, Boxes 313–3154, Meetings and Memoranda, John F. Kennedy Library, Boston, Massachusetts).

12. For President Kennedy's attitude toward Abdel Nasser—whom he had met when senator—see Mordechai Gazit, *President Kennedy's Policy Toward the Arab States and Israel* (Tel Aviv: Shiloah Center for Middle Eastern and African Studies, 1983). Gazit was Israeli minister in Washington at the time. I am also obliged to William B. Macomber, U.S. ambassador in Amman during the Kennedy administration, for a valuable talk. See also Steven L. Spiegel, *The Other Arab–Israeli Conflict*. (Chicago: University of Chicago Press, 1984), pp. 94–117.

13. Over twenty years later, Ambassador Macomber told me that even then he had sided with Hussein on both counts, although he could not, of course say so to the king.

14. The correspondence appears in full in *Jihad*, 1 April and 11 May 1961. The English abstracts in *MER, 1961*, pp. 142–44, are adequate.

15. *Ahram*, 2 April 1961, quoted in *MER, 1961*, p. 145. There is no doubt that the jubilation was genuine. Because of the nature of the case, there could be no counterdemonstration by those who viewed the correspondence with apprehension.

16. For example, *New York Times*, 29 March and 1 April 1961.

Chapter 10

1. Not the privately owned press, closely supervised as it was. Clearly there was in Jordan a line between censorship and dictation, one of the distinctions between an authoritarian and a totalitarian regime.

2. The editor of *Ahram* was eloquent after the event regarding Hussein's close relations with the conspirators, and with Colonel Haydar al-Kuzbari in particular, during the summer of 1961.

3. See Peter Snow, *Hussein* (London: Barrie & Jenkins, 1972), p. 151.

4. In the following, I have heavily drawn on *MER, 1961* (Jerusalem: Israel Program for Scientific Translations, n.d.), pp. 145–46.

5. I am following convention by continuing to refer to Egypt, even after the breakup, as the UAR, which indeed remained its official designation until the Sadat regime.

6. At a meeting with Muhammad Hasanayn Haykal (*Ahram*, 27 September 1963).

7. Muhammad Khalil, ed., *The Arab States and the Arab League* (Beirut: Khayat, 1962), vol. 1, p. 75.

8. *Jarida Rasmiyya*, no. 1494, 11 June 1960.

9. For a summary of these practices, see *MER, 1961*, p. 358.

10. Qasim had made it the official policy of Iraq not to maintain embassies in countries that had exchanged ambassadors with Kuwait, as Jordan and all other Arab countries had done.

11. Asher Susser, *Between Jordan and Palestine: A Political Biography of Wasfi al-Tall* (in Hebrew) (Tel Aviv: Hakibbutz Hameuhad, 1983).

12. William B. Macomber to me.

13. *Jihad*, 28 January 1962.

14. See also Susser, *Between Jordan and Palestine*, p. 41.

15. "The last announced plan, before the Six Day War, for 1964–1970, was a revision of an earlier plan for 1962–67, announced in 1961." (Eliyahu Kanovsky, *Economic Development of Jordan* [Tel Aviv: Tel Aviv University, 1976], p. 12. This plan was indeed composed during the premiership, and under the formal auspices, of Talhuni, but it was Tall who set it in motion, with a genuine flair for publicity. The king again cannot be held to have been more than a benevolent bystander. For the plan, see *The Hashemite Kingdom of Jordan, Five Year Program for Economic Development 1962–1967* (n.p. [Amman], 1961), and *Seven Year Program for Economic Development of Jordan, 1964–1970* (n.p. [Amman], n.d. [1966?]).

16. Figures relating to the elections are based on *Mideast Mirror*, 1 December 1962.

17. Anouar Abdel-Malek, *Egypte société militaire* (Paris: Editions du Seuil, 1962), is particularly illuminating, although the author's Marxist orientation must be kept in mind.

18. *Mideast Mirror*, 28 October 1961. The Baghdad daily whose editor interviewed the Jordanian prime minister was *al-'Ahd al-Jadid*.

19. For the agreement, see *Mideast Mirror*, 1 September 1962. The term *semi-*

union was used by Salah Abu Zayd, the Jordanian director of guidance and information.

20. *Mideast Mirror,* October 1962. A knowledgeable American diplomat told me that the unpopularity of involving Jordan in Yemen was another factor in the decline of Tall's influence from about that time.

21. The CIA "intelligence checklist" for the president, 18 October 1962 (National Security Files, Box 313, John F. Kennedy Library, Boston, Massachusetts).

22. For this, see Mordechai Gazit, *President Kennedy's Policy Toward the Arab States and Israel* (Tel Aviv: Shiloah Center for Middle Eastern and African Studies, 1983), pp. 23–26, and Steven L. Spiegel, *The Arab–Israeli Conflict* (Chicago: University of Chicago Press, 1984), pp. 102–5.

23. *Department of State Bulletin,* no. 939, 19 December 1962.

24. Harold Macmillan, *At the End of the Day 1961–1963* (London: Macmillan, 1973), pp. 275–76.

25. *Mideast Mirror,* 22 and 29 December 1962.

26. The outstanding account of the Cairo talks is that by Malcolm Kerr, *The Arab Cold War* (London: Royal Institute of International Affairs, 1965).

27. Susser, *Between Jordan and Palestine,* pp. 62–63.

28. *Falastin,* 17 March 1963; *Mideast Mirror,* 23 March 1963.

29. *Mideast Mirror,* 6 April 1963. The "measures" were taken as early as 21 March. The term *precautionary* appears in Hussein's message.

30. *Falastin,* 28 March 1963. "Country" refers to Jordan; "nation" *may* mean the "Arab nation."

31. Here, as elsewhere, I have used the excellent lists in Marius Haas, *Husseins Königreich* (Munich: tuduv, 1975), pp. 571–605.

32. *Falastin,* 28 March 1963.

33. Observers from the Israeli side of the armistice line in Jerusalem saw the beduin advance through crowded streets, wielding their lashes.

34. *Mideast Mirror,* 4 May 1963.

35. *Falastin,* 14 April 1963.

36. He died of heart failure at Amman on 12 October 1965.

37. *Difaʿ,* 21 April 1963.

38. *Difaʿ,* 29 April 1963.

39. *Mideast Mirror,* 27 April 1963.

40. *Haaretz* (Tel Aviv), 19 April 1963.

41. *Mideast Mirror,* 27 April 1963. In a letter dated 15 January 1987, Shimon Peres wrote to me "[In our talk Kennedy] spoke of Hussein with sympathy, and this was my approach too. We did not favour Hussein's abdication or his joining the above-mentioned [triple] coalition." I am obliged to Mr. Peres for his assistance.

42. *Mideast Mirror,* 18 May 1963.

43. President's Office Files, "Jordan," Box 120, 28 June 1963, Kennedy Library.

44. At a press conference in Amman, 23 April 1963 (Radio Amman, SWB, 23–25 April 1963).

45. Kennedy Library, Oral Histories: William B. Macomber. I am also obliged to Mr. Gazit for his assistance.

46. During the April riots, the Israeli army was put on the alert in the Jerusalem sector.

47. Shlomo Gazit, *The Stick and the Carrot* (in Hebrew) (Tel Aviv: Zmora, Bitan, Modan, 1985), pp. 20–23.

48. *Haaretz*, 19 April 1963. The report is clearly an appreciation of the atmosphere in Washington during those days, and as such it inspires trust.

49. For the following, I am largely indebted to Moshe Zak, "Israeli–Jordanian Negotiations," *Washington Quarterly*, Winter 1985, pp. 165–76. Mr. Zak also gave me additional information. I have also discussed the subject with Israelis who do not wish to be named.

50. There had been occasional meetings between Israeli and Jordanian functionaries since 1959, but they do not form a pattern. Ben-Gurion deprecated them as purposeless, characteristically so, too. For the tanks deal, see Zak, "Israeli–Jordanian Negotiations," p. 168. Three recently published books touch on Hussein's contacts with Israel until the Six-Day War, although this is not their main theme: Aaron S. Klieman, *Unpeaceful Co-existence* (in Hebrew) (Tel Aviv: Maariv, 1986); Yossi Melman and Daniel Raviv, *A Hostile Partnership: The Secret Relations Between Israel and Jordan* (in Hebrew) (Tel Aviv: Yedioth Ahronoth, 1987); and Dan Schueftan, *A Jordanian Option: The "Yishuv" and the State of Israel vis-à-vis the Hashemite Regime and the Palestinian National Movement* (in Hebrew) (Yad Tabenkin: Hakibbutz Hameuhad, 1986).

51. U.S. Embassy, Tel Aviv, to Secretary of State, 15 May 1964 (*DDQC*, 1980, p. 297A).

52. *Ahram*, 27 September 1963.

53. Over twenty-years later, Kennedy's secretary of state, Dean Rusk, referred to Abdel Nasser as a "scoundrel" when he recalled that period during an interview with me.

Chapter 11

1. *Ahram*, 24 December 1963.

2. For an English translation of the charter, see Nissim Rejwan, *Nasserist Ideology: Its Exponents and Critics* (Jerusalem: Israel Universities Press, 1974), pp. 195–266.

3. For Abdel Nasser's retrospective elucidation, see *Ahram*, 26 November 1965, and Avraham Sela, *Unity Within Conflict in the Inter-Arab System* (in Hebrew) (Jerusalem: Magnes Press, 1982), pp. 26–37.

4. *Hayat*, 18 January 1964; *Cahiers de l'Orient contemporain* 54 (1964): 14.

5. He settled quietly in his home town of Irbid, became a senator, and died at Amman in 1973.

6. For the gist of this episode, see the CIA's "Special Report: Nasir's Arab

Policy, the Latest Phase," 28 August 1964, (National Security Files, Country File Middle East, "UAR," vol. 2, Lyndon Baines Johnson Library, Austin, Texas). When the Six-Day War broke out, Jordan had six F-104s. (Syed Ali el-Edroos, *The Hashemite Arab Army 1908–1979* [Amman Publishing Committee, 1980), p. 330. Also see Steven L. Spiegel, *The Arab-Israeli Conflict* (Chicago: University of Chicago Press, 1984), pp. 132–36.

7. *Mideast Mirror,* 25 July 1964.

8. Throughout his career as prime minister and president, Abdel Nasser only once visited an independent Arab capital before the 1967 catastrophe. This was, significantly, faraway Rabat, Morocco, where he went for the third summit in September 1965.

9. *Mideast Mirror,* 12 September 1964.

10. This book's treatment of the PLO is restricted to aspects affecting the Jordanian Entity.

11. For details and other points, see Aryeh Bo'az, "Ahmad al-Shuqayri, a Political Biography" (in Hebrew) (M.A. thesis, Tel Aviv University, 1987). I am obliged to Mr. Bo'az for permission to quote.

12. At the Intercontinental Hotel on the Mount of Olives. This was a compromise between the Old City and Amman, the former Shuqayri's, and the latter Hussein's, suggestion.

13. *Difa',* 29 May 1964.

14. For an English translation of the 1964 covenant, see Y. Harkabi, *The Palestinian Covenant and Its Meaning* (London: Valentine, Mitchell, 1979), pp. 107–112.

15. Bo'az, "Ahmad al-Shuqayri," p. 48.

16. Ibid., pp. 48, 51.

17. *Difa',* 29 May 1964.

18. See Bo'az, "Ahmad al-Shuqayri," chaps. 4 and 5.

19. *Falastin,* 14 February 1965.

20. *Al-Nahar* (Beirut), 23 April 1965.

21. *Al-Akhbar* (Cairo), 23 April 1965.

22. At a press conference in Tunis on 11 March 65, quoted in *Mideast Mirror,* 13 March 1965.

23. *Ahram,* 23 April 1965.

24. Faysal had assumed the Saudi Arabian crown in December 1964.

25. *Ahram,* 18 June 1965.

26. At a press conference in Amman, 21 June 1965 (*Falastin,* 22 June 1965).

27. For an English translation of the treaty and a boundary sketch, see *Middle East Journal* 22 (Summer 1968): 346–48.

28. Until then, an observer standing on the shore between Elath and Aqaba could see four countries: Egypt, Israel, Jordan, and Saudi Arabia.

29. President Johnson was particularly unlucky or maladroit—at least until the Six-Day War—by seeming enthusiastically pro-Israel without pursuing such a policy in reality. Also see Spiegel, *The Arab–Israeli Conflict,* chap. 3.

30. *Falastin,* 10 June 1965.

31. *Jarida Rasmiyya*, no. 1831, 1 April 1965; *Falastin*, 2 April 1965.

32. *Mideast Mirror*, 1 April 1965.

33. *Mideast Mirror*, 13 April 1965.

Chapter 12

1. Asher Susser, *Between Jordan and Palestine: A Political Biography of Wasfi al-Tall* (in Hebrew) (Tel Aviv: Hakibbutz Hameuhad, 1983), p. 79, quoting Radio Amman, 13 May 1965; Radio Cairo, Voice of Palestine, 15 May 1965.

2. Aryeh Boʻaz, "Ahmad al-Shuqayri, a Political Biography" (in Hebrew) (M.A. thesis, Tel Aviv University, 1987), p. 76, quoting *Al-Nahar*, 12 May 1965.

3. Wasfi al-Tall in the Chamber of Deputies, 15 March 1965 (*Falastin*, 16 March 1965).

4. Syed Ali el-Edroos, *The Hashemite Arab Army, 1908–1979* (Amman: Publishing Committee, 1980), pp. 752–53.

5. Shuqayri had expressed demands in this sense in person at Amman on 25 February 1965 (*Falastin*, 26 February 1965).

6. Israelis in a position to know could offer me no clear-cut opinion on whether the new brigades put up a tougher or a weaker stand in the war; there were too many diverging factors involved. Edroos, *The Hashemite Arab Army*, and Samir A. Mutawi, *Jordan in the 1967 War* (Cambridge: Cambridge University Press, 1987), ignore the question.

7. Foreign Broadcast Information Service, Washington, D.C., 1 October 1965.

8. *Difaʻ*, 5 October 1965.

9. *Falastin*, 12 October 1965.

10. A credible exposition of these talks appears in *Falastin*, 26 December 1965, interesting also because it shows the various stresses under which the Jordanian press labored.

11. At a "People's Congress" at Basman Palace, 5 January 1966 (*Falastin*, 6 January 1966). That the PLO was "splitting the country" was, of course, an obvious charge to make, and Hussein had made it for some time. That it might also "divide the army" was less conventional, and truly slippery ground.

12. For the text of the agreement, see *Falastin*, 2 March 1966.

13. At Cairo on 22 February 1966, the anniversary of the plebiscite that confirmed the UAR in 1958 (*Gumhuriyya*, 23 February 1966).

14. Abdel Nasser did describe the Islamic alliance as an extension of the Baghdad Pact, at Damanhur, 15 June 1966 (*Gumhuriyya*, 16 June 1966).

15. For Hussein's speech, held at a banquet in honor of Faysal in Amman on 27 January 1966, see *Difaʻ*, 28 January 1966.

16. *Mideast Mirror*, 29 January 1966, cites two conspicuous examples: that of Christopher Soames, foreign secretary in the British Conservative shadow cabinet, and Winston Churchill's son-in-law, who observed at Tehran that the center of power in the Middle East was shifting from Cairo to Tehran and Riyadh and that Britain was welcoming the shift; and—more ominously, as it came from a secular source within the Arab orbit—the Tunisian *L'Action*, which in the same

context credited the Arab countries with "genuinely seeking for the first time" a new framework for cooperation that did not "necessarily" include Cairo.

17. *Falastin*, 15 April 1963.

18. The documents are pinpointed in Boʻaz, "Ahmad al-Shuqayri," p. 110; see also Susser, *Between Jordan and Palestine*, p. 79. A similar action on a smaller scale had been carried out, more discreetly, among the same groups four months earlier.

19. On 7 June 1966, (*al-Baʻth* [Damascus], 8 June 1966).

20. For the full text, see the official reprint, "Text of the Speech Delivered by H. M. King Hussein to the Graduates of the Teachers' Seminary, Ajlun, Tuesday, 14 June 1966" (in Arabic).

21. On 16 July 1966 (*Manar* [Amman], 17 July 1966).

22. Boʻaz, "Ahmad al-Shuqayri," p. 120.

23. "Voice of Palestine," SWB, 17–20 June 1966. An interesting epithet that Shuqayri bestowed on Hussein on that occasion was "half-educated," an allusion to Hussein's presumption in speaking before a teachers' seminary.

24. *Mideast Mirror*, 25 June 1966.

25. Ibid.

26. Boʻaz, "Ahmad al-Shuqayri," p. 111, quoting *Hawadeth* (Beirut), 26 August 1966; Radio Cairo, 4 November 1966.

27. For a concise essay on Sayyid Qutb, see Sylvia G. Haim, "Sayyid Qutb," *Asian and African Studies* 16 (March 1982): 147–56.

28. *Manar*, 20 February 1967.

29. For the Hatum coup and its Syrian background, see John F. Devlin, *The Baʻth Party* (Stanford, Calif.: Stanford University Press, 1976), p. 314, and the media of the time.

30. For the text, see Foreign Broadcast Information Service, 4 November 1966.

Chapter 13

1. Hussein's figure. See Vick Vance and P. Lauer, *Hussein de Jordanie, ma "guerre" avec Israel* (Paris: Michel, 1968), p. 30.

2. For a sample of American dismay, see the White House "Memorandum for the President" of 14 November 1966, signed by Walter Rostow (*DDQC*, 1984, no. 2, p. 1414).

3. Predictably, it was Shuqayri who put the case against the king at its strongest (A. Shuqayri, *Al-malik Husayn fi qafs al-ittiham* [King Husayn in the dock], [n.p. (Cairo?), n.d. (1967?)]).

4. U.S. Department of State telegram to U.S. Embassy, Amman, 23 November 1966 (Declassified NLJ 82–162), (Lyndon Baines Johnson Library, Austin, Texas). The message is a further reminder of what Hussein threw away when he joined Egypt on 5 June 1967. Yet as he saw it, he had no choice.

5. If true, the Israeli agency responsible had clearly not considered the unwisdom of adding insult to injury.

6. For instance, in a public address in Jerusalem, 25 January 1967 (*Hayat*, 26 January 1967).

7. I have also drawn for this episode on Zvi Elpeleg, "Hajj Amin al-Husayni—A Political Biography" (in Hebrew) (M.A. thesis, Tel Aviv University, 1987), pp. 192–94. I am obliged to Mr. Elpeleg for permission to quote.

8. *Jarida Rasmiyya*, no. 1966, 27 November 1966. For a translation of the law into French, see *Cahiers de l'Orient contemporain 67 (October 1967): 76.*

9. *Dustur* (Amman), 2 April 1967.

10. *Jarida Rasmiyya,* no. 1987, 21 February 1967.

11. Minister of Information Sharif ʿAbd al-Hamid Sharaf on 25 February 1967 (Radio Amman, SWB, 25–28 February 1967).

12. For an uncharacteristically outspoken criticism of the press, which is the subject of a letter from Hussein to the prime minister, see *Mideast Mirror,* 23 May 1964.

13. On this, see William A. Rugh, *The Arab Press* (Syracuse, N.Y.: Syracuse University Press, 1979), pp. 78, 82.

14. Also Mahmud Rusan, of July 1958 fame, was elected as deputy for Irbid. Here the political significance is that this man's elevation to parliament should have no political significance by 1967.

15. Radio Amman, SWB, 7–10 January 1967. The electoral law as it stood at the time specifically says that "Jordanian," as mentioned in the constitution, meant "male" (Provisional Electoral Law for the House of Representatives, no. 24). *Jarida Rasmiyya,* no. 1494, 11 June 1960; English translation in Abid A. Al-Marayati, ed., *Middle Eastern Constitutions and Electoral Laws* (New York: Praeger, 1968), p. 171.

The point is, of course, that Tall did draw the distinction between a progressive precept and a conservative usage. (Women were officially enfranchised in Jordan in 1973; see *Arab Report and Record,* April 1973, p. 156.

16. An important exception is Ephraim Kam, ed., *Hussein Goes to War* (in Hebrew) (Tel Aviv: Maarakhot, 1974). Hussein's own *Ma "guerre" avec Israel* is not particularly revealing, nor is Samir A. Mutawi, *Jordan in the 1967 War* (Cambridge: Cambridge University Press, 1987). For a general introduction to the antecedents of the war, Shimon Shamir, "The Middle East Crisis on the Brink of War (14 May–4 June)," in D. Dishon, ed., *Middle East Record 1967* (Jerusalem: Israel Universities Press, 1971), pp. 183–204, is especially lucid.

17. Abdel Nasser started to move his army into Sinai on 15 May 1967.

18. Syria went further than mere vituperations. On 21 May, the explosion of a mine, obviously destined to be smuggled into Jordan, at the Jordanian border post of Ramtha, caused great loss of life. The incident induced Hussein to break off relations with Syria, one week before his dramatic journey to Cairo.

19. Abdel Nasser's address delivered before Arab Trade Unionists on 26 May is a good example (Voice of the Arabs, Tamtzit Shiddurim, Suppl. 4, Tel Aviv, 26 May 1967).

20. Kam, *Hussein Goes to War,* p. 47; Mutawi, *Jordan in the 1967 War,* p. 106, quoting Abdel Nasser's speech of 22 May.

21. Mutawi, *Jordan in the 1967 War,* p. 107; Vance and Lauer, *Hussein de Jordanie,* p. 47; and Saʿd Jumʿa, *Al-muʾ amara wa maʾrakat al-masir* (The con-

spiracy and the campaign of destiny), (Beirut: Dar al-'Kitab al-ʿArabi, pp. 187–88, for a brief account of the visit to Cairo.

22. Shuqayri, *Al-hazima al-kubra* (The great defeat) (Beirut: Dar al-ʿAwda, 1973), pt. 1, pp. 209, 221, 237, according to Aryeh Boʿaz, "Ahmad al-Shuqayri, a Political Biography" (in Hebrew) (M.A. thesis, Tel Aviv University, 1987), p. 94.

23. According to the Israeli defense minister, Moshe Dayan, Eshkol's message ran: "We are engaged in defensive fighting in the Egyptian sector, and we shall not engage ourselves in any action against Jordan, unless Jordan attacks us. Should Jordan attack Israel, we shall go against her with all our might" (*Jerusalem Post*, 14 February 1968, quoted in *MER, 1967*, p. 223). The Norwegian general Odd Bull, head of the U.N. Truce Supervision Organization who transmitted Eshkol's request, stigmatized it as "a threat pure and simple ... from one government to another" (Odd Bull, *War and Peace in the Middle East: The Experiences and Views of a U.N. Observer* [London: Leo Cooper, 1973], p. 113). A few hours later, Jordanian troops occupied his headquarters, "the last development I was expecting." Bull asks in a footnote: "Did Israeli intelligence perhaps have a hand in this Jordanian blunder?" Jordanian soldiers also beat up U.N. employees, a detail General Bull does not mention. Whatever Israeli successes there have been since 1948, they do not include relations with U.N. field personnel.

24. Significantly, Syed Ali el-Edroos, the official Jordanian chronicler, makes much of this point (*The Hashemite Arab Army, 1908–1979* [Amman: Publishing Committee, 1980], pp. 392–94).

25. Private information.

26. Vance and Lauer, *Hussein de Jordanie*, p. 53.

27. Hussein made most of these points after the war (see ibid., passim). This might, of course, be hindsight, but Hussein's bouts of fatalism on the eve of the war are borne out by independent witnesses.

28. Ibid., pp. 65–66.

29. On Hussein's agonizing on the eve of the war, see also Kam, *Hussein Goes to War*, p. 27 (editorial footnote). Nadav Safran has a poignant formulation for Hussein's dilemma (*From War to War* [New York: Pegasus 1969], p. 233).

30. My talks with Dean Rusk, 10 September 1984. I am grateful to Mr. Rusk for his observations.

Conclusion

1. Some time ago, I came across a remark in Metternich's autobiographical memoranda: ". . . nobody's shoulders are strong enough to run away with a monarchy. If monarchies disappear, it is because they lose faith in themselves" (Metternich, *Aus Metternich's nachgelassenen Papieren*, ed. A. von Klinkowström [Vienna: Braumüller, 1880], vol. 7, p. 626). The Habsburg monarchy of 1848, to which Metternich was referring, was tougher than the Hashemite Kingdom of Jordan between 1955 and 1967. If Hussein had "run away" then, he would probably have "run away with" the monarchy. But he did not run away, and he did

not lose faith. (I found that quotation in Henry A. Kissinger, *A World Restored* [Gloucester, Mass.: Peter Smith, 1973], p. 207. The English translation there is somewhat misleading. I am obliged to Professor Walther Mediger for providing me with the original.)

2. As early as 1956, Ambassador Duke reported on an audience with Hussein: "The king stonewalled steadily in the bland and expressionless manner which he so often adopts ..." (27 March 1956, FO 371/121544).

3. The association with this term as understood in English constitutional history is, of course, absurd, but it fits the Jordanian case in its own right.

4. I wish to refer again to the research by Amnon Cohen, Moshe Ma'oz, Shaul Mishal, Avi Plaskov, and Avraham Sela, mainly concerning the West Bank.

5. This may lie at the bottom of Muhammad Hasanayn Haykal's reported denial that "Nasser ever wanted to overthrow Hussein," of which I can make nothing otherwise (Peter Snow, *Hussein* [London: Barrie & Jenkins, 1972], p. 71).

Name Index

203